# TRUTH FLIES WITH FICTION

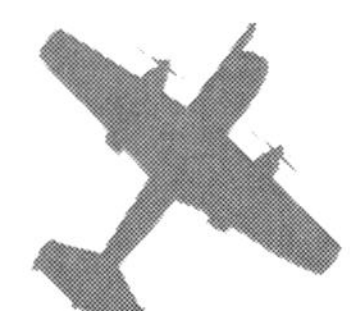
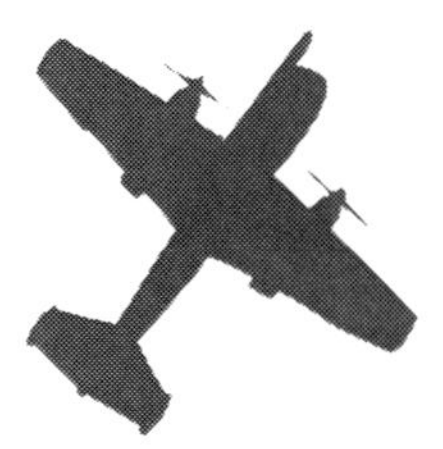

# TRUTH FLIES WITH FICTION

★ ★ ★

*Come into the cockpit on B-25 missions to Italy and France during 1944. The air war comes alive in this newly written pilot's narrative with a unique perspective. Possibly the last highly detailed story related first hand by a WWII airman. Learn details of The Allied and Axis air war never before revealed.*

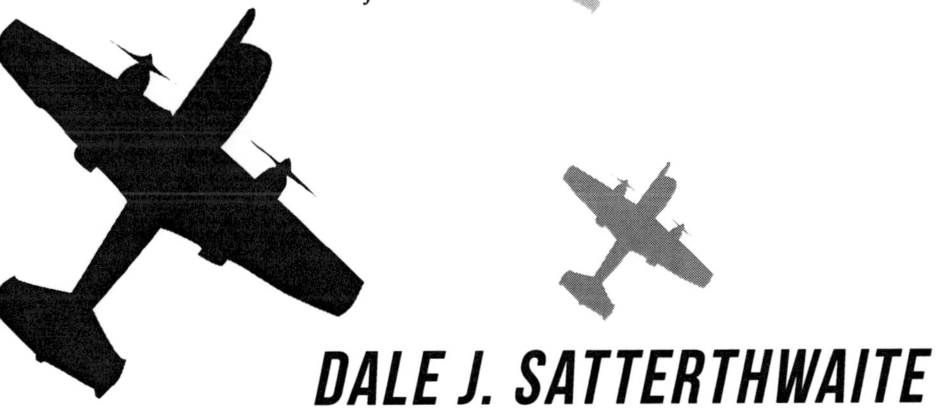

**DALE J. SATTERTHWAITE**

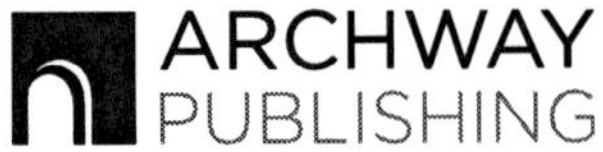

Archway Publishing books may be ordered through booksellers or by contacting:

Archway Publishing
1663 Liberty Drive
Bloomington, IN 47403
www.archwaypublishing.com
1-(888)-242-5904



The author would like to gratefully acknowledge the pictures and material contributed by Dan and Cyd Setzer and other source material from the 57th Bomb Wing. Their father Hymie Setzer is pictured on the left on pages 79 and 95. Links and other material are available on line at Hymie's War – Comcast.net. Thanks also to Don Kaiser, whose father Quentin Kaiser also served with the 340th. Don's invaluable material can be seen at http://www.warwingsart.com/12thairforce/57thoncorsica.html



ISBN: 978-1-4808-0484-5 (sc)
ISBN: 978-1-4808-0486-9 (hc)
ISBN: 978-1-4808-0485-2 (e)

Library of Congress Control Number: 2014901993

Printed in the United States of America

Archway Publishing rev. date: 3/3/2014

**I flew the North American B-25 Mitchell bomber into war.** The most amazing year of my life was spent as a bomber pilot based in Italy and Corsica during 1944. My fellow airmen and I fought pitched battles against very dangerous and committed forces. Let me share some of that year with you.

Public interest in the WWII air war is very strong seventy years after the epic battles. This is as it should be. Yet, the missions and daily lives of airmen who fought on the southern European front have not been given much attention. I hope my journal will shed some light on our experiences and the use of the B-25 as a tactical bomber.

I will detail missions where the B-25 and Norden bomb sight were used to deliver munitions on heavily defended small targets. One example of this bombing precision was a carefully planned attack which sank the German light cruiser Taranto. This mission earned the 340th Bomb Group a Presidential Unit Citation. I will provide information about little known Allied weapons deployments including delayed timer skip bombs and poison gas. There is a description of the major nighttime Luftwaffe attack on the 340th airbase in Corsica. This raid killed and injured many American soldiers and destroyed dozens of B-25s. It was one of the last major Luftwaffe missions. Photos and notes will illustrate the eruption of Mount Vesuvius which destroyed the 340th's airbase at Pompeii, Italy along with eighty-eight aircraft. There are also descriptions and photos of recreational junkets to Capri, Cairo and Rome. My story of that year includes details of the 10,000 mile flight from the United States to Italy via South America and Africa.

All pictures that are not otherwise noted are my own.

My journal is written from a personal perspective, and includes a number of letters that I wrote to my fiancée Eleanor. Notes from the various squadron diaries of the 340th Bomb Group refreshed my recollections. I relied on them heavily to provide details about bombing missions and life in the combat area. A full representation of the Allied air war can be found elsewhere. This is simply my take on that significant year. The combat awards which are interspersed throughout the book are part of my personal military records. They are not a complete history for the members of the 340th Bomb Group.

The title of my journal stems from a book called *Catch-22*. The famous novel was based on real events and actual airmen. One of the characters in the story is named Colonel Cathcart. There is little doubt that this is a characterization of Colonel Willis Chapman, the Commanding Officer of the 340th Bomb Group. Colonel Chapman flew six missions as my copilot. I believe that revelations of true events and real people rival the amazing yarns related in the novel. Joseph Heller who authored *Catch-22* was a bombardier with my outfit. I met him while flying missions from Corsica.

*Catch-22* is written from the perspective of a bombardier named Yossarian. His assessment of the war was to avoid it as much as possible because it was dangerous and crazy. The war certainly was dangerous and crazy, but most of my fellow soldiers accepted the premise that our participation was necessary and honorable. For that reason we put our full effort into ending it as soon as possible. We also took whatever opportunity we found to frolic as young men do and I have included some of the enjoyable times that we shared.

As an introductory point, let me begin with the first days of training on the B-25. My earlier life including enlisted experiences as a P-40 crew chief are separated from this body of the story in a back section entitled **"Before......"**

In my last few weeks of pilot training at Seymour Indiana, my mother came down and stayed for three or four days. While she was there I took her up in a twin engine AT-10. It was only her second airplane flight. Upon graduation, I received my commission and orders for the B-25 school in Greenville, South Carolina. My friend Herm Grub got orders to train in the new super bomber B-29. Fortunately, I had enough travel time to spend a few days at home in Detroit. My girlfriend Eleanor and I announced our engagement. I borrowed money from her mother to buy the engagement ring. I initially had saved enough to buy the ring, but spent it on a 1936 Ford Club Coupe. I was able to pay the money back in a couple of months.

*June 9, 1943*
*(Greenville, SC)*

*Dear Eleanor,*

*After a rather trying trip I arrived here at one o'clock this afternoon. I was able to obtain reservations yesterday on the fast overnight train from Washington DC to Greenville. The late departure allowed a few hours for sightseeing in Washington. I walked around the beautiful capital buildings, the parks and the Washington*

*Monument. Warm weather made the brief tour very enjoyable.*

*Greenville is a big post, and I had a lot of running around to do. This is a pleasant place; the base is a rambling affair in the midst of sweet smelling pines. It is not far from the Great Smoky Mountains. Some of the mountains are visible from the Bachelor Officer Quarters (BOQ) where I am living.*

*It looks as though I will be here at least five months. The flying course is ordinarily about three months long, but there aren't sufficient airplanes and there is also a shortage of gasoline for the planes we have. It looks as though I won't do any flying for almost a month. This break will allow me to see the area and enjoy the country club which is close to the base. The people at the club have invited us to use it when we can. All our meals are served there, and we pay about $1.50 a day. A local bus shuttles us back and forth. That's all for tonight. I had a wonderful vacation. Your folks have been so good to me and you most of all. I love you.*

*Dale*

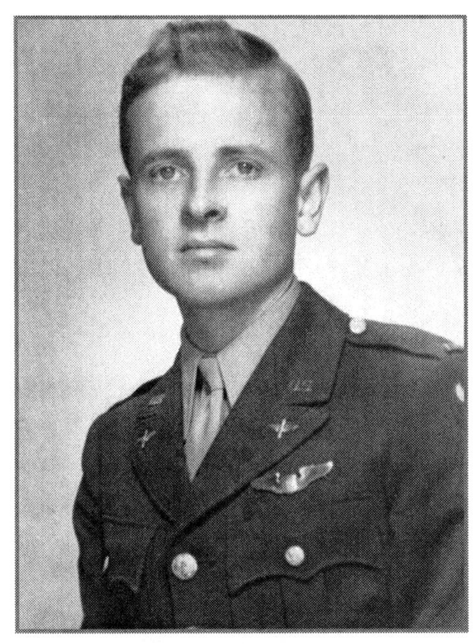

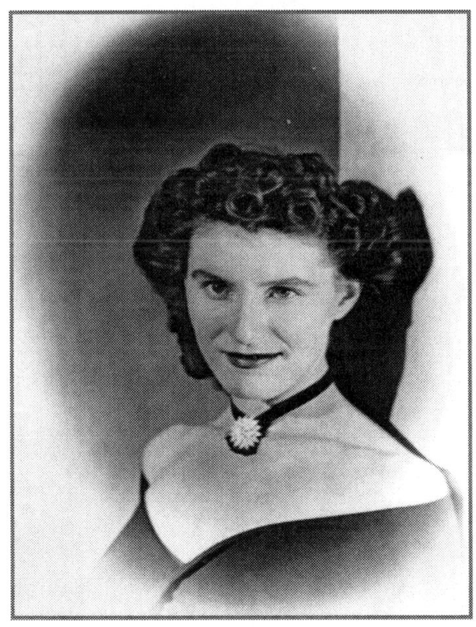

At the beginning stages of my training in Greenville I was not comfortable piloting the B-25. The flight controls were heavy and I had to put a pillow on the seat. The control column would hit me in the stomach when I brought the plane in for a landing. Smaller pilots were challenged by the cockpit layout. I had completed about ten hours of training when a directive came out stating that any pilot who was five foot seven or less could put in for fighter school. Fighters were what I really wanted to fly.

They sent the shorter pilots down to the field headquarters and the Flight Surgeon there checked our leg length and height. He told three of us, "You might as well go pack your stuff, you're gone." We returned to our unit and talked to the School Commander. He said, "Well, OK, you three will keep on going to ground school, but you won't be doing any flying until these orders come through."

The three of us attended ground school in the morning after which we were free to do as we pleased. We all had convertibles, and in the afternoon we would drive our cars out to the country club. I had my '36 Ford Club Coupe, my friend Fred Dieckmann had a '37 Packard, and Jeff Cantle had a '37 Cadillac. While there we would play golf, tennis and swim. We did this high life for quite a while and the orders never came through. Finally, the School Commander whose name was Capt. Charles Willis asked us "Well fellows, do you want to start flying again?" We all told him yes because we were about to lose our flight pay.

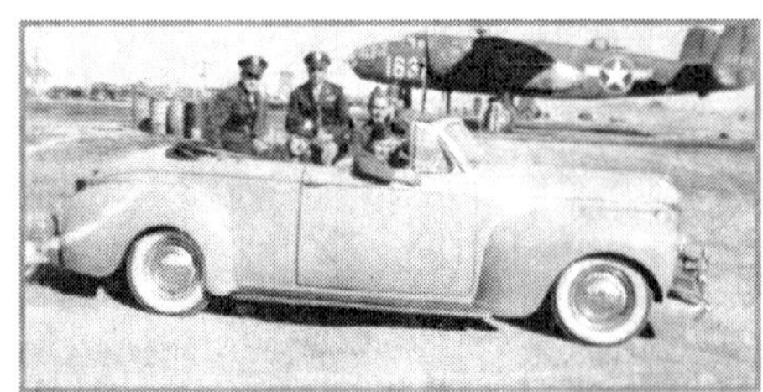

After we started flying again I started to appreciate the good qualities of the B-25. The twin tailed design was safer because a plane could sustain battle damage and continue to fly. They were also well built and rugged. In addition, B-25s were fairly fast for a bomber and later versions were well-armed. The three of us flew extra training flights to catch up with our class and we all qualified as pilots. With time I found that the design was easy to fly and performed predictably in difficult situations.

The B-25 Mitchell was named after Col. Billy Mitchell, an early stalwart proponent of bombing planes. He ran afoul of the brass with his strong public statements about the necessity of a strong Air Corps. He was demoted after ignoring orders not to sink a WWI German cruiser. I thought Mitchell was an appropriate name for the plane which would prove to be a versatile and effective tactical bomber. The beautiful lines of the plane belied its deadly nature.

*July 12, 1943*

*Dear Eleanor,*

*As I write this, it is dusk. I am sitting at my window overlooking the field where planes are always moving on the runways. There is a soft light coming through the window with a little glow from the lights down the hall. It is a little hard to write in the semi-dark, but I don't want to spoil it with harsh unshaded light. There is good music coming from the radio.*

*I have been flying occasionally. It will be slow going because there is so much to learn. The pilot must know how to operate every piece of equipment on the plane. Flight officers often teach technical details to the other members of the crew. The flying part is the least difficult, although accuracy is required, especially in the instrument and "beam" work. Today we began ground school and it will be a long grind. With this in mind, we went out to Paris Mountain for a swim. We all enjoyed it very much.*

*The B-25 is a powerful weapon and is very well equipped. The firepower on one of these models is impressive. There are three radio transmitters and five receivers aboard – enough radio equipment to fill a truck. The guns on board could fill another truck. These planes carry tons of bombs.*

*It's possible that I will be gone before Thanksgiving. There are crews moving out regularly. If I am a copilot, I will leave sooner. Of course I am trying for the first pilot. Anyway I may have a chance to fly up to Detroit sometime soon.*

*Best regards to your folks*

*Love, Dale*

Capt. Willis was a West Point graduate. His nickname was "Chicken Charles." He got that nickname because he was a bit of a ramrod and always went by the book. Despite this, I got along with him very well. One day he said to three of us, "I want to fly to Tulsa, Oklahoma this weekend! I need a copilot; do you guys want to go?" Tulsa was about a seven hour trip by B-25. Lewis, the guy who went overseas with me as copilot, and Edward G. Spray, who went over with me as bombardier/navigator went to

Tulsa with him. We put up at a hotel and Charles stayed with his girlfriend's family.

Tulsa was blasted by the sun, and was particularly noisy on the south end of the field where the Douglas Aircraft Company made bombers. Capt. Willis suggested that we buy tickets to the evening dance at the Blue Moon Club. He said the dance floor was in the open air as was the bandstand. The marque outside the club proclaimed that the Mills Brothers were playing that night.

We escaped the afternoon heat in a little tavern close by. Show-time found us wedged against each other in the club. The dance hall was filled with wildcatter's from oil rigs, Douglas assembly-line workers, GIs and dressed-to-the-hilt high rollers. A fair number of young ladies were present, and three of them were agreeable to chatting and dancing with us. The ladies returned with us to the airport later and we showed them our airplane and shared a final drink.

After our weekend, we went out to start the airplane and return to Greenville. The engines had a lot of flight hours and were rather tired. After several unsuccessful start attempts, we realized that we had run the boosters (fuel pumps) so much that it had washed all the oil off the sides of the cylinders. This meant that there was little engine compression. Finally, we managed to get one engine started. We let that engine run for a while and we were then able to get the other one going.

The Wright Company engines on the B-25 are 2600 cubic inches in displacement and develop more than 1700 horsepower. The large radial design has fourteen cylinders set in two banks. To put the engine's displacement into automotive terms, it is more than six muscle car V-8 engines. Many pilots thought Pratt and Whitney engines were superior. I liked the B-25 engines, and found them to be very reliable. Several of the airplanes that we were flying in Greenville were lightly loaded and without armor. Cruising speed was close to 240 miles an hour. One day, I flew a long cross-country flight in a newer plane with low engine hours. I averaged slightly less than 300 miles an hour on one leg of the flight. That is fast for a piston engine twin.

My main complaint with the airplane was that it was so noisy. The exhaust stacks were positioned close to the cockpit windows as were the massive propellers. In addition, the twin 50 mm machine guns in the upper turret made an unbelievable din. When they were fired my ears rang even with headphones on. The sharp staccato felt as if someone were beating on the canopy with a large chain. Most pilots agree that it was the noisiest airplane they had ever been in. I undoubtedly suffered some hearing loss in the 800 hours that I was a B-25 pilot. A minor additional issue was that the landing gear came down slowly compared to other airplanes.

Back in Greenville, some of the students were nearing the completion of their training. Edward my roommate was kind of a ladies man, and he wanted to borrow my car to go on a date. I wouldn't loan him my car, but he persuaded me to take him and his girlfriend out for a drive. We got out in the boondocks and he asked me to get out of the car and take a walk, which I did. I returned about an hour later which worked out fine for them.

Edward planned out a long cross-country flight around several Caribbean islands. These long flights were preparation and training for our deployment to Europe. Part of his flight was over the area which later became known as the Bermuda triangle. He never returned from that flight and the crash site was never located. After his plane was lost, long-distance flight training was routed mainly over the continental United States.

For these non-stop cross-country flights, they installed a one thousand gallon tank in the bomb bay. On my cross-country flight, I flew from Greenville to Tampa and across the gulf to New Orleans. We then headed north, going nearly all the way to Chicago before heading back to Greenville. The total flight time on that trip was a little more than eleven hours and the flight covered more than 2700 miles. When we got back to Greenville, there was still plenty of gas in the airplane. With that additional thousand gallon tank we could go a long way.

Several weeks after my long flight, a guy named Strickland took off in that same airplane and had some kind of engine trouble. The thousand gallon fuel tank in the bomb bay was full, which made the aircraft very heavy. They made a single engine approach to the field at Florence, South Carolina. After overshooting the runway they tried to go around, but didn't make it. No one on-board survived the fiery crash.

While I was stationed at Greenville, a well-known all-American athlete named Tom Harmon was in training there. He had been a quarterback for the University of Michigan. The rumors around the squadron were that he was a rather poor pilot. Nevertheless, he was made the first pilot with overall responsibility on an Italian bound plane. The plane went down over the Brazilian jungle and he was the only guy to get out! He wrote a letter to the squadron commander at Greenville with an explanation of why he was the only one to survive. He apparently felt a responsibility for the death of the crew, and so he said that he never wanted to fly another airplane that had more than one person in it. His explanation about getting out of that airplane and not getting his people out first was pretty hard to buy.

After he returned to the United States they checked him out in P-40 pursuit planes and he was sent to Africa. While on patrol, he was attacked by an ME-109 fighter and he bailed out. He returned to the states and married his girlfriend Elise Max who was a movie star. The wedding was a big Hollywood affair. She made her wedding gown out of a parachute! The wedding made the front pages. Later, he became a sports announcer.

*August 31, 1943*

*Dear Eleanor,*

*It is warm today and there has been no change in the weather for weeks. I got a little too much sun and my nice tan is peeling. I look like a leopard or leper – I'm not sure which. The other day I flew up into the edge of the Smokey Mountains and they were very beautiful. Rocky cliffs and pine covered slopes line valleys with swift streams. I am anxious to get up there on foot.*

*We have been on several long trips lately, and I would have gone to Tulsa for the second time if the weather had not closed down. Last week we started out for San Antonio, Texas, but we had to stop at Meridian, Mississippi because of engine trouble. Sunday we went to Avon Park, Florida near Miami.*

*Today I went on a training flight firing cannon and machine guns. Our targets were in the Atlantic Ocean near Myrtle Beach, South Carolina, which is about one hour from here. Our bombing ranges are closer - about ten minutes away. I have been doing quite a good deal of bombing lately at various altitudes. We have made passes as low as 150 feet and as high as 8000. Tonight our electrical system was defective and we weren't able to drop bombs one at a time. We had to salvo them all at once, so we returned an hour early and canceled our second flight.*

*I am satisfied with my job and I believe that is what I was meant to do. Soon I will have a chance to use the training and experience of many months. Most of the pilots in Europe are flying fifty missions before they come back. I hope to fly three or four a week like some of them are doing.*

*We get a complete weather briefing before we fly, so I always know the weather is Detroit. If it improves next week, we may put on a flight to Battle Creek. If I do get up that way I will call you.*

*Love, Dale*

I flew several training flights in a B-25G which was equipped with a 75 mm nose cannon. We trained in the ocean near Myrtle Beach, SC. Firing that cannon was a real kick. At the time it was the biggest ever flown on an airplane. It had a special sight with a trigger sticking out of it. As we made our first firing pass, the sight showed the target square in the crosshairs. The projectile was easy to follow after it was fired and I could see that it was apparently going to fall short. I couldn't figure out why the aim had been so far off. My eyes had been deceived because our shot went right through the middle of the target. As the plane overflew the dropping projectile, it appeared to be falling short of the aiming point.

We started firing about a mile from the target and if everything went right, we could get off four rounds. The plane would be at 500 to 1000 feet. I think it was accurate enough to hit a car from a mile. Time seemed to compress when we fired that weapon. The shock would nearly knock my feet off the rudder pedals and black smoke would completely block the view through the windscreen for an instant. The blast actually reduced the plane's airspeed.

It was rough duty to be the cannon gunner on those planes. Recoil on the weapon was 22 inches and the gunner would have to be sure that he was out of the way. He had an interlock switch which would prevent the cannon from firing until he was ready. Out on the nose, the barrel passed through a stout aluminum plate about 18 x 24 inches which was riveted to the airplane framework. Muzzle blast shook that plate so hard that it had to be re-riveted after fifty rounds.

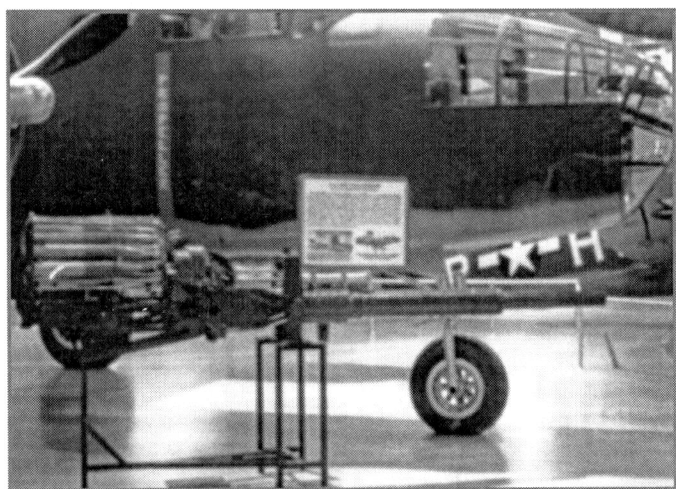

We fired three rounds successfully, but the fourth round was a misfire. The gunner waited a while to be sure that the round wasn't going to cook off. He opened the breach and the shell was stuck in the barrel. All the black powder fell loosely on the floor of the navigation compartment, so we immediately went back and landed. Any spark or flame near that powder could have been fatal. After we landed, the gunner climbed up on a ladder and pushed a long pole down the barrel to dislodge the shell. After cleaning the gunner's compartment, we went back and fired eight more rounds.

This amazing weapon system was the brainchild of Col. Paul "Pappy" Gunn. He was a retired naval officer living in the Philippines when the Japanese attacked. After being drafted into the Air Corps, he engineered changes to B-25s and other planes. One of the modified B-25s had seventeen forward firing 50 cal. machine guns! He used that massive firepower to attack ships and air bases. Some of the modified planes were successful designs, and he was sent back to the American plane factories. Col. Gunn helped them incorporate his ideas into production aircraft.

While flying on a practice strafing run I found myself in some serious trouble. At the end of the pass I pulled the airplane into a tight turn to go around for another run on the target. Suddenly the elevators felt as if they were disconnected, and we were only 200 feet above the water. I still had aileron control, and got the plane straightened out so that the elevators were again working. For a few moments it was a real pucker situation. The elevators might have been in the wake of the steeply banked wings.

Our training command had a big meet which was an inter-squadron competition. It was determined that my crew would represent our squadron. One of the scenarios involved a mock mission to drop mustard gas, which is a powerful chemical warfare weapon. The setup for the mission had a couple of big tanks attached to the wings. They contained slurry of molasses and water which apparently simulated the consistency of mustard gas. There was a three inch opening in the nose of the tanks, and glass seals were glued over the openings. Glass seals were also on the back of the tanks and dynamite caps were stuck to both the front and aft seals. When the bombardier hit the button to drop the gas, it exploded the dynamite caps breaking the seals. Ram air through the tanks pushed the slurry out. To make a target, the field crew tore up pieces of paper and positioned them in a field with a center aiming point made of a plywood sheet. After the plane made its pass they would collect the pieces of paper and determine how close the "gas" came to the target.

I figured most of the guys would come blasting over that target in a dive at about 300 miles an hour. If they came in that fast, it would really spread that stuff around but not be very accurate. We made a very slow approach over the target with the flaps down about halfway. Our speed was only 150 miles an hour which allowed the bombardier to carefully judge the release point. I heard the blasting caps fire as we passed low over the field. The sticky brown fluid plastered the center of the target. We won the event and got a trophy for it. If an airplane made an attack run in combat at that speed and altitude, they would undoubtedly be targeted with heavy and accurate fire.

At the time we knew that mustard gas was a prohibited weapon. Widespread use of chemical weapons in World War I had killed thousands of troops and permanently injured many thousands more. To use these weapons in this war seemed unthinkable. Nevertheless, a secret Allied chemical weapon stockpile was positioned in Italy in 1943. Details about this program point to a willingness by the Allies to counter any potential German chemical attack with an attack of their own. I will substantiate these claims in a later section of the journal.

At the Greenville airbase there was an altitude chamber which crews preparing to go overseas were trained in. It was big enough to hold six guys at a time. We all put on oxygen masks and the operators set the chamber pressure to equal 25,000 feet. They gave us pads of paper and told us to write our names continuously. At some point our oxygen supply would be deliberately shut off, and our writing would degrade to an unreadable scrawl. Then we would pass out. They would turn the oxygen back on, and we would pick right up and start writing again. It was good training for high-altitude, but when we arrived in Italy they took all the oxygen equipment out. The word was that oxygen tanks would explode and burn if hit.

It was clear that I would not be able to return to Detroit before my deployment, so Eleanor came down to Greenville and stayed for four days. We had a wonderful time together and I was able to take her for a flight in a B-25. It was her very first flight. The weather was pleasant, but a little bumpy as was typical on those warm days. She seems a little quiet, and I looked over and saw that she was struggling with airsickness. I was wearing my class "A" uniform rather than flight clothes and I realized that the only thing I could hand her was my officer's cap. I needed a new cap after the flight.

Herman (Herm) Grub became my friend when I enlisted the Army Air Corps in August of 1940. We both attended crew chief training school and were then assigned to P-40 pursuit planes. During our enlisted service we pooled our money and bought a car. The shared car was used to explore Florida on our off-time. Herm had been a bit of a ladies man before he went in the service. He had had some minor scrapes with the law in that regard. While we were attending school in Chicago he met and married Nell, a beautiful young lady. After that he was a changed man with no eye for anyone else.

She visited him while we were still in basic flight training, and they made a fine couple. Nell had my address in Greenville, and wrote a letter filled with chatter about Herm's training. My heart sank when I read the second letter that she sent. Herm had been killed while taking off on a B-29 training flight. Apparently one of the engines lost power as they left the ground and the plane crashed and exploded. No one survived. Early B-29s were particularly dangerous during the takeoff phase of flight. It was very difficult to relay that news to Eleanor. We both thought of him as a best friend.

My Ford convertible was a really nice car. The maroon paint had faded a little in places, but it was mechanically sound. The heater was made by Stuart-Warner and was powered by gasoline! It was so hot that it would melt the soles right off your shoes. However, it didn't put any hot air on the windshield. On one very cold trip I was forced to stick my head out the window to see. I stopped at a gas station and purchased some small tubes of salt which were designed to stick on the wipers to melt the ice.

The car had a flathead V-8 with 85 horsepower. Tires were hard to find, but I managed to scrounge around and find several usable spares. I somehow got an allotment of fuel to take the car back to my home town which was listed as Oaklawn, Illinois, a suburb of Chicago. Lou Stolt, my radio operator, lived in Chicago. The two of us decided to take the car up there just before we were to go overseas.

We were about one hundred miles from Greenville when the car blew a head gasket. It was nighttime, and we didn't have any tools. We found a Ford agency and there was a watchman inside. We banged on the door and got the watchman to sell us a new head gasket. The fellows at a nearby gas station loaned us some tools. We made repairs, and afterword a friendly policeman said we could use some jail cells to sleep. At the crack of dawn we set out for Chicago. At the end of that tiring trip, we put the car up on blocks at my parents place.

In early November we started getting ready to go overseas. Crews were formed which consisted of pilot, copilot, bombardier/navigator, two engineer/gunners and a radio operator. I had a feeling about one of our engineer/gunners. He was a little guy, about five foot one. I told the guys in the crew "that guy is a hard luck case." I don't know why I had that feeling. While he was boarding the airplane a folding ladder crushed his hand and put him out of business. They replaced him with another engineer/gunner.

We flew down to Savanna, Georgia where they issued us a brand-new B-25. We did a lot of flying locally calibrating all of the instruments. We checked the airspeed indicator by measuring miles along the railroad track. We also checked for compass accuracy. After a week in Savanna, we gathered all our gear and got ready to go. They put a 500 gallon fuel tank in the bomb-bay. Underneath the fuel tank sat a basket full of spare B-25 parts. The bomb-bay was completely full.

This airplane was the first B-25J model to go to the European theater. It was equipped with a new armament package which included extra machine guns in the nose. We thought it looked pretty mean, and Edward Spray and I decided not to name it after a girlfriend. We named the plane Tare Sugar which was an analog for Tough Sh*t. One of the sergeants at the Savanna Air Depot had done nose art on other ships, and he generously agreed to decorate Tare Sugar. Working overnight, he emblazoned the name in bold letters.

I don't know if the airplane was slightly out of trim, but Tare Sugar was a real pig for gasoline. Parasitic drag from the additional guns probably did not help. We flew from Savanna to West Palm Beach, Florida and from there to Borinquen Field, Puerto Rico. I was supposed to be leading six airplanes. We got so widely separated that we were really flying on our own. Because of the high fuel consumption on my plane, I ran the engines at low throttle settings. The other pilots did not want to fly that slowly and they went ahead.

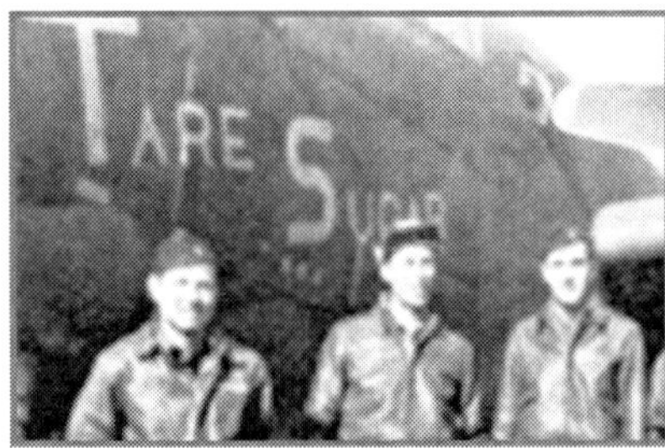


(Courtesy 57th Bomb Wing)

I complained about the fuel consumption and a North American Aviation Co. engineer looked over Tare Sugar when we arrived at Atkinson field, British Gianna. North American designed and built the B-25. He checked the carburetors and other systems aboard. No engine adjustments were required. The only thing that he could suggest was that we put as many of our supplies as we could in the nose. He thought that changing the center of gravity might get the airplane up on step so to speak. That didn't help. The legs of the South American transit were well within the range of the plane even with the higher fuel consumption. I knew that the trip out to Ascension Island might be a problem however. At regular cruise settings we should have been using 125 gallons an hour and we were using closer to 135 gallons an hour.

Our next stop on our way down the South American coast was Val-de-Cans field near Bel'em, Brazil. We spent a restless night under mosquito netting in nearly suffocating heat. At daybreak we departed the rain soaked runway and climbed out over the massive muddy Amazon. Below, the airport clearing quickly became a tiny hole in the enormous jungle. I thought of my early days flying Stearman trainers, and how the instructor constantly had me searching for a possible emergency landing place. Nothing of the sort was available here.

Our brightly colored aeronautical charts were surprisingly accurate and detailed. We navigated by dead reckoning, and some use of radio compass within several hundred miles of the fields. Approaching Fortaleza, Brazil, we saw vistas of the rugged jungle coast which sometimes disappeared behind the giant cumulous clouds. We took a dip in the ocean after preparing the airplane carefully for next flight. The 250 mile final flight to Natal, Brazil was the shortest leg of the trip. We remained in Natal for five days preparing for our ocean crossing.

Natal was a very busy place, with dozens of bombers preparing for their flight to Africa and beyond. There were also many four engine cargo planes of a variety not yet common in the states. There were Douglas C-54s, and a cargo version of the B-24 called the C-87.

Because I was in "the lead airplane," Operations assigned an Air Transport Command (ATC) navigator for our crew at Natal. Edward Spray, the bombardier/navigator, had really worked hard on his celestial navigation courses. He had all the charts, and equipped himself with an octant which wasn't standard issue for flight crews. He was gung-ho to navigate us out to Ascension Island. When they put that ATC navigator in the airplane, he went up in the nose and sulked.

*December 19, 1943*
*Somewhere in Brazil*

*Dear Eleanor,*

*I know it is been a long time since I wrote. So much has happened that I will have to send it to you in snatches. I have been in many strange places, most of them quite beautiful. I have picked up coconuts from beneath palms and eaten them. Here we have fresh pineapple which is very good indeed. Food and liquor is good and very cheap. At one stop I bought a beautiful pair of riding boots lined with white buckskin. They only cost eight dollars. I like this country and plan on returning someday.*

*We have been working long days which usually start at 4 AM. The crew members have spent many hours getting the airplane ready. They are all experienced and conscientious fellows who know their jobs well. Our flight tomorrow is a long jump. The people in charge know their business and everything is ready.*

*This is probably the last letter I will be able to get off for a few days. If it reaches you in time, I wish you a Merry Christmas and you know where my thoughts will be at that time. I pray that we may spend the next one together. Best regards to everyone.*

*Love, Dale*

*Lt DJS 0-804516 APO 12587 – BT New York NY*

**On the flight out to Ascension Island we were flying above** a thick cloud deck. This leg of our trip was 1700 miles, and favorable winds gave us enough range. We picked up the signal for the radio compass when we were about 300 miles out. The ATC navigator made an arrival time estimate to Ascension based on sun lines that he was shooting on an easterly heading. A navigator could shoot the sun with an octant and supposedly get the longitude. With that information he could calculate speed and time to destination.

I had already received information that the ceiling level over the airfield was down to 500 feet. Edward suddenly poked his nose into the cockpit and said "When are you guys going to start letting down?" Just then I saw the radio compass needle suddenly swing 90 degrees, and we made a sharp diving turn through the overcast to follow it. Several moments later we broke out of the clouds about two miles from the runway. To my right in the direction we had been flying was a 3000 foot mountain in the center of the island! The ATC navigator was twenty-two minutes off on his ETA. Fortunately, Edward was tracking our route on his own. His warning alerted me to follow the radio compass. Without turning, our course would have put us on a collision path with the mountain. Edwards saved his biting criticism until we were out of earshot of the ATC navigator.

The runway at Ascension could be dangerous on takeoff. As they accelerated, aircraft were climbing a gradual rise till about midpoint. We were warned to watch our airspeed so that we did not become airborne before we had attained flying speed. There had been some rather bad incidents at the field when planes mushed back down and crashed. It wasn't a good place to be stuck with aircraft damage. There was nothing there except the field.

One of our six airplane crews discovered what it was like to be stranded at Ascension. On takeoff, they had a bird strike which broke the windscreen. They went back and landed and the mechanics got in touch with American suppliers who sent out a new windscreen. It took several weeks to get there. They took off after the repair and hit another bird; breaking the windscreen again! This added to Ascension's reputation for having many birds around the runway.

From Ascension Island we flew to Roberts field, Liberia, a 1500 mile flight. We were not far out from Ascension and saw a U-boat on the surface. Lewis, the copilot, sent a message back to the airport tower. Several weeks after we arrived in Italy, we heard from newly arriving crews that the English had sent a destroyer out and sank it. We happily parted ways with the ATC navigator at Roberts field. His estimates were no better on that portion of our trip.

The field was located some distance from the capital city Monrovia, so we didn't go into town at all. A gigantic Firestone rubber plantation was the main feature outside. Local men approached us with notes written in English asking for work. Their notes stated that they were trying to earn money to attend the missionary school which was not free. We hired three or four of them to wash our airplane at five cents apiece. The plane wasn't very dirty, but it was the only work we could think of.

We were planning to fly to Takoradi Airport, Gold Coast the next day, but learned that the field there was unusable, and we were stuck in Liberia while they were repairing it. The heavy B-24s were making it across in one shot from Brazil to Takoradi, a distance of about 2400 miles. Torrential rains at Takoradi had softened the fields. Metal plates which lined the runway would shoot straight up in the air when the big bombers landed. The engineers built a parallel runway and we arrived there December 23.

Fourteen hundred miles separated us from Casablanca, Morocco. If we ran low on fuel during the flight, the ATC briefing officer said that we could stop at a base manned by the French Foreign Legion. This remote desert outpost named Tindouf is on the western tip of Algeria. Headwinds slowed our progress as we proceeded north. It was clear that we weren't going to make it to Casablanca without refueling. As we approached Tindouf, I misread the signs marking the dirt runway and landed next to it. Fortunately, my mistake did not result in a blown tire. We were warmly greeted by the Legionnaires who didn't give us a hard time about the landing mistake. The French Commander offered only 300 gallons because fuel had to be hauled seven hundred miles from the coast. It was Christmas day when we landed, but I expected it to be hot in the desert. A steady breeze made the forty-five degree air very chilly. I got back in the airplane and grabbed my jacket.

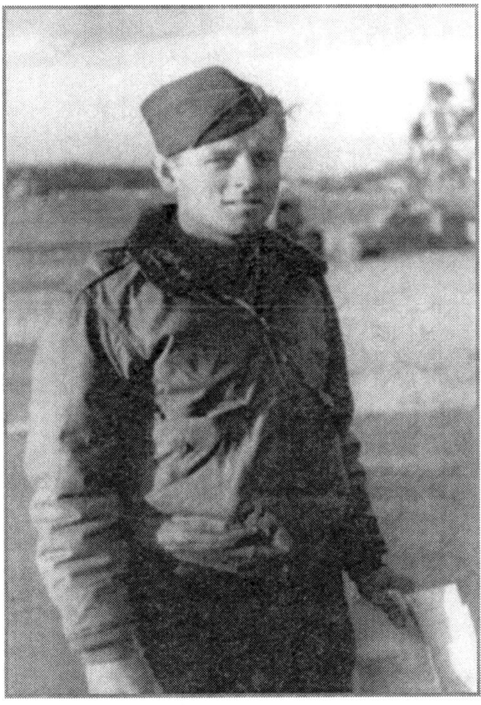

The ATC officer had also briefed us on several possible courses northward from Tindouf. A route through the Atlas Mountains was our preferred choice. Although the canyon entrance was difficult to spot from the air, it was the most direct path to Casablanca. He told us that if we found the canyon entrance right away, to proceed on through the mountains. If we were not able to quickly spot it, he emphasized that we should not to waste fuel looking for it. Our alternate instructions were to head out to sea and fly along the coast.

We found a bone dry canyon that matched our charts and began the ascent. In short order we were above 13,000 feet with impressive mountain tops on either side. To surmount the summit safely required in instrument altitude of 15,000 feet. A high layer of clouds sat on the peaks. I throttled up the engines to climb into the cloud bank on instruments. Lewis, the copilot grabbed my shoulder and pointed at the wing. A coating of ice was quickly forming on the wings and engine nacelles. Ice accumulation reduces lift, and can cause an airplane to stall. We descended back down and saw that the clouds were sinking lower while the canyon elevation was going up.

The approach into that pass was the most rugged, inhospitable country that I have ever seen. Directly ahead of us were peaks that seemed to block the canyon. My confidence began to evaporate as I wondered if we had misread our charts. Our course could not be reversed for two reasons. There was no room to turn, and our fuel would not last for a coast detour. Rather suddenly, the narrow canyon revealed a 90 degree bend to the left. Our charts did not show the bend, and the ATC officer had not mentioned it. If we had been flying in the clouds on instruments, a mountain impact would have been the inevitable result. We managed to squeeze through the pass with about 500 feet between the ceiling and the ground. Once again we narrowly avoided a crash against a mountain peak. Later on, we found out that none of the other planes which left the States with us took the mountain route. Lush green vegetation covered the peaks on the Morocco side.

We went in and landed at Casablanca. My orders ended at that point and we reported to Casablanca Command. The Headquarters there assigned crews to operational units. The next day I went down to the flight line and bumped into a guy that I'd gone through basic flight training with. He was a B-24 pilot, and his plane had made an emergency landing there. He told me that they had narrowly avoided a fatal crash over the ocean.

While the plane was on autopilot, an engine had suddenly quit. Unbalanced thrust caused a yaw, which tumbled the gyros and the autopilot. Before the pilots could react, the plane rolled upside down and did a violent uncontrolled split S maneuver. Enormous stress from this acrobatic turn put a permanent bend in the wing. The pilots managed to regain control and then administer first aid to the crewmen who were thrown around inside the plane. This also happened to a B-25 in the states, and all the autopilots were removed from our planes.

Our delay in Casablanca stretched to about one week. There was transportation available to go into town. We were cautioned to be on our guard if we went because some soldiers had been mugged. We did go into town and went inside the enormous Hassan II Mosque. It was one of the biggest in the world, and could hold 25,000 worshipers. A friendly cab driver showed us the Anfa hotel where F.D.R. and Churchill met to formulate a plan for the war at the beginning of the year. He dropped us off at a nightclub where we had drinks and dinner. There was a station just outside of town where soldiers could catch military transportation back to the field. As we approached the station there a soldier was standing there with no uniform. The unlucky man was barefoot in skivvies. He had been rolled, and they took everything from him.

Donkeys were everywhere around Casablanca, and they would start heehawing early in the morning. Between the donkeys and roosters it was a noisy place. We had our own animal which caused some issues. It was a spider monkey that one of the crew had picked up in Brazil. This monkey was a real nuisance, and had fouled the airplane. He got away in the ship and no one could catch him. I insisted that Casablanca was his end destination. Someone finally used food to entice it out of the plane and into our assigned Quonset hut.

One morning I noticed that the monkey was hanging suspended from a thick power chord that was exposed in the ceiling. Suddenly, he shot across the room on the chord and grabbed a large spider. Maybe they call them spider monkeys because they like to eat them. In Liberia there was a chimp that lived at the air base. Every afternoon the C/O would be chauffeured to the PX five miles away. When the car headed for the gate, that chimp would race behind it and jump on the back fender. Apparently he got handouts there.

We got our orders to report to the 340th Bomb Group near Naples, Italy. The other five airplanes went different directions. We flew to Oran on the Algiers Coast. Oran's airport was a hub of activity with P-38s, B-26s, A-20s, B-25s, B-17s and Spitfires continually landing and taking off. Wrecked French warships lay at odd angles in the harbor, victims of a British attack. Oran had been home to most of the French fleet and the British made a preemptive attack to keep the warships from falling into German hands.

Our long day ended with a late afternoon approach into Tunis, Tunisia. Edward Spray and I took a rolling cab tour of the downtown area. The driver assured us that the streets were reasonably safe, and we walked through part of the Medina; a marketplace. Many shops lined densely packed alleys and covered passages. Pungent smelling spices and brightly colored weavings were for sale along with leather, tin and fine filigree.

Continuing east at daybreak, we were impressed with views of Mount Etna which pierced through the overcast and was spectacular. I had never seen a large volcanic mountain before. The area around Naples was also overcast. I saw a hole in the clouds and dove steeply through it. We broke through the cloud base at 600 feet and leveled off. Four large barrage balloons blocked our forward view, and I banked the plane sharply to avoid them. Both the Axis and Allied forces used large balloons tethered with strong metal cables to prevent low level air attacks. I asked the crew to keep a sharp eye out so that we did not snag a balloon cable. Capodichino airport was visible north of the town and we flew over to the field and landed.

We went inside operations and asked them where the 340th Bomb Group was. They said, "Oh, they are over at Foggia." We got back in the airplane and made the fifteen minute flight. There were several runways in the area, but the primary airport was called Foggia Main. It was lined with steel mats, which could be a little slippery in the rain. After touchdown I hit the brakes, and one side grabbed harder than the other. The airplane spun around and we were going down the runway backwards! I pushed the throttles to full power and we quickly came to a stop.

Every inch of the Foggia field sat in a large brown puddles or calf deep mud. A mud caked Sergeant said, "They pulled out of here four days ago and relocated south of Naples some place." We flew south, and looking toward Mount Vesuvius, saw a big airfield full of B-25s. We went in and found out we were at the right field.

Our assignment was to the 486th Bombardment Squadron based at Pompeii airfield. The other squadrons assigned to the 340th Bomb Group were the 487th, 488th and 489th.

After a warm welcome, several pilots told us about the situation in the Italian war zone. They also bought us up to date on the 340th Group and its part in the hard fought African and Sicilian campaigns. The 340th ground crew did not go overseas with their planes. Instead, they embarked from San Francisco on a round the world cruise which took them through Australia and India. Their forty-two day voyage ended at Suez, Egypt.

The pilots and some crew members flew their planes on a similar route to our journey through South America, Ascension Island and Africa. A tragedy struck the group on the flight from Khartoum to Cairo. A heavy sand storm greeted them on arrival. Several planes were able to land safely, but as the storm intensified, one crew could not find the field, even with the help of flares fired from the ground. The crew was ordered to bail out, and four of them successfully parachuted. Three men went down with the ship.

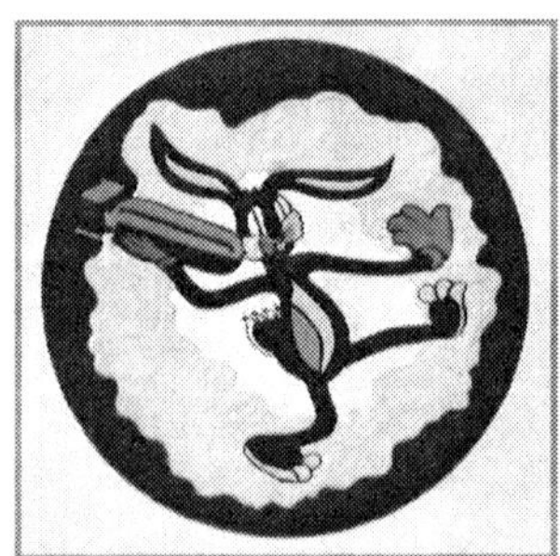

**486th Bombardment Squadron Patch**

After the ground and air crews were reunited at Kabrit, Egypt, they discovered that their supplies were many weeks behind them. Rumors were that the supplies had not yet left the states or that their equipment had been diverted to front line units. The time in Kabrit became a battle for supplies and equipment of any kind. Scrounging was the order of the day.

In late April another blow struck the 489th squadron. Two planes had a midair collision while flying in close formation. Both planes crashed, and the bombs aboard exploded killing eleven crewmen. During this time there was a push to conclude the Tunisian campaign and the unit flew as many missions as possible. German antiaircraft was deadly and accurate causing many crashes. Fighter opposition was also intense. The Luftwaffe was still a very potent force during those battles.

In mid-June the unit relocated to Hergla, Tunisia, one of the driest wind-blown places in North Africa. Hergla proved a good place for watching air raids. With the harbors of Sousse and Tunis nearby, as well as convoys passing just off the coast, the Germans did not take time to give the Hergla airfield any personal attention. The German air raids with the defending Allied antiaircraft fire could be watched from a comparatively safe grandstand seat.

Following the invasion of Sicily, the Group relocated to Comiso, Sicily in early August. It was a much more pleasant situation than Tunisia. The group regretted the efficiency with which it had bombed that area. Hangers, barracks, swimming pools and tennis courts were ruined. The runway and parking areas were cleared off to make a nice landing field, and the beautiful surrounding countryside more than made up for the destroyed luxuries. Comiso was located in the most fertile valley region of Sicily. Orchards and vineyards abounded, and eggs and vegetables could be purchased.

Comiso proved to be a short waylay as the group was relocated to Catania, Sicily at the end of August. Constant German air raids mainly targeted the harbor there, and the only Group ground injuries came from falling antiaircraft shells. Catania and the surrounding area proved to be heavily mined and booby-trapped. Sappers were constantly busy trying to clear areas for personnel to move into. Despite these problems, Catania was for the most part a good location. The nearby towns sold gelato and good wine. Some of the soldiers befriended young ladies in the area and hospitals also were staffed by American nurses. The nearby sea afforded swimming facilities, and Mount Etna provided a place for sightseeing.

Early targets from that field were over southern Italy. On September 8th they received the exciting news that Italy surrendered unconditionally. On the first Group night mission, two planes crashed on takeoff with only one survivor. On the following evening another crew made a water landing, and all aboard returned safely.

Targets in Albania, Greece and Bulgaria occupied the Group in November. They observed P-38s tangling with ME-109s on several of those raids. Gunners on their planes were credited with three enemy fighters on one mission. Thanksgiving saw the group relocating to Foggia. The field was a complete quagmire when they arrived. It was nearly impossible to operate there, nevertheless, they were credited with some successful targeting. They had only moved to Pompeii airfield a few days prior to our arrival. When we caught up to the Group they had flown about 120 missions.

Tare Sugar garnered more than a little attention since it was the first ship of its type. Our squadron notes had the following comments regarding her: "The plane which arrived on January 6 is well-heeled with guns. There are three in the nose and two on each side of the pilot's compartment. There is also a tail gun, plus top turret and waist guns. It is called Tare Sugar and has the Morse code symbols for Tough Sh*t on the side. It has only 85 hours on it and is straight from the States."

William Gans, one of the fellows in my living quarters, was a real nice guy who had an arctic style sleeping bag. The two of us made an arrangement that if I were shot down, the leather boots that I bought in South America would go to him. If he were shot down, I would get the sleeping bag. I got the sleeping bag. He went down three or four weeks after I got there. Edward G. Spray was killed on his first mission which was the bridge at Pontecorvo, Italy. They took three direct 88 mm cannon hits, and no one got out of the airplane. The following accounts are from my diary, and detail missions and events in all four squadrons. Squadron notes helped me reconstruct this history.

January 5 Capt. William Shealy, the 486th X/O, returned from Naples today with good news. Yesterday he talked to 2nd Lieut. Patrick O'Leary who has been missing in action since Nov. 17th. O'Leary was assumed to be either dead or a P.O.W in Greece. He and Lieut. John E. Smith bailed out after their plane was crippled by three direct hits from antiaircraft guns (ack-ack or A/A). Both were found and hidden by Greek patriots. Lieut. Smith was badly injured in the jump. The Greeks turned him over to the Germans so that he might receive medical attention. O'Leary was successfully slipped out of the country with the patriots help. He asked Capt. Shealy to keep the story quiet so that he might walk in on his friends unannounced. O'Leary is of the opinion that the other four members of his crew are dead.

January 6 The weather is clearing, but still cold, and there is a general scavenger hunt for fuel which is rather sparse in this vicinity. Lieut. O'Leary returned to duty today, and he failed to surprise his friends because the rumor of his safe escape traveled faster than he did.

January 7 Combat crews are busy with a week of intensive training which includes practice missions each day, weather permitting. Rumors circulating the flight line have shipped us to England, Siberia, or China.

January 8 A briefing set up a simulated bombing attack on a road bridge south of Potenza. Eight planes participated, dropping their practice bombs in a good pattern. On the return, the area south of Vesuvius was covered in mist and the field was difficult to find. One of the huge barrage balloons over Torre Annunziata was snagged by one of our ships and nearly dragged down. Our planes were flying around in the heavy haze straining to see each other. Flying from this field is going to have its difficulties. Squadron personnel are having some trouble with Italians who are employed at the base. A number of them were apprehended while helping themselves to property in our quarters.

January 9 A practice formation was to have dropped bombs on a range located on the famous Salerno invasion beaches this morning, but dull skies and intermittent rains canceled the mission. Lieut. Col. Charles D. Jones, new 340th Group C/O, visited the squadron this afternoon. He insisted upon being personally introduced to every man in the outfit, clerks and cooks alike. The general opinion expressed was that he would be "a good man to work for." He succeeds Lieut. Col. Adolf Tokas who in turn replaced Col. W.R. Mills who was shot down last May in Tunisia.

January 10 Latest rumor: the 12th Bomb Group, not us, will be the ones going to the Burma area. The squadron is now fairly well supplied with coal which Capt. Shealy and a crew swiped down by the docks in Naples. There are many advantages to being near a port; the chief one being that at least for now we are eating better than many other outfits. Several men visited the lavish Orange Garden Club in Naples tonight. Upon return, they told us that the place has an atmosphere of a nightclub at home, serving gin, vermouth and several other mediocre drinks. There are enough women (nurses and Red Cross) to make the place ornamental.

When we were returning from missions, we would typically approach in an echelon shaped flight at very low altitude over the field. The lead plane would do a steep turn to line up on the runway. The rest of the planes would make a similar turn, leaving vapor trails off of the wing tips. We would land about ten seconds apart. The airplanes would be staggered, one on the left side and one on the right side. Prop wash from the plane ahead could be dangerous, and the direction the wind blowing was important. For example, if the airplane ahead of you was on the left and the wind was on the left, it would blow that prop wash right into you.

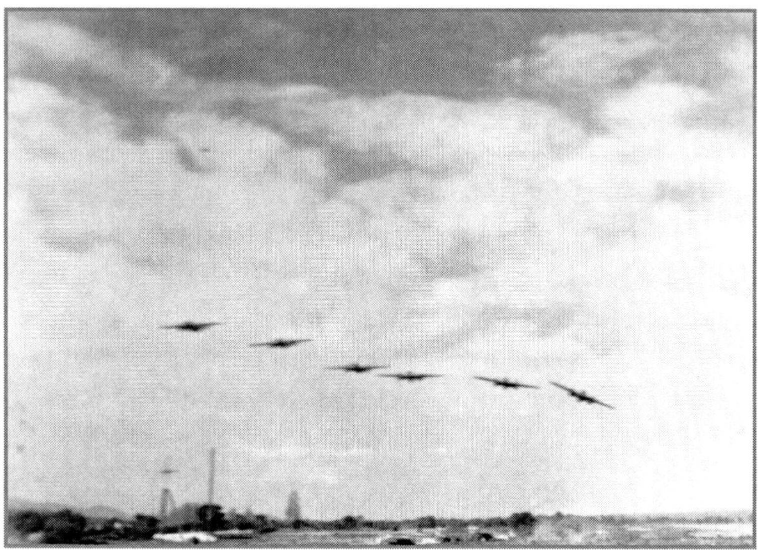

January 11  1st Lieut. George A. Smith, 2nd Lieuts. James L. Black and Frank T. Saunders Jr., S/Sgts. Dean Bryant and Roland O. Lowder were instantly killed this afternoon as their plane was making its approach to the Pompeii airfield after a practice mission. I witnessed this disaster. Prop wash combined with wind caused their plane to suddenly roll to the right while on final. The low wing caught the ground, and in an instant the plane flipped over on its back, hit the ground and exploded. Apparently 100 pound practice bombs blew up inside the airplane. Lieut. Smith, the pilot, came across with the original flight echelon in early 1943 and had completed 42 combat missions over enemy territory.

January 12  Funeral rites for the crew killed yesterday were held at 1300 hrs. this afternoon. The bodies were taken to Naples for burial. Chaplain Cooper officiated. We were issued heavy protective flak suits today which contain money purses and escape kits. Fifth Army has continued its slow advance, and is now less than four miles from the Cassino, Italy.

January 13  Tare Sugar went up with the mission today to Guidonia airfield, about twenty miles east of Rome. We showered the airbase with fragmentation bombs which exploded among hangers and parked aircraft. Other Group planes bombed the dispersal area east of the airfield with good results. The field was evidently an important target because 130 bombers took part in the attack. Three Bomb Groups were assigned the same mission. Ack-ack was intense, but not very accurate. One of our ships took some flak as we banked away from the target. All of our planes returned safely, but a crew from the 12th Group was shot down. After we returned from the raid, I talked to Lieut. Steve Puckett. He told me that he had dreaded the mission, possibly because he had not flown in a month. He said he almost got sick until the A/A began to pop, but curiously he felt better after they began shooting at him.

January 14 Some of the boys got down and kissed the good earth when they returned from today's mission. It was rough, and some of the men were comparing it to the hectic raids around Solomon, South Tunisia during the climactic days of that campaign. Nine planes from our squadron took off at 1315 hrs. The target was the marshaling yards and bridge at Pontecorvo, Italy. We were told it is a vital link in enemy supply line. Ack-ack was accurate and intense while we were on the bomb run. Damage to our flight was particularly heavy. One of our planes was seen to go down over the target, a wing shot off and burning. Edward Spray was aboard.

A second shot up plane limped back across the battle line, with the entire crew bailing out successfully. Maj. Lewis E. Keller, squadron C/O, made his third forced jump, bailing out from that airplane. In a third ship, radio/gunner Tech Sgt. Moran could not communicate with the rest of the crew in his heavily damaged plane. His intercom was shot away, and he bailed out over enemy territory. 2nd Lieut. D. L. Glade succeeded in bringing the crippled plane and the rest of the crew safely to the home base. A fourth plane was also crippled by the ack-ack, and the pilot, 2nd Lieut. C. J. Clark was blinded in one eye by flying glass. They landed safely at Pomigliano airfield. Our squadron losses were seven men and two planes. Of the seven airplanes returning from the mission, all were holed (damaged by bullets, cannon shells or flak), and five men were injured, but none critically.

This is a portion of Maj. Keller's mission report: "As soon as we dropped our last 1000 lb. bomb we received a near miss which wounded the pilot, Lieut. Swope. I was on board as copilot. The flak burst hit the left engine, causing the propeller to run away.

Lieut. Swope's left arm had been hit, and I took over flying the plane. Lieut. Swope immediately feathered the left prop. He took the ship back and made a right turn toward friendly territory while taking evasive action. We took additional near misses, damaging the right engine. I noticed the oil pressure was fluctuating seriously but as this was our only engine, we coaxed it across the bomb line at which time I ordered everyone to abandon ship.

Just as Lieut. Swope left the ship, the right engine ran away at uncontrollable speed and I feathered the propeller. I then realized how quiet it was with no engines, but time was wasting. I made two turns, one to the right and one to the left. Then I looked at my altimeter, airspeed and rate of climb instruments. My altitude was 5000 feet; my airspeed was 185 mph and my rate of climb about 1000 feet per minute down. I decided to jump, so I moved over to the left pilot seat which was pushed back. After trimming airplane, I bailed out."

January 15 Six 486th squadron planes joined with twelve others to target the marshaling yards at Foligno. We encountered ack-ack just before the target, but in contrast to yesterday's ordeal, it was light, scattered and inaccurate. The bomb pattern had a fair degree of accuracy on the marshaling yards. Some of our crewmen saw three enemy fighters on the way back. The gunners were rather disappointed that they offered no opposition. All planes and personnel came back safely.

Sgt. Greg Moore, the squadron PX man, has inaugurated a new set up where cigarettes and candy are meted out every other day, thus conserving the rations. The movie tonight was "Omaha Trail."

January 16    We destroyed the marshaling yards at Terni today. Large explosions in the target area were the result of a perfect bomb pattern which started at the north side of the tracks and continued to the sea side. There was no ack-ack over target with the only light A/A south of Ancona on the return. All planes and personnel returned safely.

Romance has blossomed in the bosom of the war weary 486th squadron. Cpl. Bill Dunnerman asked permission of Maj. Keller to marry one of the local signoras. She's lovely, but can't speak English nor can he speak Italian. However, Bill claims that she can understand him; perhaps it's the international language of love that every human understands.

January 17    The marshaling yards at either Sulmona or Giulianova were the designated primary targets today, but both targets were completely obscured by clouds. The formation sought the alternate target at the marshaling yards at Chiaravalle. The bomb pattern landed in the yards southwest of the town and extended through the town.

A sage observer of squadron activities put this note in the daily file: "It was with mingled emotions that we received several letters concerning two of our members. Everyone in our squadron will raise a farewell glass this evening, while the First Sergeant exhales a huge sigh of relief. The letters both came from hospitals. One of the letters informed us that Cpl. Lionel Levin was to be transferred to the Zone of the Interior (U.S.A.) for "further observation" and treatment. The other letter told us that PFC D. W. Cameron had been admitted to the hospital with a diagnosis of amnesia.

To call these men characters would be an understatement of classic portions. Their presence in the squadron has been made conspicuous by their frequent absences. Since their arrival in Italy, the Army has been a mere side line while they followed more lucrative pursuits. While the squadron was based at Foggia, they passed themselves off as realtors and succeeded in selling some property to a gullible Italian for $400. They sold a parked auto to another trusting Italian for $100. These were the stories that were making the rounds and neither one of them denied the allegations. It would appear that Cpl. Levin has succeeded in his determined vow to 'get home somehow', and it would appear that his business affiliate will be right on his heels. We will miss these men."

January 18 Six 486th planes took off this morning at 1020 hrs. to bomb a railroad viaduct at Terni, Italy. Reconnaissance photos showed that bombs from all four squadrons narrowly missed the target, with the 486th pattern coming closest. We did damage a part of Terni which is occupied by the Germans. Two planes were holed, but the damage was not serious.

For tonight's movie Capt. Shealy rented the theater in San Giuseppe, a nice little pocket-size cinema house replete with balcony and a bar in the lobby. We had chicken and dumplings for dinner tonight, an illustration of how well the 486th is eating since moving near to Naples. Rumor has it that a warehouse in Naples is stocked to the roof with bottled Coke.

On our guided trips through the ruins of Pompeii, the guides seem to rush through most of the ruins, but they linger long and dramatically at the building which had been used as a bordello. One of our stray bombs made a direct hit on that section of the ruins. The irony of this is not lost on us. Some surprising discoveries on the tour are: That the unearthed town is so large; that artifacts predating Pompeii been found, and that the towns were buried under ash carried by the wind rather than lava. A WAC being escorted through the ruins was seen blushing outside the love room of the ancient bachelor brothers! Tickets for the tour are five lire.

Maj. Lewis E. Keller, the squadron C/O, was in my estimation a bit swell-headed. He was anxious to fly Tare Sugar. We loaded the machine guns and put three crewmen aboard. I went along as copilot. Our flight path proceeded over Naples Bay and out to sea. All the 50 caliber guns were ready to fire. The bombardier's flexible gun was converted to a fixed gun operated by the pilots.

The Major fired the five cockpit operated guns at bursts in the water. The turret gunner was also firing his guns in the same direction. It was indeed a noisy and impressive amount of firepower. He would then try to hit the froth made by first burst with a second burst. After a while he tired of that, and flew low along the coast. We passed by a fishing boat and he circled around it. He called up to the overhead turret gunner and told him to shoot up that boat, but the gunner wouldn't do it. He knew better.

I never saw Maj. Keller much after that. His "mission" was to drive around in a Jeep and try to get try to get connected with girls. He would come into headquarters and sign reports or whatever paperwork was needed and then disappear for a week. Consequently, Capt. Charles Nathan, the Flight Surgeon, was basically running the outfit. He was a good officer, and an excellent physician.

This was the last flight that I took in Tare Sugar. She was assigned to the 487th squadron next to us. Col. Jones took the advice of several experienced pilots who thought the extra guns on Tare Sugar were the reason for her extra fuel consumption and were not needed. Lt. Col. Tokas had told them that they would have to get permission from 57th Wing Headquarters to take the extra strafing guns off. Col. Jones told them, "You have to fly these planes into combat. They should be set up for the best performance. Take the guns off if you don't want them."

January 19 The frost was really on the pumpkin this morning. Six 486th planes targeted the airport at Rieti. The leading box of planes made a wide turn from the initial point, which threw our 486th flight slightly off the assigned heading. The bombs fell among the hangers on the east side of the field. One of the hangers and the workshop were hit and an explosion, probably from oil storage was observed. No planes were seen on the field. There was no opposition and all planes returned safely. Lieut. Coleman was not so fortunate. His plane dropped bombs on the practice range near Foggia and was shot at by American A/A. They returned with some fresh flak damage, and Col. Jones said he would send pictures of Allied planes to the gun crews.

The Group Officers Club opened for the first time tonight with a celebration that lasted into the early hours. It is in a requisitioned house made comfortable with furniture acquired in Naples and elsewhere. Italian liquor flowed freely, and a band from Naples played with considerable spirit.

Two trucks loaded to capacity departed for the San Carlo opera house in Naples to hear La Traviata. Both trucks arrived at Naples in time for all to have a bite to eat and drink some vino before the performance. Cpl. Bartkowski's opinion was, "I enjoyed the opera very much, but there was too much singing! It gets monotonous hearing them sing all the time. I think they should talk now and then." Other opera goers included S/Sgts. Prichard and Hausner who returned in a festive mood after consuming two bottles of vermouth. They said it was really good, and it must've been. Both men insisted on serenading around their tent area at much too late an hour.

January 20 Six 486th planes bombed the railroad bridge east of Carsoli. Apparently every Group in the theater had the same target. Visibility was poor due to smoke and explosions caused by bombs dropped earlier in the morning. After our attack, we made a 360 degree turn about two minutes off the target and the bridge was still standing. There were however hits on the tracks. A/A was nil, and all planes returned safely.

Maj. Hackney took a plane to Cairo and will fetch back a stock of liquor for the Group Officers Club and also a supply for our own party. A $10 donation was put up by each officer. For several nights Mount Vesuvius has been flashing brightly, with streams of lava flowing down the upper flanks of the mountain. The usual small, dull patches of red have also included occasional showers of sparks which ride up into the air. From Naples, lava can be seen flowing a third of the way down the mountain. Naples is off-limits because of a typhus scare.

January 21 Two missions were flown today. The first target was the marshaling yards at Foligno. Targeting was done via a timed attack because of the heavy overcast. There was no A/A, and all planes returned safely. My plane departed on the second raid to the Avezzano marshaling yards almost as soon as the first mission returned. Clear weather helped the bombardiers, and we saw several hits on the west end of the yard. There was no opposition.

Col. Jones revealed to combat crews in the evening that shortly after midnight the Allies would launch an amphibious landing on the Anzio beaches south of Rome. The planned objective was to take the high ground facing the city. Two divisions and specialized troops using eighty-three landing vessels protected by five cruisers would do the job. Col. Jones said that our medium bombers had completed their part of the job eleven days ahead of schedule. The missions succeeded in cutting communications to Rome, and it appeared that this was done without arousing German suspicions. He wound up his comments by criticizing today's morning bomber formation. He was aboard one of the planes, and told us that the formation was spread out over five miles.

Assembling a formation of planes was a bit of a challenge for the pilots. The first flight of planes would take off one after the other and fly out about three minutes. The lead plane would turn back toward the field. Then the aircraft behind him would make their turns so that they formed a box-shaped grouping called a flight. There could be six, nine or twelve planes in a flight. It was kind of a trick to judge when to start turning, so that your aircraft was correctly positioned behind the leader on the downwind leg. The next flight of planes would take off as that was happening, and they would join up with the first box. It was repeated one more time for a typical sized formation of eighteen airplanes.

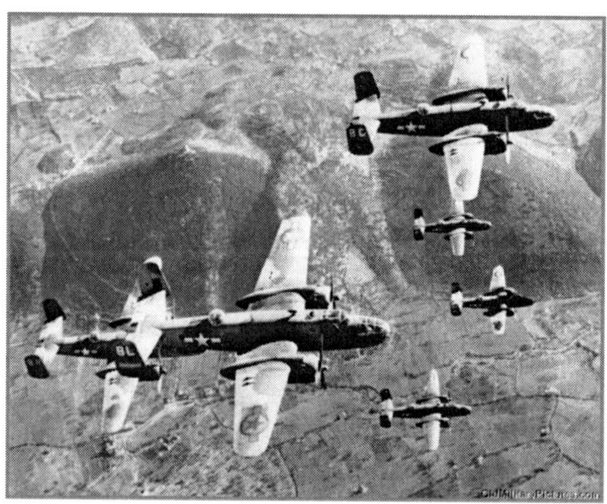

(Courtesy 57th Bomb Wing)

Our Group had four squadrons with twenty-four planes in each squadron. On a typical mission, three squadrons would put up six planes each and one of the squadrons would be on stand down. During an all-out attack, the Group would occasionally put up as many as seventy-two planes. I was the leader in the front flight on two of these mass formation missions.

January 22 We flew an afternoon mission to bomb a railroad junction north of the little town of Segni. Later photos showed direct hits on the railroad, and crews reported an explosion which came from nearby buildings. The A/A was pretty rough, and all planes from the 486th flight were holed. Ship 7H had the nose wheel door blown off, but returned safely.

The return route home brought the formation close to the Allied invaded beaches just twenty-eight miles south of Rome. Lieut. Hallahan said the operation appeared to be proceeding smoothly and in good order. "It was not like Salerno," he said. "There were no plumes of smoke and no confusion. The boats were lined up neatly and the cove looks like Naples harbor." Some of our planes also dropped 50,000 leaflets telling of the landing and asking the Germans to surrender. The leaflets said the following in German:

> *"Allied landing near Rome! Strong Fifth Army divisions with tanks and heavy artillery now stand between you and Rome. Your main line of defense in the South is turned. Whether you face to the North or South, you have the enemy in front of you and to the rear. The battle in this area becomes a battle of encirclement. Under the protection of heavy naval units and with the superior Allied air arm, a ring is closing inexorably. With one stroke your situation has become a desperate one. Every attempt at relief or escape can only lead to bloody losses, as at Stalingrad. The immediate future will lead you into*

*a cruel gauntlet under a hail of bullets from British and American planes."*

Only scattered A/A was reported by the three planes that dropped leaflets and all returned safely. One of our ships -Tuff Stuff, is the subject of lots of wagers. The engines have over 550 hours which is the second-highest in the Group. The wager is whether or not they'll reach 600 or 700 hours.

## Air Medal, Eighth Cluster Awarded

Fred W. Dyer, 066-4548, Capt., for meritorious achievement while participating in an aerial flight as pilot of a B-25 type aircraft in an attack near the town of Segni, Italy, on January 22, 1944. Denver, CO.

*January 22, 1944*

*Dear Eleanor,*

*As I have probably told you before, it is very difficult to write when there is no possibility of receiving mail for a month or more. The only consolation is that I will probably get five letters at once from you. Yesterday, I went on my third mission. Our Colonel tells us the news before it happens. It is very much more exciting and interesting to know why we bomb each target, and what use the land forces make of our operations. So far, our missions have been fairly easy except for one.*

*Combat is our only interest as it should be. Transportation is difficult, and the surrounding towns have little to offer. There are some interesting places with historical background. For instance, I have seen the ruins of Pompeii and Mount Vesuvius is next to us. If we stay in Italy I will probably have a chance to visit the Isle of Capri.*

*Every mission puts me closer to home. I would go on two a day if they would let me. I know that the best part of our lives will begin when we are together once more. That is what I am fighting for, and that is why I pray that peace will come soon. Until I return I am sending all my love.*

*Dale*

**January 23** **Our target was the crossroad at Avezzano. Five** ships were over the designated area at 1025 hrs. and returned with a sad story. Their bombs landed in town starting from the southwest corner of the large square and extended through the town on 120 degree heading. This result was not according to plan. Planes from the 489th had better luck, and laid down an excellent pattern which was verified by photographs.

The show tonight was "Jane Eyre" with Orson Welles. It was not very popular. The Dance Committee spent the day in Naples buying $3000 worth of liquor, and making a door-to-door campaign inviting women to the upcoming evening event. The Colonel succeeded in getting new American tents for the Group, and they can be seen popping out here and there. He also got some galoshes, but they are all size 8 and are appreciated by those like me whose feet happen to be the right size.

Two planes were sent to Bizerte, Tunisia for modification. Ship 6S is a B-25D, with 285 hours and 45 combat missions to her credit. She has neither name nor picture on her nose.

There is armor on the floor of the bombardier's compartment and in the turret as well. She is well-liked, a fast ship. This plane has given little trouble, and hasn't had an engine change. An ME-109 cannon shell went through one of the vertical stabilizers while over Athens in November. The crew was able to bring her back safely. The other plane, 6P, a B-25C, was named "Leaky Lucy" by Maj. Hackney. She has 333 hours and 52 combat missions. Her armor, armament and characteristics are similar to 6S. The picture on her nose is a nude woman on a latrine.

January 24 Intermittent rain caused the squadron to stand down today. Fifteen minutes after the stand down was declared, there wasn't a vehicle to be had within the squadron. Experienced joyriders concoct some "official" business to transact in the restricted city of Naples. Officers PX rations went on sale today and we were quite pleased with the variety and quantities after this week's disappointing mess meals. Capt. Hurley flew to Catania today to purchase fresh vegetables and fruits to supplement the quartermaster issue.

Lieut. Herman has an Italian houseboy who was apparently descended from a long line of landscape gardeners. This young man enlisted the help of several friends to lay out a drive lined with trees to the entrance of Lieut. Herman's tent. They did an excellent job, with several trees forming an arch to the door of the tent. After many favorable comments, the boys decided that their "mansion" should have a name and christened it "Villa Maria." Rumor has it that Maria is the name of Lieut. Herman's favorite signora.

January 25 We targeted a road junction at Artena this morning. It was completely obscured by clouds and our planes returned to base. Over our field, the formation leader asked operations if we should go back and he received an affirmative answer. Two airplanes landed, but I returned with four other ships and bombed through the clouds. Photos were not good, but served to show that the pattern probably fell near Gennaysano, which is about three miles northeast of the target.

Last night Sergeants Bunn and Padon fell into a well getting a cold bath on a cold night. No injuries were suffered.

Everyone put on their best uniform and went to Naples for our planned night on the town. There was plenty of liquor, and plenty of it was drunk. In a spirited effort, nine officers went down the street to a hospital and lugged a piano down three flights of stairs and up the street for two blocks so that we would have music. The girls were not noticeably beautiful, but some were good dancers. The hall itself was an elaborate affair of gold leaf, painted ceilings, crystal chandeliers, and brocaded walls.

Our squadron area is in the little town of Poggio Marino. Inhabitants say the buildings bordering the road were dynamited by the Germans. The population is poor. There is a little marketplace laid out each morning with handmade baskets, chairs, letters, etc. Baskets of oranges and apples are placed atop attractive leaves. The small shops are cluttered with cheap merchandise. The women seem to be hard-working and cheerful. All the men, young or old, appear cynical and without initiative. The newborn babies look undernourished, but the other kids have plenty of vigor. The village buildings look as if they were molded in wet lava by a giant child who tried, but couldn't quite get his corners square and lines straight. Roofs are of different levels, sprouting old thin chimneys at odd intervals. A few of the roofs are tiled, but most are just rounded off lava. All the structures are old.

Other 340th squadrons have their headquarters on the road which winds past the landing field, toward the town of Terzigno. The road is busy, filled with G.I. vehicles, carts and horses. Women walk by with vegetable baskets on their heads. We also see kids, and soldiers stringing wire or carrying typewriters. There is a general noise of woodcutting, hammering, yelling children, and the slush of vehicles going through.

There seems to be a considerable amount of pilfering by our fellows from the storehouse behind the mess Hall. Canned chicken, fruit, and fruit juices disappear right and left. Bread is a favorite item because it is a basis for late snacks in tents and rooms. The mess hall boys themselves often cook up a few pork chops late at night, or at least there have been pork chops smells emanating from the kitchen.

January 26 Icy patches caused several falling injuries this morning, and a stand down was declared. The Germans are putting up stiff resistance at Anzio. They counter-attacked, and drove our forces back across the Rapide River. Losses on both sides have been great. Rumor has it that a bunch of Allied tanks were wiped out when they tried to break out on the plains back of Cassino.

A drive is underway to clear some of the Italians from the base. Telephone wires have been cut, (once during a red alert), and much of it has been stolen. This will be hard on those who have been keeping women in their rooms. Mail hasn't been coming in regularly for the last week, probably because of the invasion. Tonight the cinema house in San Giuseppe presented "In Little Old New York" with Alice Faye, Fred McMurray, and Richard Green.

January 27  Todays combat missions may have caused us more headaches than the Germans. Our morning target was the railroad junction at Colleferro. Bombs landed in the field south of the target for another near miss. Heavy and accurate A/A was encountered over the defended hill south of Rome, and two airplanes were holed. The afternoon mission was to the marshaling yards at Orte. Ship 6P piloted by Capt. Willhite ran into trouble shortly after takeoff when due to hydraulic failure, two 1000 pound bombs dropped through the closed bomb bay doors, ripping them off. The bombs detonated harmlessly in a field. Capt. Willhite flew the plane out to sea and jettisoned the remaining bomb. He warned the crew to be ready to bail out. After the landing gear lowered normally, he brought the plane safely back to base.

The standby plane took his place in the formation and they proceeded to target. A small percentage of bombs struck the yards, but a greater percentage landed beyond the target. All planes returned safely with no A/A. A radio/gunner accidentally jettisoned his hatch on the afternoon mission. There is little real news from the landing at Anzio. The word from headquarters is that General Ira Baker has a plan to pick out an area and pound the hell out of it.

January 28  We went back to Orte today. The three squadrons had at least six hits on the tracks. "It couldn't have been better if we had dropped the bombs from a six foot ladder," said Lieut. Hayes. Several bomb bursts were observed on the railroad bridge north of the target which crosses the Tevere River. A/A was not accurate, and all planes returned safely. The day was warm and sunny, with ash from Vesuvius blowing toward the west. The local citizens say that you can tell the weather by the direction of the ash plume. South means it will be colder; east means rain, and west or north means warmer weather. Rotation of combat crews has come to a halt for the time being. The reason may be that they are waiting for General Baker to take command.

We had hamburgers for lunch with second helpings. Lieut. Forrester, our new athletic director, is getting all kinds of equipment ready. A volleyball court was set up today and soon the guys will be getting more than enough exercise. Capt. Brooks decided to throw the ball around for a while and wound up with a sprained ankle and a decision that he would stick to cards and other "sit down" forms of relaxation in the future. The movie tonight was "Ox Bow Incident" with Henry Fonda and a good cast. It was hardly a show for soldiers, but it was liked in some quarters.

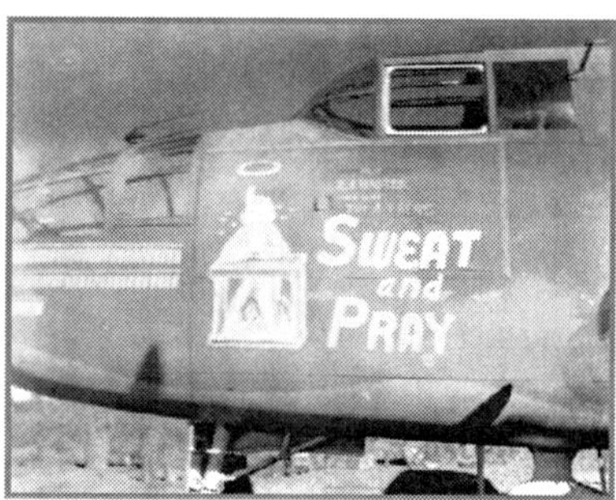


January 29 When early morning missions are flown, we sometimes are given a mission briefing on the prior evening. Last night we were assembled and given information for a morning mission to Perugia. Just before take-off, an alternate target, San Benevello, was rushed in. There were no instructions about just what in or around the town was to be bombed. The formation went over to the east Italian coast and flew up over the water. Most of the target was obscured by clouds, and the bombs were released early. They detonated in the water off San Benedetto. Some flak was encountered after "we woke up everything in southern Italy." All planes

returned safely. Pistols belonging to the combat enlisted men have been collected from them. They will be issued when missions are flown and returned to the armory afterward. Some of the men stand accused of shooting up the little towns nearby.

There is some justifiable grumbling going on because our APO has been changed four times. These changes are screwing up the mail. Lately, it has taken several months to give or receive mail. The Officers Club served a watery beer this evening. It came from Africa, and old-timers tell me that it was the first beer the group has had since July.

January 30  A road junction at Frascati was hit by twelve of our planes this morning. Considerable confusion exists about the results of the raid, but the opinion seems to be that because of nearly complete cloud cover they missed the junction. All of our 486th planes returned safely, but 7N, "Flying Jenny," a plane from the 487th was hit, damaging the left engine and hydraulic system. The flak hit them while they were on the bomb run, but they still managed to drop their bombs with the formation.

Flying Jenny was brought back to the base for a belly landing by Lieut. Forrester. It wound up a twisted mess of aluminum well off the end of the runway. The most serious injuries were the photographer's broken leg and arm. The other crewmen were shaken up but not badly hurt. T/Sgt. Paul Hoffman, the crew chief for Flying Jenny took pride that it was one of the best ships the 487th had. He almost cried when Capt. Coyle told him that Flying Jenny had crash landed and could not be repaired. Col. Jones has ordered the erection of several large black and yellow signs reading: "340th, Bombardment Group, The Best Damned Group There Is Product of the USA." He says he means it.

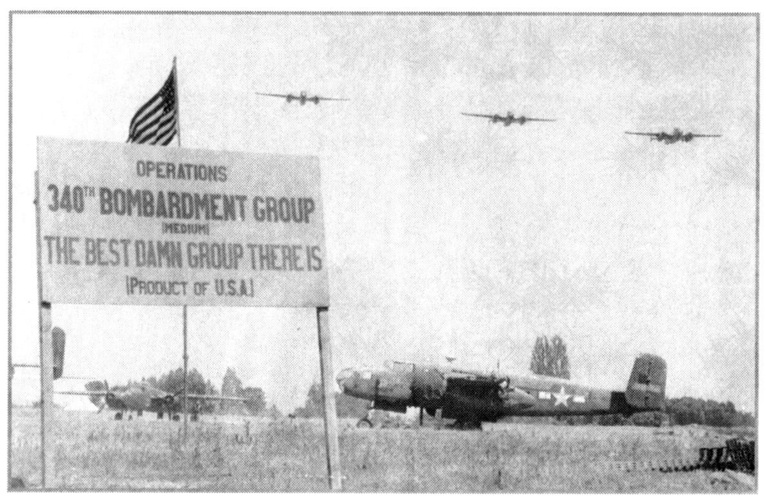


Courtesy Daniel Setzer

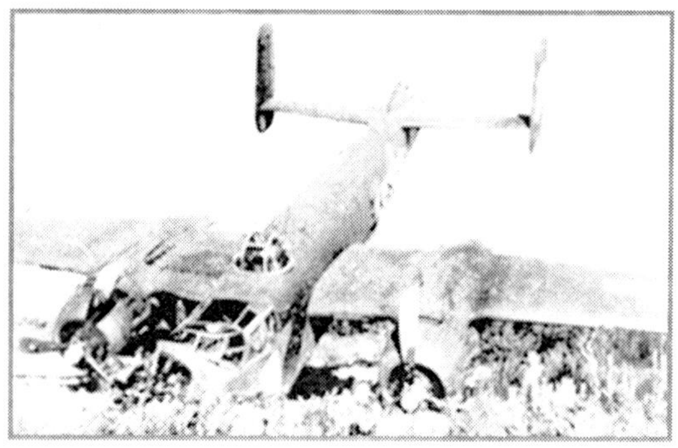

Courtesy 57th Bomb Wing

## Air Medal Award, Fifth Cluster Awarded

Harold L. Carson, 354-75834, T/Sgt., for meritorious achievement while participating in an aerial flight as a radio/gunner of a B-25 type aircraft in an attack upon a road bridge at Frascati, Italy, on 30 January 1944. Louisville, KY.

January 31 We were up early, and had a fine breakfast of fresh eggs. The eggs were our first in three weeks. We were getting a daily supply from a farmer in exchange for our transportation of agricultural supplies for him. This practice was discontinued after being frowned on by our inspectors. In an unrelated incident, a couple of lads got in trouble for working on their own in the grain hauling business. The vicinity of the volleyball court took on the appearance of a slaughterhouse today, with Lieut. Samuels butchering the cow recently purchased by food scroungers. The next few days will be a holiday in the mess hall from normal army fare. Geese have been landing near the runway at Foggia, but no one has gone hunting for them.

A morning mission to Valletri was canceled because our troops probably took care of the target on their own. Three of our planes braved a cold rainy morning to drop leaflets in the Cassino area. We have inherited those duties, called nickelling missions from the 12th Group because they will soon be leaving.

Part of the problem with our early bomb accuracy was that the lead bombardier used a British Mark Nine sight. The sight was basically a protractor. When the sight got lined up with the target, the bombardier pushed the button on the pendant which caused the bombs to drop. The bombardiers in the trailing airplanes would drop their bombs on cue from the front ship. There was of course a human factor, and the bombs were scattered quite a bit. The outfit had a reputation for plowing up graveyards all over southern Italy. For this reason, the morale was low when I arrived.

Lieut. Col. Tokas was in command of the 340th Bomb Group when I got there. In my estimation, he just didn't have it as a leader for that outfit. We were flying practice missions for formation flying when I arrived. We were also dropping dummy bombs. In early January a Lieutenant Colonel quietly joined the staff. Nobody knew who he was or why he was there. He would spend his time down on the line chewing the fat with the crew chiefs, and with the cooks and so on. This went on for a week. Suddenly, orders came up that he was going to be our new commanding officer. His name was Lieut. Col. Jones.

Col. Jones was a West Point graduate and shortly after his appointment to the 340th was made a full colonel at the age of 32. He was really on the ball. One of the first things he did was take an airplane down to Africa. He came back with a portable shower. It was immediately put to use and could handle six guys at a time. Sometimes there was a double line of men twenty deep queued up to use it. Before that, the squadron had no shower except for one that I had rigged up. The other fellows had to go twelve miles into town to the USO where there were showers. That situation had a very negative effect on squadron hygiene.

My assembly consisted of a showerhead made from aluminum tubing in which the aircraft shop drilled holes. We put a gasoline fired stove in an overhead room, and ran plumbing from the basement up to this room with a valve. We would fill several five gallon cans and put them on the stove. After the water was warm, we poured it into a third five gallon can which was connected by tubing down to the shower. The other guys in the squadron thought it was funny, but it worked. The commanding officer, executive officer, and squadron surgeon lived across the street and they would come over and use it.

One of the other things Col. Jones brought back from Africa was a large generator to provide power for the shop and lights for the living quarters. Up to that point, our only illumination came from carbide lamps which we purchased from the locals. Our accommodations were "borrowed" homes. All the buildings had high domed ceilings and were made of poured concrete. We were spread out along the street that was adjacent to the airfield. The houses had no windows, and during daytime the only light available was through the front doors which were left open. At night, the houses interiors resembled mine shafts, with faintly glowing carbide lamps.

The generator that Col. Jones brought back didn't have a power source to drive it. He took it down to the motor pool and told them to hook it up to a truck engine, which they immediately did. We had some pretty good mechanics. They connected power lines to the houses and from then on we had evening lighting. Those two improvements were really good for morale and Col. Jones' "stock" went up pretty high.

He caught a sergeant urinating against a wall and he cautioned him about it. Not long afterward, he caught the sergeant again doing the same thing. There was a latrine not far away and he was just too lazy to walk down and use it. Of course Col. Jones could have busted him, but he didn't choose to do that. Instead, he had the sergeant send his entire paycheck to his wife stateside, and the guy didn't have any money after that. We all thought that was good justice fairly met.

In October, 1943 the Luftwaffe bombed the Pompeii area and particularly targeted the harbor. They did a pretty good job of it, and the harbor docks were unusable. To offload supplies our guys were using Duck amphibious vehicles. The engineers were busy trying to clean up the clutter in the bay.

On the day following our arrival in Italy I was at Headquarters talking to the Operations Officer and a lieutenant walked in. It was O'Leary. Everyone gathered around and after greeting him warmly, wanted to know his story. German A/A hit his plane from below, setting both engines ablaze. After bailing out, he came down in a pasture near a rock wall. An ME-109 fighter strafed the wall while using the parachute as a target, and he jumped on the other side. The plane reversed course and strafed again on his side, so he again jumped over the wall. After the fighter left the area, he gathered up his parachute and warily proceeded toward a nearby village. There were no vehicles in the center square which meant there were probably no German soldiers. He moved into the square and saw a kid standing there. O'Leary threw the parachute to the boy who ran away with it.

He got connected up very quickly with the Greek underground. The Greeks would walk through pastures several hundred feet ahead of him. If the coast was clear, they would give the signal to come forward. He worked his way into Athens that way. He was sworn to secrecy about the rest of his journey back to our squadron. They sent him home right away. This often happened with returning pilots to ensure that their knowledge of the resistance would not be revealed if they were again shot down behind lines and taken prisoner. I don't know how many missions he had flown.

At that time pilots typically flew about fifty missions before being sent home. The Flight Surgeon would decide exactly how many you would fly. There was one fellow in the squadron who had been made a warrant officer instead of a lieutenant when he was commissioned. A certain percentage of graduates from cadets were made warrants. He was a good pilot. Before reaching the fifty mission mark, he went into Capt. Charles Nathan's office and said, "I'm not going to fly anymore missions." Capt. Nathan said, "Oh?" He said, "Yeah, I want to go home." The reply was, "I can't make you fly anymore missions, but you're not going home." Capt. Nathan arranged with Air Force Headquarters to have him assigned to Naples as kind of a courier pilot flying tiny L-4s. He came over and visited us one day. He made a pattern on the field and landed that L-4 crossway on the runway!

The broad runway at Pompeii was wide enough to handle four B-25s taking off at the same time.

While he was in Sicily, this warrant officer got access to an ME-109 fighter. It was in good shape except for the landing gear. He managed to scrounge parts from wrecked airplanes and make the plane flyable. A large crowd of pilots cheered when he boldly climbed in the plane and flew it off the field. Of course, there was a great clamor amongst the pilots to fly it. The first officer who attempted to fly it cracked up while landing. Those fighters had narrow undercarriages, and they were easy to ground loop. A Hawker Hurricane was sometimes flown by our pilots at Pompeii airfield, and I let it be known that I wanted to be checked out in it. I had high hopes that it would happen. The Vesuvius eruption destroyed that airplane, so I never had a chance to fly a fighter.

February 1 Pelting rain caused yet another mission cancellation. Even with the poor weather I was able to fly twenty missions this month, a good accumulation. The word is that Cassino has been surrounded by our troops on three sides. Today was payday, and gambling started early. The guys usually go at it for three or four days following payday. We got a generous supply of PX rations, with two cartons of good cigarettes, matches and candy. Beer was on our wish list, but was not available. Two teams were formed, and played a baseball double header while dodging raindrops.

The Italians just bundle up when it gets cold. They run around barefoot in this weather, not appearing to mind. If they have any shoes, they are simple wooden clogs, with a piece of canvas across the instep. We are amazed by the industry of the Italian girls. They drive cattle drawn carts, wash clothes, and appear hardier than the menfolk. The boys in one tent have adopted a sweetheart. Her name is Angelina, and she is the youngest (four years old) of ten children. She is full-faced, and has a low husky voice. They have donated food to her elderly father and urged him to take better care of her. They also bought her a dress which they claim "cost us plenty."

February 2 Our target today was the road junction in the village of Marino which is on the road to Rome. We formed up with several other flights, and it was difficult to define any individual bomb patterns. The intelligence team called it "an excellent Group job." Flack was intense and accurate, holing four airplanes.

Donuts and coffee were served at Operations for the first time. Crews returning from missions were debriefed on the line, and this will probably become standard practice as long as we have the donuts. There was some criticism, the men saying they would rather go to the squadron for a hot meal. Jell-O was served for the first time. It was found in an open case at a 5th Army salvage dump. This warehouse operates on such a scale that it cannot bother with cases of canned foods which have broken open. Our Mess Sergeants make weekly foraging trips to the warehouse to which we have been generously allowed access.

I joined a party of men on a trip to Caserta, which is the Royal Italian Palace. Due to restrictions, the entire palace was not open for inspection. Our jaws collectively dropped when we entered the rooms which were available for viewing. The palace and grounds are a spectacular homage to royalty. Patterned after Versailles, it rivals it in the opulent use of gold. Sculpted gardens extend out to the distant horizon. Allied headquarters is based there. Whatever future location that they are housed in almost certainly will be more modest.

February 3-4 No missions were flown either day because a late winter storm coated the area with ice. We had good thick steaks for lunch on the 3rd. We had chili tonight and one comment was, "It's worse than starving."

The fellows who go to Naples report the black market is rampant, especially in liquor. Further, Sgt. ____cciolo (name withheld) is rumored to have more than a passing connection to the black market. While the 340th Group was based in Sicily, he is believed to have befriended one of the mayors. These men were selected to replace the Fascist leaders kicked out after the invasion. These new mayors were associates of the American mobster Lucky Luciano. The famous criminal was in jail in America, but nevertheless had strong influence in Sicily. Luciano parlayed these connections in support of the Allied invasion in return for a reduced jail sentence. In effect the US government replaced the old mayors with the powerful men who had connections to Luciano.

Sgt. ____cciolo may have been the basis for Lieut. Milo Minderbinder in Catch-22. He was our supply sergeant, and he had access to many things that could be sold on the black market. The brass kind of ignored his activities because they may have reasoned it was easier to let him supply basic needs to the civilian population than to do it themselves. He never seemed to get in any trouble.

February 5 Despite a threat of snow we returned to combat, and our six plane flight led a thirty-six plane formation. Airborne frostbite is a consideration for gunner crewmen with reported temperatures aloft of -20 below. Open gun ports funnel the frigid air directly into the aft part of the plane and any exposed skin freezes in seconds. The target was the marshaling yards at Terni, but due to slight errors the bombs fell to the southwest of the yards. We did have a good pattern on the tracks. There was no opposition, and all planes returned safely. We had ham for lunch (more 5th Army surplus) and bologna for supper, also a first.

February 6 Today was one of those days which all of us would like to forget. A tragic accident killed five men from the 489th. The day broke clear, sunny, and cold. The morning was inexplicably wasted. A mission got underway at 1310 hrs. to bomb the road junction at Alfadina. As is customary, three standby planes took off and circled while the formation was being made up. Those planes were not needed on the mission and started back to the field. Near the ruins of Pompeii, plane 9K flown by Lieuts. Willtshire, Capson and Karvel with Sgts. Luczak, Miller and Wellington crashed. Bystanders said a wing appeared to come off, as if the ship might have struck a barrage balloon cable. Shortly after it crashed, the four 1000 pound bombs detonated. Somehow Lieut. Wiltshire survived and will recover from his injuries.

Our formation found the inland route clouded over, so we made a bomb run over the water at Frascati. Three squadrons, including the 486th, hit the junction squarely on the nose. A/A on the way out was scattered but fairly accurate. Lieut. Duchannan got a large hole a few inches from the seat of his pants.

The innumerable lights in Naples Harbor every night intrigue and mystify those of us who are blackout conscious. From our perspective, the illumination makes Naples an easy target to find. The engineering tent burned today, destroying a good typewriter. A newcomer to our squadron says he likes us. He commented that, "The older hands welcome the new ones as old friends."

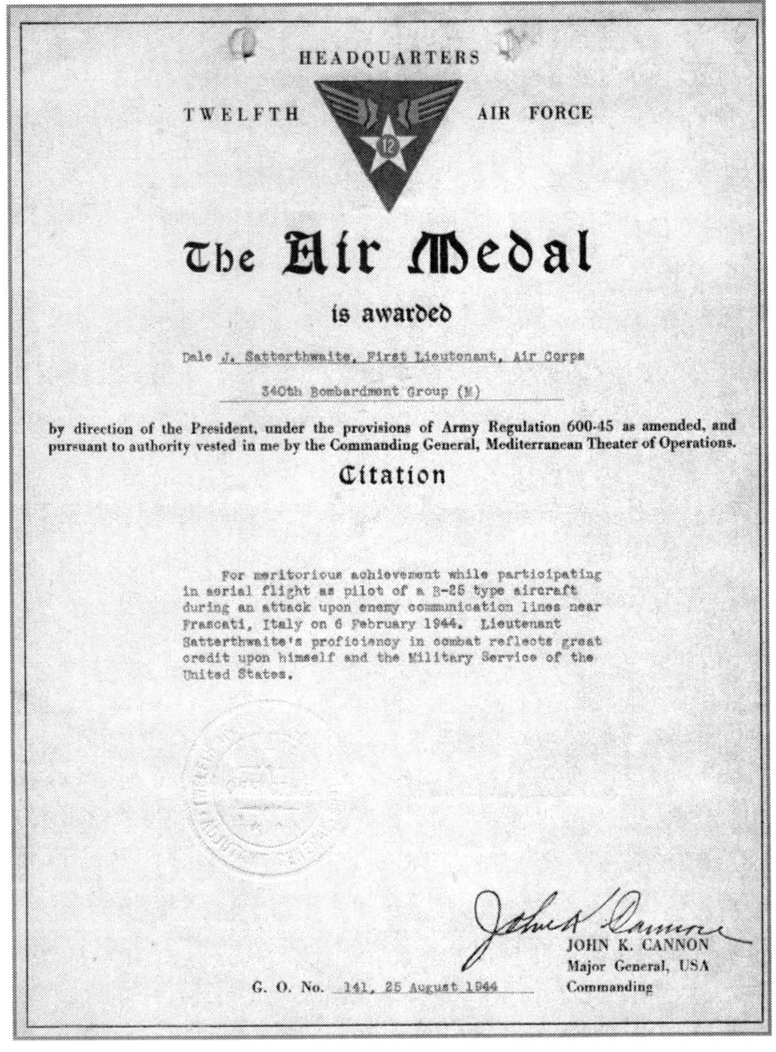

HEADQUARTERS

TWELFTH AIR FORCE

# The Air Medal

is awarded

Dale J. Satterthwaite, First Lieutenant, Air Corps

340th Bombardment Group (M)

by direction of the President, under the provisions of Army Regulation 600-45 as amended, and pursuant to authority vested in me by the Commanding General, Mediterranean Theater of Operations.

Citation

For meritorious achievement while participating in aerial flight as pilot of a B-25 type aircraft during an attack upon enemy communication lines near Frascati, Italy on 6 February 1944. Lieutenant Satterthwaite's proficiency in combat reflects great credit upon himself and the Military Service of the United States.

JOHN K. CANNON
Major General, USA
Commanding

G. O. No. 141, 25 August 1944

February 7 Twelve planes of the 486th took off at 1410 hrs. to bomb the marshaling yards at Viterbo. Our planes led the mission, with Col. A. C. Agan, a member of General Baker's staff riding as observer. We hit the yards squarely, and also laid a pattern across the road and railroad south of the chokepoint. Four German fighters circled at a distance, but they did not close in and Spitfires chased them back north.

More guys have been going to the opera and enjoying it. One sergeant said, "I never was an opera lover in civilian life, but I do enjoy the ones that I have seen. When you come right down to it, I would much rather see a good jazz band, but we can't afford to be too choosy out here."

## Air Medal Awarded

Harvard F. Stewart, Jr., 067-3290, First Lieut., for meritorious achievement while participating in an aerial flight as a bombardier of a B-25 type aircraft in an attack upon the marshaling yards at Viterbo, Italy on 7 February 1944. West Chester, PA.

February 8 Our instructions today were to flatten the town of Cisterna di Roma and we did. We were told that the Germans were preparing to hide tanks inside some of the houses. Two flights with eleven planes each were over the town at 1010 hrs., and dropped 88 1000 lb. bombs. Both patterns landed squarely in the center. Lieut. Stein said he could see people scampering down the streets. Five planes were holed, but all returned safely. Intelligence reported that our Allied artillery guns blasted enemy anti-aircraft positions when our planes came over. Three planes from the 486th dropped pamphlets in the Avezzano area this afternoon. There was no opposition. The rumor is that we will soon start a drive to capture Cassino and Cisterna.

February 9 The mission assignment was to lend close support to embattled troops fighting at the Anzio bridgehead. The target was a triangle formed by a railroad and two highways near Carroceto. Twelve 486th planes hit the area at 1420 hrs. and dropped their bombs with good effect. A/A was heavy and accurate. 7V, piloted by Lieut. Foster, had its brakes and flaps shot out. 7M, piloted by Lieut. Puckett, sustained damage to the hydraulic lines.

Both ships returned safely to the field and made successful emergency landings. Everyone else returned safely. A sizable amount of mail came in today, including some Xmas packages which were apparently lying around in some remote spot since the early part of December.

A packed party celebrated the completion of the new Day Room. It is a wood structure, walled with insulating material. Located on the line, it has several neat homemade pieces of furniture, a bar, and two stoves. Those who helped in its construction are very proud of it. This warm quiet room is ideal for reading and chess games. It is a nice place to while away a few hours on non-mission days.

February 10 Morning skies were crisp and clear, nevertheless a stand down was declared with no apparent reason. We quickly understood when the wind shifted, which brought a deluge of rain lasting all afternoon and evening. The usual vehicle shortage occurred immediately after the stand down was announced. In addition to Naples, Pompeii and Torre Annunziata are frequently visited by off-duty troops who have transportation. Those not fortunate enough to get a vehicle content themselves with the local vino emporiums in Poggiomarino. Five lucky airmen left for the states today after completing their combat tour. Lieut. Bill Mayor, one of the five, was so excited about getting everything together that he forgot his orders. A messenger chased him all away to Naples with the precious documents.

February 11 Rain, thunder, lightning and a downpour of hailstones made take off impossible. Troops at the front are badly in need of our support. Despite the unfavorable weather, combat crews were on the alert until 1230 hrs.

Men returning from Capri are sold on the island. During winter months the boat trip to the island can be rough. There is no heat or hot water, but real sheets and innerspring mattresses are compensation enough. The food is said to be good and the hotel bar never closes. Enlisted men are only permitted a three day stay. The short sojourn is barely long enough to get a look at Tiberius' Castle between bouts at the bar. Combat crews have seven days leave. The Blue Grotto is often impossible to see by boat because sea conditions are too dangerous for small craft. Overall, the island is a pleasant escape from the warring world.

February 12 Twelve ships took off at 1030 hrs. with capacity bomb loads aimed at a railroad junction at Campoleoni, Italy. They flattened the railway junction and station. Ack-ack was heavy, intense and accurate. Eleven of our ships were holed, and 6R went down over the target. The plane was last seen banking away from the formation with damage to the right stabilizer. Crewmen in the ship closest to her saw one parachute opening. Other formations reported seeing all six parachutes in the air as they left the target area. Time alone will assure us of the fate of our absent comrades. The plane was by crewed by Officers Jim Boston, Charles Chandler, Rob Alexander, and Sergeants William Isaacrowitz and Paul Ruppert.

The little red funicular railway runs up to the base of the cone at Vesuvius, but most visitors ride up to the base in a Jeep and walk the remainder of the way. They are accompanied by guides who make ashtray souvenirs by planting pennies in hot lava. Lately, we have felt the rumble when the cone is about to cough. Steam can be seen coming from crevices. Pompeii airfield is only ten miles from the mountain which dominates the southern sky. Some daring souls go up to where they can look into the crater. They run the risk of having a piece of hot lava wrapped around their necks. Sgt. Parrington says he did it, but wishes he hadn't.

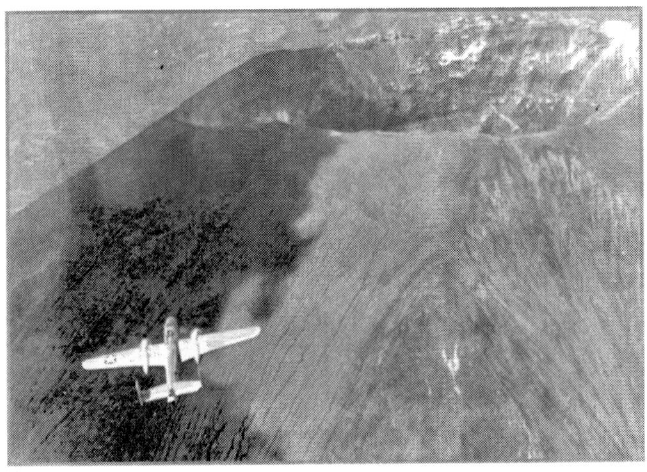

(Courtesy 57th Bomb Wing)

February 13 Mount Vesuvius appeared this morning in a garb of snow, reaching from the lower slopes to merge with the white cloud cover. The Lattar Mountains, which rise out of the sea at Sorrento, were equally beautiful in their winter dress. Ten planes of the 486th loaded with 500 pound bombs attacked a vehicle and car park located between Lake Albano and Lake Lemi. All the bombs fell in the target area, and we witnessed and felt four or five massive explosions. One copilot saw a single motor vehicle on the main road going like a bat out of hell. The ack-ack was intense and accurate, with four ships holed. 7M, "Tuff Stuff" received a direct hit in the bomb bay, and was seen to crash on the beach, a blazing inferno. The fate of officers Chet Keough, Larry Lewis, Charles Klujaza, and Sergeants Rob Rosado, John Weber and Dale Click is unknown. Our other planes did return with Lieut. Hayes slightly injured by a piece of flak.

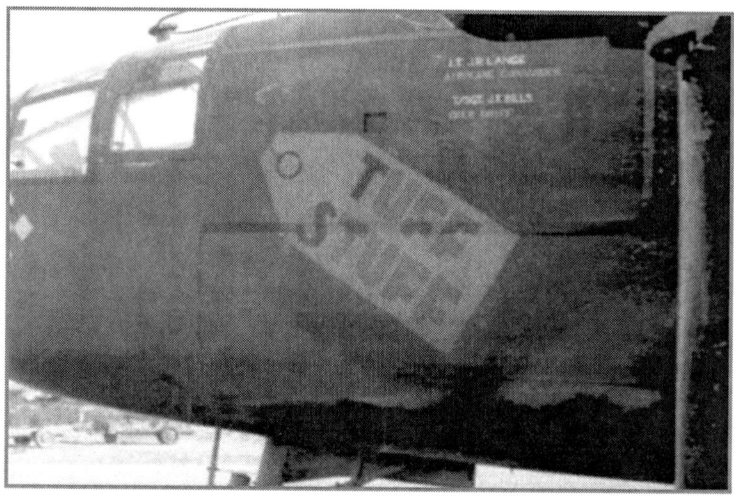

(Courtesy 57th Bomb Wing)

The 488th also flew a mission that day. Here is a report about one of their officers:

## Distinguished Flying Cross Awarded

The Distinguished Flying Cross is awarded to the following named personnel, Air Corps, United States Army: George L. Wells, 040-5510, Capt., 488th Bomb Sq., 340th Bomb Group. For extraordinary achievement while participating in an aerial flight as pilot of a B-25 type aircraft. On 13 February, 1944, Capt. Wells, in support of the Anzio Beach head, Italy, led a formation against a heavy enemy troop, gun and supply concentration near Campoleoni, Italy. While on the bomb run, the formation was met by a withering barrage of heavy, intense and accurate antiaircraft fire. His plane was holed in many places, including a burst in the left rudder which severed the cables and controls. Displaying superb flying ability, he managed to keep the formation intact, thereby enabling the bombardiers to drop their bombs in the target area with devastating effect. Unable to maintain the crippled aircraft in formation, he returned unescorted and landed safely at his own base. His aggressiveness, courage, and devotion to duty on this and many other combat missions have reflected great credit upon himself and the Armed Forces of the United States. Cedar Brook, NY.

February 14  My airplane was with five other B-25s over the Perugia marshaling yards at 1013 hrs. today. We dropped a good pattern of 1000 pound bombs over the highway and tracks. A/A was scattered and fairly accurate, and three planes were holed. One twin-engine enemy aircraft was sighted, but after receiving fire from one of our gunners it turned away. All returned safely with no casualties.

Lieut. Lewis and Lieut. Klujaza and Flight Officer Keough, who bailed out of their crippled ship yesterday, returned to the fold today. They were none the worse for their harrowing experience. They and Sgt. Click were picked up by a destroyer after swimming around in the cold water for an hour. Sgt. Click is in the hospital. No word is been received on Sergeants Rosato and Weber.

Someone in the cook's tent located a fiddle and music of the barn dance variety was heard coming from their tent. We don't have a lot of enthusiasm for this music and would prefer some sophisticated swing.

February 15  There was an evening briefing on today's target, which was the highly publicized monastery at Monte Cassino. Two flights with twelve planes, was over the Abbey at 1100 hrs. We dropped forty-eight 1000 lb. bombs, with a majority of them landing on or near the buildings which caused fires and explosions. The buildings were obscured by smoke, and photographs did not reveal much. With massive damage to the visible areas, it appeared that Monte Cassino was turned to rubble. There was little A/A and all our planes returned safely.

A new portable Victrola, which Sgt. Stellato happened upon during one of his many excursions, was purchased for the Day Room. It's a neat little Italian made job, and no doubt will get much use. Cpl. McBride suffered an embarrassing moment today. While driving a weapons carrier on some mission, he became annoyed at the driver of an Italian sedan. Upon passing the sedan, he put forth language unbecoming a member of the Air Force. Much to his discomfort, a shiny gold star adorned the shoulder of one passenger. He now has a new list of unpleasant assignments.

The Allied Command thought that the Germans were using Monte Cassino as an observation point and as a hardened battery for their artillery. Our troops were positioned in the valley below. For whatever reason, the Germans had not occupied Monte Cassino. They were in the hills next to it. After we bombed it, they did occupy the site, and they felt justified to do so. In retrospect, it was a mistake to bomb it because it created a lot of protected positions for their 88 mm cannons. The Germans also used the shattered masonry as shelter for their snipers. This was a very old structure with historical significance. The Germans had allowed the monastery leaders to move many of their artifacts out of harm's way sometime earlier.

Before we arrived, there was a monstrous big attack there. B-24s, B-17s and B-26s had spread bombs all over that mountain. On my first Cassino mission I was able to see our bombs go down to the target. The crude Mark Nine sight worked well enough to aim our bombs right into the center. Our formation circled to the right, which presented a good view of the collapsing roof. Unfortunately, this mission didn't help our ground troops around there very much.

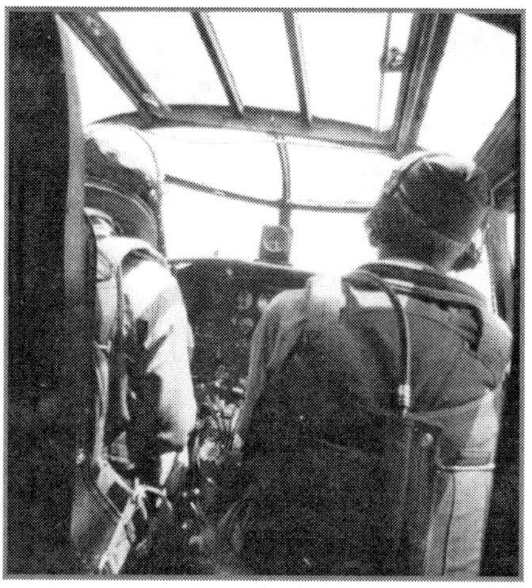

## Over Cassino

I was still flying as copilot on these missions, but treated with easy consideration by the first pilots and allowed to perform takeoffs and landings. On the second mission to Cassino, we had what might be my closest call. My ship must have been flying on the right side of the formation because Nelson Dozier, the first pilot had his seat pushed way back so that I could see the aircraft on my left. We got into heavy and accurate antiaircraft fire on the bomb run. Nelson slid his seat forward and said, "I'm going to take it."

Suddenly there was a hell of a bang, and some of our instruments went dead. There was a continuous roaring wind which whipped paper and other debris around like a tornado inside the airplane. I knew that we had been hit, but didn't know the entry point or the extent of damage. As far as I could tell there was no fire. We finished up the bomb run and Nelson said, "Is anybody hurt?"

Courtney the bombardier said, "I am." Nelson had me go check on him. As I moved towards him, Courtney threw something and I caught it. It was hot. He pulled his flak jacket out of the tunnel and it was torn and smoking. He was bruised, burned and cut from his chest down to his belt. The tail end of an 88 mm shell came through the Plexiglas in the nose. It went right over the top of his flak jacket while he was looking through the bomb sight. This four-inch piece of metal stopped next to his belt! Fortunately the Plexiglas had stopped most of its velocity. It may have been falling when it hit us.

The thing that made all the noise and made the instruments go dead was a second big flak hit. It entered from the bottom and exited through the top of the airplane. The blast made a four inch hole where Nelson had been sitting before he slid his seat forward two seconds earlier. If he hadn't moved, it would have hit him under the seat and in the legs. It cut a bunch of wires and cables which caused the instruments to go dead. When the flak exited, it took out a dinner plate sized piece of the top turret glass. Somehow the turret gunner's injuries were limited to cuts on his neck and a slight concussion. Air rushing in through the shattered nose and out the gun turret caused the whirlwind and noise.

After rendering some first aid, I returned to the cockpit amazed that we were still in the air. Nelson said the ailerons were OK, but the rudders were very stiff. We cycled the landing gear early to make sure it was working. Nelson released a red flare over the field and made a standard slow approach rather than our usual high-speed turn. The landing was fairly normal, and we climbed down to survey the damage from the outside. Courtney was in hospital for a couple days and the ship was moved to the shop where it remained for two weeks.

## Air Metal, Second Cluster Awarded

Courtney G. Pitkin, 040-4535, First Lieut., for meritorious achievement while participating in an aerial flight as a bombardier of a B-25 type aircraft in an attack upon military installations Cassino, Italy on 15 February, 1944. Denver, CO.

Dale J. Satterthwaite, 080-4516, 2nd Lieut. for meritorious achievement while participating in aerial flight as pilot of a B-25 type aircraft in an attack upon enemy military installations Cassino, Italy, on 15 February 1944. Oaklawn, Illinois.

February 16 The lead plane on today's mission was from the 488th. While over the marshaling yards at Campoleone it was hit directly by an 88 mm shell and went down in flames. We reported seeing one open parachute. The copilot of the ship was assistant Group Operations Officer, Maj. Gersky. Flak also hit two planes from our flight. 6J made an emergency landing at Pompeii with the plane shot full of holes. S/Sgt. Kelsey was wounded in the right arm and believed to have suffered a fracture. 6M returned with a large hole in the fuselage near the tail, created when an 88 mm shell went through without exploding. Many drinks were shared by that crew in the evening.

February 17 Our target today did not have a name. It was a pinpoint near Highway #8, which parallels the Tiber out of Rome to the sea. The six planes dropped their bombs slightly to the right of the pinpoint. A/A was light and all returned safely.

A little diversion was added to the opera today attended by thirty of our men. "Cavellerio Rusticana" was a short opera with two ballets," Bolero and Dance of the Hours." All comments were favorable and everyone seemed to enjoy the performance.

February 18 Six of our ships attacked the marshaling yards at Foligno. Shortly after takeoff, 7S returned to the base due to mechanical failure. The remaining ships were over the target at 1000 hrs. and dropped their bombs with a fair degree of accuracy. One building in the target area just south of the aiming point was observed to be on fire. No ack-ack or fighter opposition was encountered and all ships returned home safely.

The rest camp on the Isle of Capri has been reopened after being "off-limits" for several weeks due to the typhus epidemic. Several crewmembers departed for a few days of well-earned rest. A catholic memorial service for all lost 340th Group personnel was held this morning at one of the local churches. Members of all faiths were invited to attend. In our squadron, those who were not on duty attended to a man. The church was heavily draped in deep mourning and displayed an American flag. Chaplin Cooper conducted a short service afterword and we sang some hymns.

February 19 We flew two missions today over the fierce battle raging at Anzio beachhead south of Cisterna. The 321st Group led both missions over the target. They lost a total of eight planes in the hail of flak which came from German positions. Most of the fire came from the cliffs over the beachhead. This unbelievable loss of thirty-eight men was the highest single day casualty count by one of our B-25 equipped Groups during my deployment.

One of their planes bellied in on our field and burned. All crew members got out safely, and in a hurry. Our ships dropped their fragmentation cluster bombs in the target area which was full of troops and supplies. The bombardment left many vehicles ablaze and we could only guess at the number of Axis soldiers killed or wounded. We made a sharp right turn after the bomb run and avoided some of the flak. The Germans may have been holding their fire from the cliffs. While we were making our bomb run, dive bombers were overhead looking for targets. Despite our good fortune, all the planes in our flight had fresh damage, but returned safely.

Maj. Hackney is now the C/O of the 486th. Maj. Keller has become Group Operations Officer. Lieut. Gibson finished his 50th mission this afternoon, and is about ready to turn in his tools. The show tonight was Barbara Stanwyck in "Lady of Burlesque." A fellow viewer's opinion was, "I disliked it as much the third time I saw it as the first."

February 20 Anzio again received several visits from us. I flew with the morning group and we dropped a nice pattern along the road bordering the woods. Flak was moderate, but inaccurate because they were deflection shots. Enemy fire came from the dreaded area around Lake Albano. Our planes were the only ones to hit the target, and we put all bombs in the target area. The thirty-six planes on the afternoon mission brought their bombs back. We got a thank you telegram from the Commanding General in the beachhead which expressed his appreciation for today's air support. He stated that, "Bombing was the deciding factor in the repulse of the enemy's attack. Lost ground has been recaptured."

February 21 A stand-down was announced late last night; a little too late for the heavy drinkers to take advantage of it. Three full bags of mail came in today which ends the recent postal drought. Several former boogie artists are trying to brush up their skills on the piano in the Day Room.

February 22 I attended a predawn briefing for an attack on the marshaling yards at Foligno. We carried 1000 pound bombs today, and our box of planes led the other flights to the target. The flight path took us close to Perugia where flak was heavy and accurate. All six of our planes were struck by enemy fire before we pulled away. Because of this, the 489th led the squadrons in. Despite the damage to our airplanes, our bombs hit the target dead center in a concentrated pattern. "I followed the bombs all the way down," said S/Sgt. Hunt. "They seem to converge and go down as a single bomb." Lieut. Somers, in 6J, was hit by a piece of flak in the forehead. The copilot, Flight Officer Leggett, took over while the bombardier gave first aid. They brought the ship in nicely, and Lieut. Somers was taken to the hospital. Capt. Sethen announced later in the day that he had died.

## Distinguished Flying Cross Awarded (Posthumous)

Wilber E. Somers, 043-7070, Second Lieut., 486th Bomb Sq., 340th Bomb Group, for extraordinary achievement while participating in an aerial flight as pilot of a B-25 type aircraft. On February 22, 1944, Lieut. Somers flew in an attack upon the Foligno marshaling yards, Italy, a vital link in enemy supply lines. Despite heavy, intense, and accurate antiaircraft fire which heavily damaged his aircraft on approach to the target, Lieut. Somers courageously continued in formation, enabling his bombardier to release his bombs with devastating effect upon the objective. Turning from the bomb run, Lieut. Somers was fatally injured by a burst of antiaircraft fire. His selfless devotion to duty, and his outstanding proficiency as a combat pilot reflect highest credit upon himself and the Armed Forces of the United States. Mr. W. Earl Somers, Sr. 1308 5th Avenue. Coeur d'Alene, ID.

## Air Medal, Second Cluster Awarded

James E. Turtle, 078-9073, First Lieut., for meritorious achievement while participating in an aerial flight as pilot of a B-25 type aircraft in an attack upon the marshaling yards at Foligno, Italy February 22, 1944. Pensacola, FL.

Joseph B. Ross, 081-5392 First Lieut., for meritorious achievement while participating in an aerial flight as pilot of a B-25 type aircraft in an attack upon the marshaling yards at Foligno, Italy February 22, 1944. New York, NY.

February 23 A dark sky and intermittent rain brought a stand-down today. At 1330 hrs. Chaplain Cooper conducted a brief ceremony for Lieut. Somers. The body was taken to the American military cemetery in Naples where, on a pretty hill overlooking the city and its harbor and snow-Covered Vesuvius, Lieut. Somers was laid to rest.

February 24 The recently constructed ME-109 base at Fabrica north of Rome was our target. These planes have been attacking the Anzio bridgehead. Five of our planes were over the target shortly before noon, and dropped frags (fragmentation bombs) and 250 lb. bombs on each runway and dispersal areas. Sgt. Todd reported seeing many fires, easily identified as burning planes. Allied strategy was to flush the planes into the air, and then bomb them when they return for refueling. It seemed to work, and eighteen planes were claimed by intelligence officers to be destroyed. All our planes returned safely, reporting only a single burst of flak.

The bombardiers will begin using Norden bomb sights very soon. The crews who aren't familiar with the Norden sight aren't happy. They point to recent heavy losses of the 321st Group, and blame the Norden sight. Today's mission was the 100th for 6D, "Cow Town Avenger." Lieut. Pilloway and S/Sgt. Hart have been eager to run up the record for her, and she's the first In the Group to reach the century mark.

Last night's show "Kid Rookie" starring Sterling Holloway, was a walloping success. "The best stage show I've ever seen," said one man. "Worth five dollars," said another. The band was tops and the pacing was swift and smooth. The performers were amongst the best.

February 25 High winds were accompanied by sheets of rain. Opera has taken the squadron by storm. Many men are going for the first time and are getting a kick out of the performances. Their opinions of the performances are remarkably good. "Barber of Seville" was fairly popular. "Aida" was liked for splendid sets and good singing. "Pagliacci" was best liked for its pleasant, familiar music.

Sgt. McKivisson suffered a concussion in last week's motorcycle accident and is suffering from amnesia. He only remembers recent experiences. McKivisson seems eager to return to flying status, and may be allowed to do so. Doctors hope that flying will help jolt him back to normal.

I only went to the opera one time and the performance was La Bohème. The sold out show was on a Saturday afternoon, and the predominantly Italian crowd was boisterous. They were a critical bunch when it came to opera, and alternately booed and cheered the troupe. Mimi the female character is supposed to be a slightly built woman, further emaciated by tuberculosis. At the conclusion of the opera, Rodolfo is supposed to pick her up and carry her to a divan. The woman playing Mimi was closer to 200 pounds and there was no way Rodolfo could pick her up. She collapsed back on him, and he dragged her across the stage. The crowd objected mightily to this story variation.

Opera was a part of our daily lives however. The 486th cooks were Italians who sang opera arias while they worked. Beautiful baritone and tenor voices would fill the squadron area, and some of the fellows grew so accustomed to these frequently sung tunes that they would whistle or hum along.

February 26 A steady downpour continued until afternoon. One of the fellows had some harsh criticism for the Red Cross, saying, "I don't see the point in sending five civilians over here to give donuts and coffee to their friends." He thinks the Salvation Army is the only organization worth a hoot. The guys on the line are preparing the basketball court. The next few days should find a game in full swing. The motor pool has become a favorite lounging spot since it was learned that they mysteriously acquired a barrel of vino. Lieut. Tom Bowden says, "At last we're getting on the ball around here, but we should find out the donor's name and address so the barrel can be refilled at regular intervals."

February 27 Take off was delayed, and then abandoned altogether by freezing rain. Sergeants Clarkson, Casey, and Bradley returned from an extended stay on the Isle of Capri. They left the squadron with seven day passes, but they "accidentally" missed the return boat and couldn't catch another one for four more days. All were much impressed by the meals, conveniences etc. offered on the Isle and were sorry that they finally had to get out. Our mess hall supply was broken into sometime after dark and relieved of a large amount of flour and spam, which in these times is hard to procure. The Provost Marshal is hot on the trail of the culprit. If caught with the goods, he will be severely dealt with.

February 28 We were determined to end the recent stand down. Eighteen planes departed Pompeii field in route to Camino which is located north of Rome. Cloud cover prevented them finding the target, and some crews dropped their bombs through the clouds with uncertain results. Seven planes returned with their bombs. On the way home, S/Sgt. Crosby received a severe cut on the head which was caused by flak fired from Gaeta point. Restrictions on the sale of grain and meat are off, and shops are displaying their wares. Pork chops sell for about a $1.20 a pound. Some black market sales continue; the underground price for wheat is $1.00 per kilo.

February 29 Sunshine parted the clouds at noon, and a mission to dropped frags north of Cisterna was dispatched on short notice. No doubt the generals want to let our enemy know that we are still around. Heavy and intense ack-ack holed five of our ships, but all returned safely.

GI stoves have been supplied to the squadron now that spring is here. As they say, timing is everything. A number of men have purchased locally made cameos, and are pasting them to their letters and sending them home. One cameo carver works at his home in Torre del Greco. His shells are first glued to a stick for easier handling. With a tiny chisel he cuts the soft outside into a bas-relief figure. Cameos are sold by their size, and a nice one about an inch wide sells for seven dollars.

In early March I had flown about twenty-five missions, and was experienced enough to qualify as a first pilot. A more modern job title for first pilot would be Aircraft Commander. When pilots arrived from the states, they were assigned to fly and train with various squadron pilots as a copilot. After flying some missions, they were judged for their suitability as a first pilot. These decisions were left in the hands of the experienced pilots. If the pilot arrived in a combat zone flying as copilot, they usually transitioned to first pilot after a greater number of missions. Every pilot joining the B-25 combat units had a chance to make first pilot, and thereby be promoted to first lieutenant. The heavy bomber pilots were treated in a different manner. Crews of B-17 and B-24 bombers who deployed to Europe stayed in their respective pilot, copilot designations throughout their tour.

Nelson Dozier took such a personal interest in my progress that it was almost like being in school again. The rub was that he expected me to match his skill. He was the one who was vested with the business of putting a final seal of approval on my transition to first pilot. He was decent and thoughtful enough to commend my performance on our rough Cassino mission.

In early March Col. Jones called all the flight crews into an assembly. He asked, "Who has experience with the Norden bomb sight?" There were a scattered number, perhaps a dozen pilots and bombardiers of which I was one, who had used the Norden sight. He put the Norden sight in lead airplanes and we were designated for those crews. In truth, I had only flown two training missions with it, but that was enough experience. Thus, my transition from copilot to flight leader took the space of two weeks.

I needed a new bombardier, and I was coupled up with a fellow named Cyril Staub. He stood about six feet four inches and was very slender. While off duty Cyril wore cowboy boots in which he loped along with easy grace. He was younger than me, of dark complexion and generous with his magical smile. The two of us traveled around a good deal together. We were once sketched by an amateur cartoonist in the squadron who thought we looked like Mutt and Jeff from the comics. I was five feet six inches and weighed 125 pounds. Pilots and bombardiers were the only crew members who were teamed together. Engineer/gunners and copilots frequently changed ships. Cyril and I went up and practiced bomb runs together, and then we were assigned a target.

On our first mission we missed the target by a long ways. On most missions the lead ship would have a Norden sight and the fourth ship would have one as well. On the bomb run the pilot would get the ship straight and level. The bombardier would level up the bubbles in the Norden sight. On this first attack he forgot to level up the bubbles, causing our aim to be way off. When we returned, we were debriefed, and they asked us how we missed the target by such a wide margin. Cyril admitted to them that he had not leveled the bubbles before the bomb run. After that, this man who stood six feet, four inches had the nickname Bubbles!

In preparation for a mission, the bombardier would install a cam in the bomb sight before we took off. The cam described the drop characteristics of whatever bomb we were using. There was a telescope on the Norden sight which was motor driven. The bombardier would elevate the scope so that he could see target from some distance out. The telescope would start rotating down at a rate that was supposed to keep the crosshairs on the target. The bombardier had two knobs on either side. If the crosshairs drifted either direction, he would turn the knobs to bring it back. Information from the bombsight operated an instrument on the pilot's panel called a Pilots Directional Indicator (PDI). There were also adjustments for the rotation rate on the telescope to keep it centered and that data was shown on the PDI. If the Norden sight was correctly set up, and the pilot followed the PDI and had his ship straight and level at the correct altitude, we hit the target.

Without good sight adjustments by the bombardier, the pilot might end up chasing the needle on the PDI. The pilot's job was to center the PDI, keep the needle and ball in the middle, and keep the airspeed and altitude at what had been predetermined during planning. If the needle and ball weren't centered, it tended to throw the bombs because the plane was skidding. I felt that this was a heavy workload, so I always had the copilot handle the throttles on the bomb run. His job was to maintain our airspeed. It didn't make any difference who was riding in the right seat. Col. Chapman handled the throttles on the bomb run when he flew with me.

With a little practice, we became skilled enough to hit pinpoint targets consistently. We really started to knock down some of the masonry bridges. They had arches that were twelve feet thick at the thinnest point, and we had to hit them with two or three 1000 pound bombs to do any serious damage. We got good enough that the squadron next to us had ninety-six percent of their bombs in the target area over July and August. The 486th wasn't quite that good, but we were still rated exceptionally accurate.

We were typically bombing at an altitude of nine to twelve thousand feet. "Within the target area" meant being within a radius of 200 feet of the target. We always carried cameras with us so that we got good pictures of the hits before we left the area. The bombardier or gunners generally snapped the pictures. One of the ships had a fixed mounted camera in the fuselage, and the gunner would operate it. Sometimes they would send out a camera ship to photograph what we had done.

Prior to the initial Anzio assault, we hit targets that had nothing to do with the landing. The Allies had to be cagey enough to hit targets without alerting the Germans to their real purpose. By severing the rail and road connections, the allies limited the Germans ability to supply troops at the Anzio beachhead.

On missions to locations which had not had prior attacks, there would often be a couple of defensive gun batteries near the target. If we hit the target successfully, the Germans would often repair it. This was especially true if it was an important supply line.

They would augment their defense at the same time. When we came back to knock it out again, heavy and accurate antiaircraft fire would be waiting. That increase in enemy firepower meant that we had a heightened sense of danger on those missions.

Once the bombs were released, we would usually dive to try to get below the antiaircraft fire. If the ack-ack was above the formation, especially if it were behind us, we felt pretty safe. If it was in front of us, we got worried. The other advantage in diving was that the German gunners were used to slower airplanes like B-17s and B-24s, and often they couldn't quite track us. In our evasive dives, the airplane would usually be going about 300 mph indicated which meant about 325 mph true airspeed, and the pilots would initiate a pretty significant turn. The controls were very stiff at that speed even with hydraulic boosting. It was hard to move the control column.

We practiced making our bomb runs as short as possible and the typical bomb run from the initial point (IP) was 30 seconds. Unlike the bomb runs that the heavies made, we approached our IP making evasive turns and changing altitude. The altitude was predetermined at the IP point however, and that was set into the sight. On the final gyration approaching the IP, we wanted to roll out at that altitude and proper heading. Of course, the ack-ack gunners would have their best shot at that point. Immediately after pickling bombs, the bombardier's announcement of "Bombs away" would be quickly followed by a gunner's yell "Bomb bay doors closed. Let's get the hell out here!"

All pilots had their own methods of coping with the stress of combat. I knew that if I survived, it would be based partly on skill and partly on luck. On one hand I knew I could handle my flight leader duties, and I trusted Bubbles to put our formation on the target. I knew that he trusted me to have the airplane on the correct heading, speed and altitude no matter how much opposition we faced. We both knew it was our job to make sure that the certainty of a successful mission outweighed the risk to those assigned it. On tough missions, the shells from 88 mm cannon and heavy machine gun bursts were often close enough to be lethal. I saw stricken ships with crews bailing out over occupied territory and knew fate would decide if I would join them. The expression aptly stated by others that "only a fool would not be afraid" rings true. On every mission where we faced opposition, those feelings were always in the background. Nevertheless, most of us kept a brave and quiet face.

Capt. Charles Nathan, the Squadron Surgeon, was someone I considered a friend. He understood combat stress very well. One day after the funeral of one of my good friends, he struck up a conversation with me and told me he thought I was a stoic. I humbly took that as a compliment more meaningful than any decoration or award. I ask the reader to remember and consider that emotional fabric when reading these daily mission reports.

The Pompeii airfield was not very far from the Anzio beachhead; about thirty-five minutes at most. Many of our missions following that landing were in support of the troops there. The intense fighting at Anzio was something to behold. It was like the front cover of a magazine with fighters in dogfights, antiaircraft shooting all over the place, and airplanes going down in smoke and flames. As one can imagine, it was a pretty exciting and dangerous place to be.

We always approached from the landside, never the water. The Germans controlled the high ground, and they had excellent A/A on the bluffs. There were many airplanes shot down there. The battle went on for months, finally ending in May. I went over the beachhead eleven times, and my plane had fresh bullet holes on every mission.

Some squadron activity information was lost due to the Vesuvius eruption. My flight records for March can at least show the dates that I flew and hours.

INDIVIDUAL FLIGHT RECORD

(1) SERIAL NO. O-864516 (2) NAME SATTERTHWAITE, DALE J. (3) RANK 2nd Lt. (4) AGE 1919
(5) PERS. CLASS 01 (6) BRANCH Army Air Force (7) STATION Pompeii L/G, Italy
(8) ORGANIZATION ASSIGNED 12th A.F. 12th B.C. 340th 486th Gaudo L/G, Italy
(9) ORGANIZATION ATTACHED
(10) PRESENT RATING & DATE Pilot May 28, 1943 (11) ORIGINAL RATING & DATE Same
(12) TRANSFERRED FROM (13) FLIGHT RESTRICTIONS
(15) TRANSFERRED TO (14) TRANSFER DATE
(16) PERS. CLASS | RANK | RTG | A. F. | COMMAND | WING | GROUP NO. | GROUP TYPE | SQUADRON NO. | SQUADRON TYPE | STATION | MO. | YR.
(17) MONTH March 19 44

| M-S Day (18) | Aircraft Type, Model & Series (19) | No. of Landings (20) | Flying Inst. (incl. in 1st Pil. Time) S (21) | Command Pilot C CA (22) | Co-Pilot CP (23) | Qualified Pilot Dual QD (24) | First Pilot Day P (25) | First Pilot Night P N or NI (26) | Rated Pers. Non-Pilot (27) | (28) | (29) | Non-Rated Other Arms & Services (30) | Non-Rated Other Crew & Pass or (31) | Instrument I (32) | Night N (33) | Instrument Trainer (34) | Pilot Non-Mil. Aircraft Over 400 H.P. (35) | Under 400 H.P. (36) |
|---|---|---|---|---|---|---|---|---|---|---|---|---|---|---|---|---|---|---|
| CT 2 | B-25D | 0 | | | 1:30 | | | | | | | | | | | | | |
| T 5 | " C | 0 | | | 1:00 | | | | | | | | | | | | | |
| A 6 | " | 0 | | | 0:30 | | | | | | | | | | | | | |
| A 7 | " D | 0 | | | 1:15 | | | | | | | | | | | | | |
| C 8 | " | 0 | | | 2:30 | | | | | | | | | | | | | |
| CT 10 | " | 0 | | | 1:10 | | | | | | | | | | | | | |
| T 11 | " | 1 | | | | | 1:30 | | | | | | | | | | | |
| C 13 | " C | 0 | | | 3:00 | | | | | | | | | | | | | |
| T 14 | " D | 0 | | | 1:00 | | | | | | | | | | | | | |
| C 16 | " | 1 | | | | | 1:45 | | | | | | | | | | | |
| T 17 | " | 1 | | | | | 1:00 | | | | | | | | | | | |
| C 17 | " | 1 | | | | | 1:50 | | | | | | | | | | | |
| CT 18 | " | 1 | | | | | 1:35 | | | | | | | | | | | |
| T 19 | " | 1 | | | | | 1:00 | | | | | | | | | | | |
| C 19 | " | 1 | | | | | 2:40 | | | | | | | | | | | |
| C 30 | " | 1 | | | | | 3:30 | | | | | | | | | | | |
| T 31 | " | 1 | | | | | 2:15 | | | | | | | | | | | |
| COLUMN TOTALS | | | | | 11:55 | | 17:05 | | | | | | | | | | | |

Certified Correct:

NELSON L. DOZIER
Captain, Air Corps,
Operations Officer.

| | (42) TOTAL STUDENT PILOT TIME | (43) TOTAL FIRST PILOT TIME | (44) TOTAL PILOT TIME |
|---|---|---|---|
| (37) THIS MONTH | | 17:05 | 29:00 |
| (38) PREVIOUS MONTHS THIS F. Y. | | 241:15 | 359:40 |
| (39) THIS FISCAL YEAR | | 258:20 | 388:40 |
| (40) PREVIOUS FISCAL YEARS | 253:00 | | 259:00 |
| (41) TO DATE | 253:00 | 258:20 | 647:40 |

AIRCRAFT 19 | NE. 20 | CARD NO. 1: 21 22 23 24 25 26 | CARD NO. 2: 27 28 29 30 31 | CARD NO. 3: 32 33 34 35 36

March 1 It was raining this morning as usual, and we suspected there would be no mission. Nevertheless, I was with six crews who appeared at Group Operations for a 0745 hrs. briefing. We returned to the squadron area to await the call for takeoff. The weather worsened, and finally at 1500 hrs. a stand down was declared. Waiting to be called for missions is almost as trying as flying them. Crews must stay close to Operations in order to be able to leave on a moment's notice.

March 2 Our mission today was in close support of troops in the Anzio area. It was a rough mission with five ships holed and a gunner slightly wounded. A ship from the 489th made a belly landing after the wheels refused to come down.

March 3-5 We are grounded by nonstop rain showers. Italy's reputation as a place to escape the northern European weather is clearly exaggerated.

March 6 Contemplated targets remain clouded, so a practice mission was flown.

March 7 The marshaling yards on the outskirts of Rome saw action from our bombers today. Eighteen planes dropped a very neat and excellent pattern. A newsreel cameraman came along and took pictures of the formation and explosions over the target.

March 8 Orte Marshaling Yards received a repeat visit today, and we left scores of burned and derailed freight cars, twisted rails and gaping bomb craters.

March 9 Scheduled stand down day.

March 10 The biggest calamity of the day was the loss of Col. Jones in 6M, the lead plane just ahead of us. They were hit by flak on the bomb run which was near Rome. A moment later, they called May Day. The plane remained on a level course for several minutes after it was damaged, which allowed five visible parachutes to deploy. Then it nosed over and plunged to the ground in a mass of flames. Two other crewmen on board did not get out. It will probably be some time before we find out if the Colonel was amongst the five who jumped. As mentioned, he is very capable and will not be an easy man to replace. Everyone likes his affable personality and easy leadership style. He was later awarded a Distinguished Flying Cross for that day's mission. Two other 486th ships experienced a mid-air collision over the target. They both limped back to Pompeii airfield with damage to their wings.

Three days later the Deutsches Reich radio reported that a 32-year-old Colonel on board a B-25 shot down near Rome was taken prisoner. This was undoubtedly Col. Jones. In the absence of more definite information, it is safe to assume that he is alive.

March 11-12 The Day Room had lots of visitors. Local weather remains completely socked in.

March 13 Eighteen Group ships dropped 48,000 pounds of bombs on the Perugia marshaling yards. One train left the station with burning cars streaming behind it. All our planes returned safely.

## Air Medal, Fourth Cluster Awarded

Edwin L. DeCamp, 120-3391 Sgt., for the meritorious achievement while participating in an aerial flight as gunner of the B-25 type aircraft in an attack upon the marshaling yards at Perugia, Italy on 13 March 1944. Brooklyn, NY.

*March 13, 1944*

*Dear Eleanor,*

*I received two V mail notes from you tonight. At least three of my letters must be lost or in transit based on when you last heard from me. I went on my 24th mission today, and tomorrow they are sending me to rest camp. I flew the last three missions as first pilot. Everything is going well with me-health, spirits, and work. The only shortcoming is a cramp in my love life. I will stick V mail notes in between letters so it won't be so long between times.*

*I will write you when I arrive at Capri. It is a famous place and I remember hearing a ballad about the island. Strange, awesome, and censored things are happening outside our airbase tonight. Nothing to do with the war, but perhaps even more spectacular. Wish you were here to see it.*

*Love, Dale*

My letter's censored comment refers to the increasing volcanic activity of Mount Vesuvius. As mentioned, there were guided tours to the rim of the volcano, and they would get pretty close to the edge of the cone. A captain from the 340th was up on the summit with a guide when a rock was ejected from inside the mountain. It hit him in the head and killed him. None of the fellows that I knew risked going up there. On one occasion I flew right through the ash cloud coming out of the mountain. The plume was not very thick. I didn't realize that ash could be hazardous to the engines. The mouth of the volcano was several hundred yards across.

The engineers made a taxi strip from Pompeii airfield to another field some distance away that was closer to Naples. When Vesuvius blew its top that night in March, we heard that the seismologists stationed there had warned the American officials that a major eruption was imminent. I always wondered why they didn't taxi the 340th aircraft over to that other field. The adjacent field was spared major damage because the winds blew most of the ash the other direction. Many of the destroyed aircraft would've remained flyable if they had done that.

March 14 Terni Marshaling Yards was accurately targeted by the front flight of planes today. Flights two and three hit buildings in the town, which set off some big explosions. Major Hackney talked to combat crews yesterday about the risk of malaria at what may be our next port of call. He warned everyone to avail themselves of all precautionary measures which might prevent the disease. This of course increased speculation that we could wind up in China or India.

March 15 Earsplitting explosions from defensive cannons shook us out of bed about 0100 hrs. The northwestern sky on our side of Vesuvius was streaked with red tracers, accompanied by a flight of Allied fighters which droned overhead. This action heralded a German air attack on Naples. At dawn, we learned that their barrage had been a heavy one lasting about forty minutes.

The report is that they sank a hospital ship and damaged a naval vessel in the harbor. An Allied smokescreen was so quickly laid with the help of an off-shore wind that the harbor was thickly blanketed in a few minutes. Most of the bombs landed in town. They damaged the transient Officers Mess, the apartments nearby and an Italian bomb shelter. Several hundred casualties resulted. At least two German planes were shot down. Our earlier suspicions that the bright lights coming from Naples would attract German bombers proved true.

Today the heat was turned on Cassino. We ran two missions over the hills above the abbey where fighting has raged unabated for weeks. Allied troops were removed from the immediate vicinity of the town in anticipation of a concerted aerial bombardment aimed at completely obliterating it.

### Air Medal Awarded

Edward F. Murray, 074-400, First Lieut., for the meritorious achievement while participating in an aerial flight as bombardier of B-25 type aircraft in an attack upon enemy military installations at Cassino, Italy on 15 March 1944. New York, NY.

### Air Medal, Third Cluster Awarded

Joseph D. Ross, 074-1700, First Lieut., for meritorious achievement while participating in an aerial flight as pilot of a B-25 type aircraft in an attack upon enemy military installations at Cassino, Italy on 15 March, 1944. New York, NY.

### Air Medal, Fifth Cluster Awarded

Joseph A. McGinnis Jr., 079-5797 First Lieut., for meritorious achievement while participating in an aerial flight as pilot of a B-25 type aircraft in an attack upon any military installations at Cassino, Italy on 15 March 1944. Philadelphia, PA.

March 16 Our planes were over Cassino again. It is difficult to believe that there can be much left of the abbey after the devastating raids of yesterday. Over 1400 tons of bombs were dropped within an area of less than one square mile. The brass is of the opinion that it lies directly in our path to Rome.

March 17 We plastered the Roccasecca town center with 250 and 500 pounders today. It was a nice change from Cassino and we faced no opposition from ack-ack.

March 18 This morning our planes paid a visit to Foligno, hitting the city with 1000 pounders. Tonight Vesuvius presented one of the most beautiful sights I have witnessed. A mass of wildfire poured down from its open top. It vividly outlined the western slope of the mountain and ran down to the sea. Drifting away to the southwest were huge clouds of smoke. It was a most awe inspiring spectacle.

## Air Medal, Fifth Cluster Awarded

Vincent Myers, 066-3652, Capt., for meritorious achievement while participating in an aerial flight as bombardier of a B-25 type aircraft in an attack upon a road bridge at Foligno, Italy on 18 March 1944. Apache, OK.

Colonel Willis Chapman was assigned as 340th Group Commander. He came directly out of Bomb Training Command in the states and had never flown in combat. We initially resented him for that reason, but it turned out that he knew what it was all about. He ordered us to practice a simulated bomb run on every mission before we arrived at our actual IP. We would make a practice run on something selected as a target, and this allowed us to get all the crosswind drift computed. When we made the actual bomb run, it was unusual for us to be straight and level for more than twenty seconds. This change made a big difference in our accuracy, and decreased our exposure to antiaircraft fire. With his changes we really started hitting our targets.

At Col. Chapman's request, a talented team was given the task of figuring out a way to use a radio link between all of the airplanes to trigger the bomb release simultaneously. What they came up with was truthfully the first squadron based precision bombing method. The lead bombardier's bomb release switch also released bombs from the rest of the airplanes. There was an unused channel on every plane's high-frequency radio which was tuned to receive a signal from the lead plane's bomb sight. The radio was connected to a device called a marker beacon, which in turn would electrically operate the bomb release mechanism. It was a brilliant stroke of engineering. This technological advance eliminated the human element, and vastly improved our accuracy.

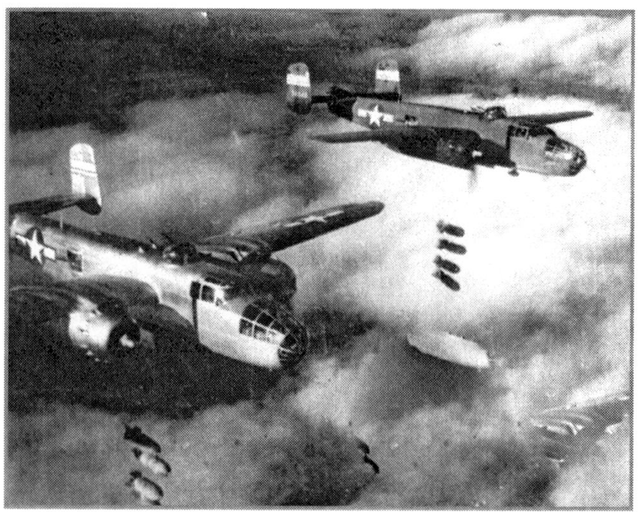

(courtesy 57th Bomb Wing)

After the system was augmented, pictures of bomb patterns were so tight that you could tell where each airplane had been in the formation. Our planes were capable of carrying five 1000 pound semi-armor piercing bombs. When the lead bombardier prickled the bombs from fully loaded six ship formations, 30,000 pounds of bombs went out instantaneously.

One of my interests there was photography. No color film was available, but someone came across a cache of British aircraft camera film which was about ten inches wide. It was black and white high-grade film, but not very fast. They set up a jig with razor blades and this film could be cranked through it and split up into 620 and 127 widths. When we developed this film we would save the paper backs and reapply it to the new roll. That system worked out pretty well.

There were some pretty serious photographer types in the squadron. I remember this one fellow had his tent a long ways away from the rest of the camp. I don't know why they let him do that. I went over there to visit him one night and he had a low fire of dimly glowing coals burning. He was sitting there with a helmet full of fixer between his knees developing film. Some of the guys in intelligence shared their film developing chemicals with us.

I had a professional quality, Government Issue photographic kit. The kit held a Speed Graphics press type camera, flash, tripod and all kinds of other stuff. My recollection is that someone had this dedicated case full of supplies. When he went back to the states, he gave the whole thing to me. The camera was outstanding, and it had a synchronizer which was used to take flash pictures. I used it to photograph the devastation caused by the Luftwaffe raid on Alesan field. The fellows nicknamed me "Satchel" because I often had that case with me.

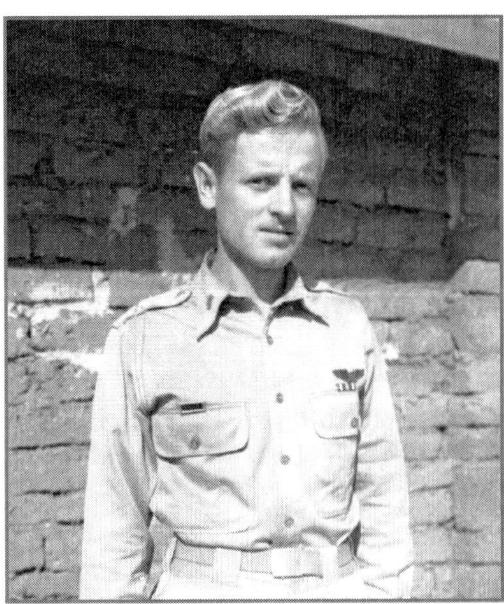

Some of my fellow shutterbugs and I made a photographic studio inside a tent. I constructed an enlarger which worked well. The lamp and 24 volt battery for the enlarger was "borrowed" from the airplane bone yard. It had a precise on/off switch, which made exposure control easy. Other airplane bits and pieces made up the lamp support and film drive. I used the optics in the press camera to focus the negatives. Sometimes we would send our undeveloped film along with the crews going to Cairo. I sent negatives to Cairo several times, and the studio did not return the finished pictures or negatives. That is why I built the enlarger.

When Vesuvius erupted, I was over in Capri on R&R. I arrived there three days prior to the eruption. We stayed in a beautiful, very elegant hotel and had lunch on the terrace. The staff served us our meals on silver plates and we drank from embossed crystal. No menus were offered, but our appetites were whetted by the finery. While waiting for our first meal, my new friends and I strongly anticipated an entrée that was commensurate with our surroundings. The main course arrived on a large covered platter, and with a flourish, our server removed the lid to reveal Spam!

Capri was the playground of wealthy people from Caesar's time and many beautiful structures from that time remain. Large villas dotted the highest peaks with impressive views of the water. We hired a horse drawn carriage as our conveyance. Some of the shops sold beautiful housewares and antiques that came from the villas on the island. I went into a shop and briefly chatted with a woman who was the store owner. She was a British subject who was unable to return to England after the hostilities started. I purchased two champagne sized flutes embossed with a royal crest. She said they had belonged to a wealthy family on the island. Somehow those delicate glasses survived all the events that I will relate. We hired a boat with the idea of going into the Blue Grotto, a famous cave which is carved from the rocky coastline. Not surprisingly, weather prevented us from entering the cave.

On the forth morning of our stay, we came out of the hotel to find many people standing on their roofs. An accumulation of gray dust lay in the street which we realized was volcanic ash. For a time the wind blowing from Vesuvius came in the direction of Capri. A huge eruption plume filled the eastern sky. Several calls to the Operations office at Pompeii airfield got no answer. We then contacted the USO on the island and they told us that the 340th Bomb Group had been wiped out by the eruption.

A long line of GIs formed at the ferry dock. My group boarded a boat in the early afternoon for the bumpy ride back to the mainland. Enterprising cab drivers were charging triple rates for rides to Naples. Our shortened stay meant that we still had available funds to pay for a ride.

Of course, the town was in an uproar. Many of the 340th enlisted men were there. As previously noted, the officers' quarters near Pompeii were in rock structures. Enlisted men had their tents right on the flight line. Anything flammable was destroyed by the hot lava rocks which pelted down. Some of those fellows took temporary shelter underneath the wings of our airplanes. The tail surfaces of our planes were made with doped fabric covering which caught fire. On the morning of the first day many soldiers evacuated. Some went to Naples, and others headed directly to our new temporary base.

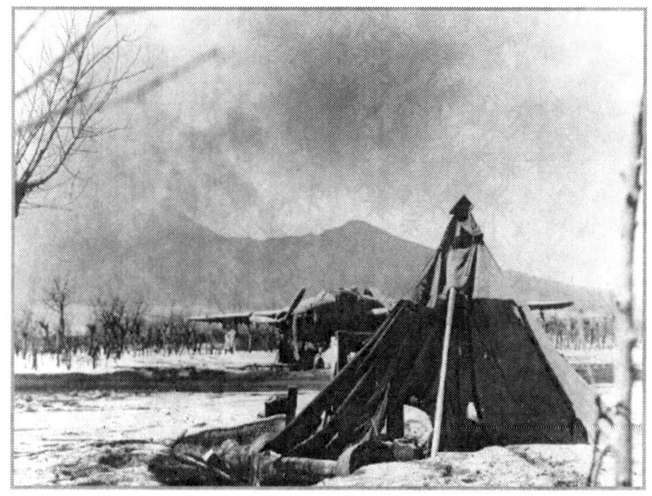

(Courtesy 57th Bomb Wing)

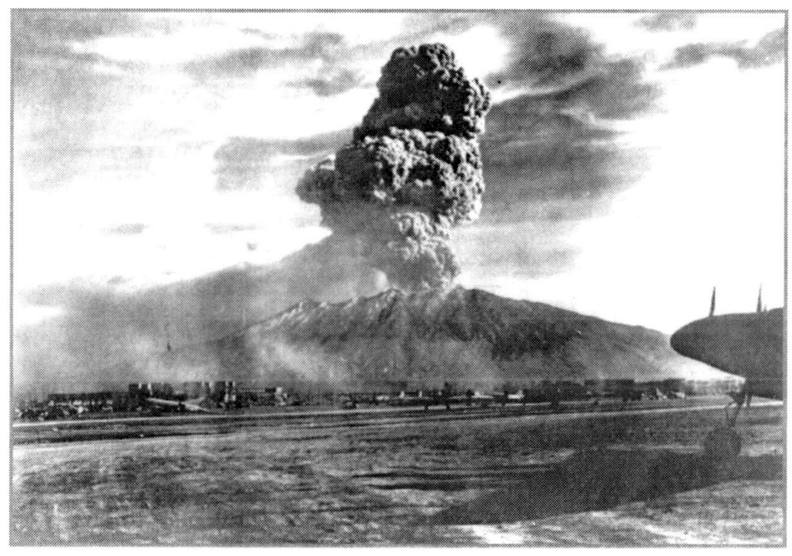

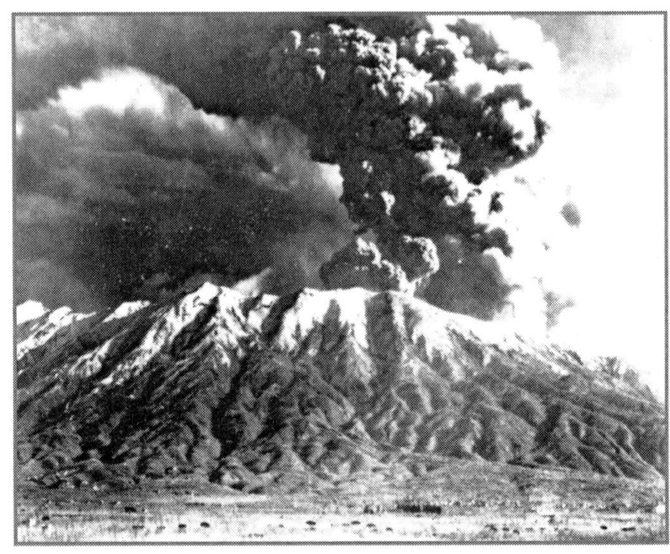

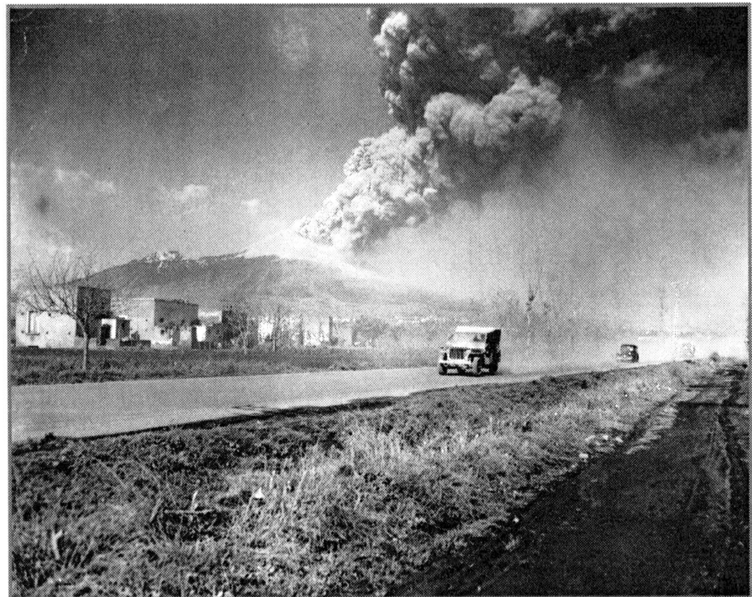

(Courtesy NARA)

One of the men who had been with us on Capri let us in on his secret. He admitted to stealing a Jeep weeks earlier. It was fortuitously parked in a garage in Naples. The rest of us were somewhat amazed by his bold misappropriation of government property. We used the Jeep to join the procession of vehicles heading south away from the eruption.

As the evacuation convoy slowly progressed, we bumped into some of our squadron members. They told us that our Group had been ordered to relocate to a converted pasture called Gaudo L/G (landing field) about fifty miles south of Naples. The other news they passed was that most of our planes were destroyed along with most of our personal property. Looking back towards Pompeii, we could see an enormous plume of ash kicked up by the vehicles on the road. Fortunately, the afternoon wind blew the ash in a different direction.

Our convoy traveled a route on back alleys through Poggiomarino, and into the gathering darkness. The lead Jeep, loaded to the gunwales and dragging an equally loaded trailer, made little progress until a truck nosed up behind it and added its power. At each village we passed, there were welcoming committees on the roofs. They showered us with shovels full of volcanic ash as we crept through the narrow streets. Ash tossed from the roofs made deep drifts on the streets that the convoy had to plow through.

Approaching a makeshift bridge, we saw a sign which said, "No Thoroughfare," but we were not in a mood to turn back. Several men crawled down the bank to watch the action of the bridge supports while we passed. As we held our breaths, the first truck gingerly made its approach and almost capsized. The driver gave it the gun and, with a dozen men hanging their weight on the top side, made it across. The rest of the passengers were ordered out of the other trucks and Jeeps. By careful approach, each of the vehicles was guided across without incident.

Around midnight a tired, bedraggled and cold bunch of men with faces like coal miners finally saw the welcome lights at Gaudo airfield. The next day "Axis Sally" announced to the world by shortwave that the eruption was an act of God for the Germans. She also stated that the 340th was wiped out to the last man and plane. She was nearly right about the planes, but our casualties only amounted to two serious injuries. One man was struck in the face which broke his nose. The other soldier was conked on the helmet by a lump of falling lava. He fell down and broke his arm.

We were reequipped with some war weary airplanes, and everyone was surprised how quickly we were able to resume operations. After the eruption subsided, our guys went back to Pompeii and scrounged the area for stoves, stovepipe, tent poles and any other stuff of any value. They also salvaged usable parts from the destroyed planes.

On the 27th we were in the air for a mission that took us to the Perugia East Railroad Bridge. We knocked out the west approach. The next day we returned to the same bridge and completely demolished it. The enemy extracted a heavy payment. Five of our flyers, all radio operators/gunners, were hit by flak over the bomb run and seriously injured. One of the casualties, young and popular Staff Sgt. Henry Waldroup died the next day. On the 29th, five of our Mitchells staged an uneventful raid on the airfield at Viterbo, Italy. Bad weather prevented any bombing on the 30th and the 31st.

The following is an enlisted man's description of the hours and days around the major eruption.

## FROM A PERSONAL DIARY

*March 20, 1944: As I sit in my tent just off the runway of the Pompeii Aerodrome, I can hear in short intervals the loud rumblings of the volcano on the third day of its present eruption. The noise is like that of bowling pins slapping into each other on a giant bowling alley. To look above the mountain tonight, one would think that the world was on fire. The thickly clouded sky glows like the illumination above a huge forest fire. As the clouds pass from across the top of the mountain, the flame and lava can be seen shooting high, to spill over the sides and run in red streams down the slopes.*

*Last night was much clearer, but the volcano seemed not as angry as it does tonight. Against the darkness of the night, the lava gave fiery edges to each side of the crater and part way down the slopes.*

*The rumblings started sometime yesterday, and have continued at a few seconds interval ever since. The lava started spilling over three days ago. Today, it was estimated that a path of molten lava one-mile long, a quarter-mile wide, and eight feet deep is rolling down the mountain. Towns on the slopes are preparing to evacuate.*

*I have just looked at the mountain through high-powered glasses. It is some sight! Flame, sparks and lava are being thrown from the crater like rice at a wedding; going high and spilling out on all sides.*

*The rumblings are now growing louder, and the flames and sparks are flying higher. The mountain is really angry tonight. This is a sight to be remembered, an ironically beautiful sight.*

*Our location is apparently safe. At any rate, no civilian or Army authorities seem worried. Lava has not started to flow down this side of the mountain as yet, but is flowing towards Naples. I can imagine that the people in that vicinity are highly apprehensive.*

*This is a feeble description. Would that I had words to really describe this location.*

*March 21, 1944: This was a rainy day, and heavy clouds hang over the mountain so that its activity could not be observed. However, the rumblings and explosions gave evidence that the fury had not abated. Towards evening the rain stopped, and the clouds cleared away. Dense smoke and heavy steam poured upwards many thousands of feet and spread out over an area of many square miles. The dense, billowy steam took beautiful forms, and was lighted around the edges by increasing sunshine.*

*At 1730 hrs. small streams of lava began running down our side of the mountain. This is the first flow on this side. Soon many swift, fiery streams were flowing in all directions. The rumbling continues and is more prolonged. This evening, it would seem that the whole top of the mountain is burning. Fiery patches here and there resemble a log which is just burning out. Heavy explosions occur followed by prolonged rumbling. Sparks and molten lava are thrown high into the air, and fall like rain on all sides of the cone.*

*The mountain is hard to describe. Eruptions occur from a cone which sets apart and inside the rest of the mountain. This inner formation rises many feet above the mountain proper. Above the cone lip, sparks are falling and fiery streams are flowing. Much of the rest of the mountain is covered with snow; a most interesting contrast. Dark clouds hang heavy above Vesuvius tonight, but they are penetrated by the red glow.*

*It is now 0100 hrs., and I am scheduled for guard duty on the airfield. My tour will end at 0500 hrs., and those intervening hours should be very interesting. I shall write tomorrow about the occurrences during the night. We are a bit concerned about the whole thing, and I imagine that many soldiers have offered as I have, a prayer for safety.*

*March 29, 1944: Eight days since my last entry. A lot has happened. I should like to report from the present and work back, but for the sake of interest, shall try to take up where I left off.*

*The early part of my guard tour was more or less uneventful. Low storm clouds made the night very black. The mountain, although invisible, could be heard. Rumblings and explosions continued. Occasionally, fine black particles fell like rain. From time to time the clouds would lift to partially reveal the volcano's cone. It was an eerie sight. It appeared as though glowing lava was flowing through the clouds. Now and then the top was visible to reveal flame and lava shooting skyward.*

*At 0115 hrs. the mountain began to pant like a mighty giant gasping for breath. This went on for about a half hour, and was followed by a continuous, deep rumbling.*

*A huge black cloud in the exact shape of a great reclining bear completely hid the mountain, so its activity could not be observed. With the rumbling, more of the fine black particles began to fall.*

*At 0200 hrs. the volcano seemed to explode. Mighty roaring occurred, and pieces of lava as large as golf balls began to fall around me - ten miles from the foot of the mountain. They beat upon the airplanes, setting up a racket in the black of that eventful night like hail on tin roofs. This rock shower lasted about 10 minutes. Then all hell broke loose. Black stones of all sizes, some as large as footballs, fell in great quantity, completely covering the ground. They broke branches from the trees, and smashed through tents to break up on their floors. They tore through the metal, fabric and Plexiglas of the airplanes. Soon, all the tents were in tatters with much of their contents destroyed by direct hits. Radios, cots and many other effects were severely damaged.*

*The storm of lava and rain continued through the morning, piling up on the ground like snow and multiplying the damage. Soldiers who ventured from shelter wore steel helmets. Civilians covered their heads with pans or heavy baskets.*

*At noon, the decision was made to evacuate the entire camp. The personnel belongings which were still usable were quickly gathered. Amidst much confusion, my truck finally departed at 1500 hrs. The eruption still raged. Small stones fell in quantity, and every fifteen minutes or so the heavens would open up with the big stuff. I say heavens instead of the mountain because that is the way it seemed. The stones were not lobbed from the mountain, but dropped from clouds falling straight down with great force. Large stones fell close to the mountain, and as we drew further away, fine ash was falling. We evacuated through the ash which was now over one foot deep.*

*After losing our way several times, we arrived at our new quarters at about 0100 hrs. on the 23rd. We were harbored at a tobacco warehouse on the airfield. It was home for the 321st Bomb Group at Paestum, near Salerno. We unloaded our things and set up cots under the drying tobacco leaves. A colder night I never experienced, and hope never to experience again. The next night was not quite so bad. I slept with all my clothes on, including a leather fur-lined cap with ear flaps pulled down. Upon rising, I had only to put my shoes on to be completely dressed.*

*After breakfast on the 25th, twenty of us were assigned to return to Pompeii airport to salvage what we could from the damaged aircraft and airfield. Upon reaching the airport on the 26th, we found almost complete devastation. Tents were torn to ribbons, and eighty-eight airplanes were a total loss. These airplanes were worth twenty-five million dollars. How Jerry gloated.*

*Axis Sally dedicated her program one evening to the survivors of the 340th Bomb Group. The following night she cracked "We got the colonel, Vesuvius got the rest." She explained how the 340th was no longer operational. How wrong she was. Within a week the 340th was bombing Jerry in northern Italy. We have bombed them every day since. Each of the four squadrons now has fifteen or more B-25s, and some now carry thirteen 50 caliber machine guns.*

*In just a few days we will go to Corsica to lead all B-25 Groups in the approaching big show.*

> *Just a few words about Vesuvius and the vicinity as we found it upon our return. The ash had completely covered the ground to a depth of about two feet. Dense smoke and brown ash billowed profusely from the mountain. We were unlucky enough to be windward of the mountain, so that the ash got into our eyes and covered our clothing. This irritating dusting was very uncomfortable. Ash completely covered the countryside with a snowy whiteness.*
>
> *As we left the place a week later, dense ash was still billowing from the volcano. The mountain had become quiet, and all danger of further eruption is unknown. Twenty-five days after the disaster, the 340th Bomb Group is again a complete fighting unit, and is still the best damned Group there is. Hitler, the self-styled "Great Rebuilder," please note.*

I think this anonymous soldier was too modest about his descriptive abilities. I can confirm how cold it was a in the tobacco warehouse on our first night at Gaudo airfield.

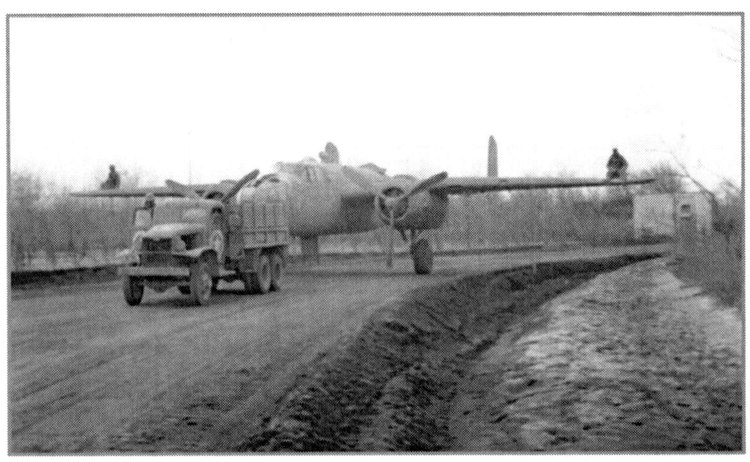

(Courtesy NARA)

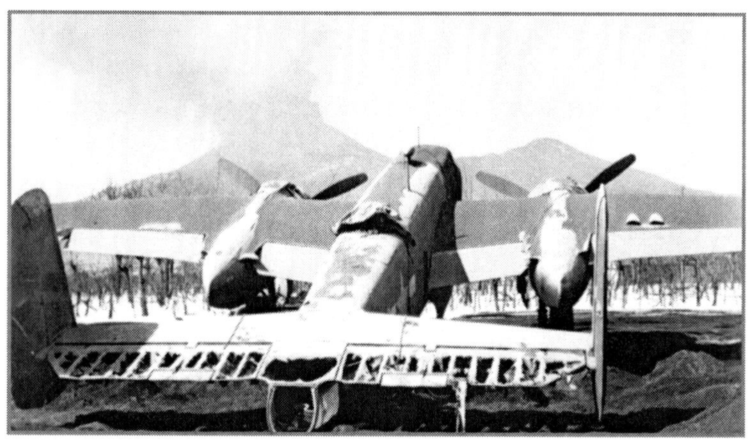

(Courtesy NARA)

**April 1** (From Gaudo landing field) Our target for today's mission was the railroad bridge six miles north of Oviedo. This bridge is important. It is the corridor for the majority of Florence to Rome rail service which passes over the Paglia River. There are many bomb craters near the bridge from earlier attacks. The 486th dropped a compact pattern 300 feet north of the bridge, but photos from the following squadrons showed no hits on the tracks.

The biggest news today is that the Cairo Cossacks will be home tomorrow. Nearly every week a B-25 packed with guys is flown to Cairo. The lucky folks who are aboard for R&R are referred to as Cairo Cossacks. Officially, the purpose of the flight is to supplement our diet and drink with items not available in the war zone. We all eagerly await our opportunity to experience life in a warm exotic city. How fortunate for the last fellows that they missed old Mount Vesuvius's rampage. Lucky dogs!

The 486th reformed with fifteen planes which consisted of two originals, seven loaned from the 321st and six new ones. The older planes were not equipped with the better hydraulic pumps on the J models. This meant they had more physical and less responsive controls. Flying those ships was a real workout. The J models took very little effort, and I could actually feel the location of airplanes behind me because they gently moved my control surfaces when they turned.

About a five-minute walk from the squadron area was an American cemetery named Mount Soprano American Cemetery where over 1000 of our men are buried. They died during the bloody Salerno invasion. The regularly spaced, simple white crosses are an impressive and thought-provoking sight. For my own part, it reminded me of the anguish I felt when my fellow airmen failed to return from a mission. It was a memory that I'll never forget.

April 2 Today we went back to finish yesterday's work. Part of target was obscured by smoke, and we still weren't able to knock the bridge down. Moderate to heavy antiaircraft fire damaged four of our ships, but all returned safely with no reported injuries.

Our Cairo boys are back and they brought beer! There is enough for the whole squadron to get at least one bottle apiece. They have some fine stories to tell. Lieut. Tipton reveals the following: One day at one of the local beer joints whilst Capt. "Catnip" Shealy was making many passes at the females, a tomcat breezed in the door. We were surprised when it made a beeline for Capt. Shealy's unoccupied hand which was dangling near the floor. With much tail twitching, he proceeded to smell our old buddy's hand. The waiter came and carried the cat out the door. Within a few minutes the cat was back, licking the other hand this time. After much shooing and sprinkling of pepper, the cat was finally persuaded to leave much to the amusement of the many female patrons and bystanders. To show he was a good sport, Capt. Shealy went to work repairing the building elevator that had been broken for several weeks. He got it done!

April 3 Today we are still tasked with the same bridge at Orvieto. It was again obscured by clouds. An alternate target was about nine miles south of there on the main line of the railroad. It was not seriously damaged, while heavy and accurate antiaircraft holed eight of the twelve ships. All ships returned without incident.

I was able to re-create my shower with the help of my friend, Tom Wheeler, who was a carpenter before the war. This contraption is a little less enclosed, and is constructed of two wooden platforms shielded with canvas walls around three sides. Besides mine, there is only one other shower for the entire Group. Money orders were being purchased over in the Group operations building all day. Most of the guys are sending a good portion of their salaries home. They're just isn't any place to spend it in this location unless some smart Italian opens a vino shop in the vicinity.

## Air Medal Awarded

Marion E. Prechutko, 324-53434, Sgt., for meritorious achievement while participating in an aerial flight as an armor/gunner of a B-25 type aircraft in an attack upon a railroad bridge at Orvieto, Italy on 3 April 1944. Newark, NJ.

## Air Medal, First Cluster Awarded

Peter Kok, 074-1654, First Lieut., for meritorious achievement while participating in an aerial flight as bombardier of a B-25 type aircraft in an attack upon a railroad bridge at Orvieto, Italy on 3 April 1944. Zeeland, MI.

Edward F. Murray, 074-4400, First Lieut., for meritorious achievement while participating in an aerial flight as bombardier of a B-25 type aircraft in an attack upon a railroad bridge at Orvieto, Italy on 3 April 1944. New York, NY.

Windurn E. Reagan, 067-7874, First Lieut., for meritorious achievement while participating in an aerial flight as a pilot of a B-25 type aircraft in an attack upon a railroad bridge at Orvieto, Italy on 3 April 1944. West Monroe, LA.

**April 4** **Weather is still deterring our missions. Today we** returned with all the bombs on twenty-four ships that were sent out. The Group Officers Club at seems to be working out nicely as the boys find it a place to shoot dice, and play cards. Of course, gamblers can win anywhere from $1-$1000. Those same players also have a very good chance of losing it. Some of the guys in our squadron have won between $300 and $500, and the next day or night they are now minus the same amount due to a little unscrupulous gaming. I occasionally played cards, but was selective about the game and the players.

Supply handed out new gas masks in exchange for our old ones. They are lighter and less cumbersome. The terrific interest in our protection from chemical weapons denotes the possibility that the Germans may use gas when the situation becomes critical. A meeting of all musicians in the Group was called this evening for the purpose of organizing a band. Little "Moe" Ferraro is sponsoring the idea and we are enthusiastic. Due to an insufficient number of musicians in our Group, the 321st is going to collaborate.

April 5 Old Man Weather is the worst enemy of any air force. Lieut. Wheeler returned from Naples with a truck loaded with canned food stuffs that came from broken cartons etc. Our sudden move left us with very little food and this resupply will augment the current K ration diet. The quartermaster invited us to return for another truckload.

The new Enlisted Men's Club opened today. Maj. Hackney, Capts. Dozier, Shealy and Wathen and a few more of the squadron's officers put in an appearance. Major Hackney made $60 on the first three throws in the dice game and seemed to enjoy taking money from the enlisted men. Free cigars and plenty of good old American whiskey were the final touches to this very fine opening night. I'm guessing that most of them had a big head the next morning, but felt it was worth it.

April 6 Our target was the Perugia airfield, where we succeeded in hitting targets around the field and taxiways. Two large oil fires were started and one plane on the ground exploded. The 487th provided a flight of six planes behind us, and they took heavy damage. 7K was hit, and only two bailed out of the plane before it exploded as it hit the ground. Officers Bart Parker, Randy Hicks and Sergeants Al Vervacke, Steve Tulin, John Raschetz and Dave Pinkerton were crew members. 7T was also crippled by ack-ack over the target, and was last seen aflame as it spiraled earthward. Four parachutes left the plane, which most probably added four more men to the P.O.W list. Officers Greg Ashmore, Henry Finnie, George Simpson and Sergeants Jim Eichner, John Kline and Brad Burton were aboard 7T. Three of our planes returned with fresh flak damage. Lieut. Wilkerson was cut slightly with Plexiglas on his face and head.

April 7 Return fire damaged three of our ships as they attacked a railroad bridge near Ficulle, Italy on the Ritorba River. It was not destroyed, but there were two hits on the bridge deck.

The outside cinema presented “Intermezzo” with Leslie Howard. The general opinion was that the picture was pretty good. Those that stayed behind passed along their orders for precious stones and other items to the guys headed to Cairo. Almost anything can be purchased there and some call it the “America of Egypt.”

## Air Medal Awarded

Howard C. McElroy, 075-0422, First Lieut., for the meritorious achievement while participating in an aerial flight as pilot of a B-25 type aircraft in an attack upon the railroad bridge at Ficulle, Italy, on 7 April 1944. Los Angeles, CA.

*April 7, 1944*

*Dear Eleanor,*

*I am in the midst of setting up housekeeping in a rather dilapidated tent. Quite a come down after my last days of luxury. I have just returned from Capri where I lived in clean sheets, with bathtub, bar, dining room, and nearby quaint shops. Breakfast in bed! There were beautiful views of the blue Mediterranean to wake up to every morning. How I wish you were along to share it with me. I enjoyed it all, even the boat trip there and back.*

*I was made first pilot just before I left, and flew as a three ship element leader. Today I will lead the squadron on our mission. Of course, this is more responsibility than*

*I have ever had. I must therefore cut this short and go to sleep early to be ready for it.*

*All my love, Dale*

April 8 (The following comments were in the 486th Squadron notes for the day. Of course Lieut. Staub, A.K.A. Bubbles, was in my airplane.)

"The briefing today called for six ships to be directed at the railroad bridge four miles northwest of Orte on the Tevere River. Three of our planes got hits on the target. The other element (three planes) could not correct for drift, so they held their bombs as Lieut. Staub, the lead bombardier, saw a marshaling yard one mile south of the bridge with a train stopped at the loading platform. They dropped their bombs which cratered the tracks and hit the train and platform. The locomotive was severely damaged. The men definitely used their heads. They didn't waste their bombs by throwing them away when it was impossible to hit the main target."

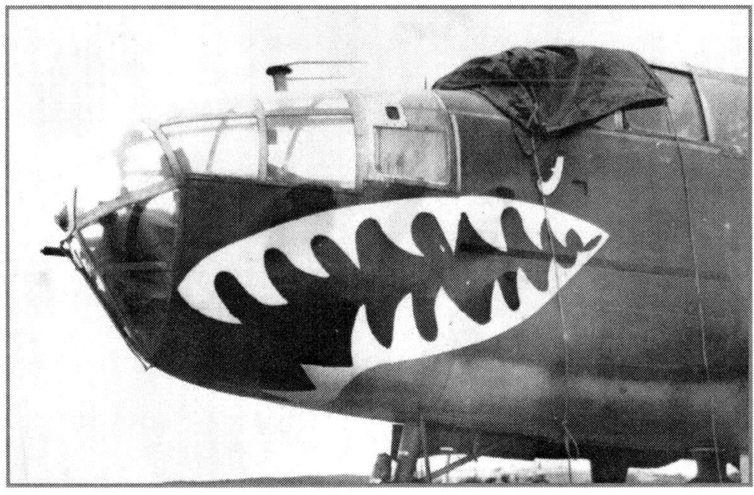

April 9 No mission today as we had the usual low ceilings and nil visibility. In spite of the weather an impressive Easter Sunrise Service was celebrated in the ancient Greek ruins of Paestum. We were informed today that we are going to move to Corsica. Naturally there were many "bull" sessions following this revelation. The comments that I heard concerned the lack of things to do on the island as well as high prices and the unfriendly attitude of the inhabitants. There is also the possibility of visits from the Luftwaffe. We hope this news will mean that the invasion is in its final stage of preparation.

Old Jocko, our squadron dog, is having a devil of a time with another pet of ours, little Penelope. His romance with her is not going anywhere. He tries and tries, but the only result is a squeal from Penelope who turns and runs with Jocko hot on her heels. For Jocko sake, we hope that he fulfills his mission someday. Forty men left the squadron this afternoon for Naples and the afternoon performance of "This Is the Army." They arrived in Naples to find Capt. Bugbee and his three associates had secured the tickets for the entire gang. The show was more widely enjoyed than any performance hitherto shown. The rest of our fellows are eager to see the show as well.

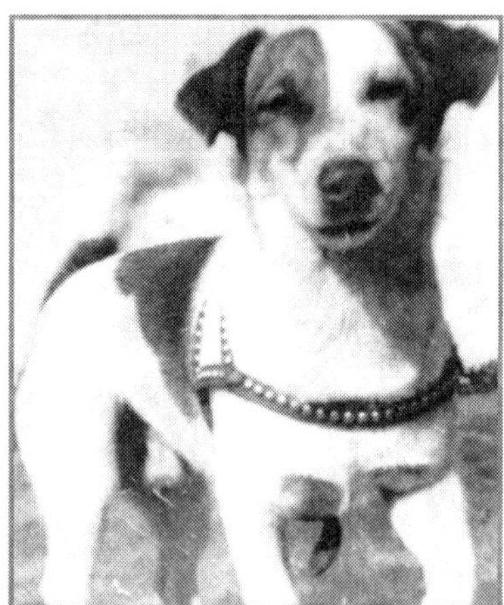

**Jocko**

The maintenance on our planes was excellent, but I may be somewhat prejudiced in that view in that they made me the Assistant Maintenance Officer. I was trained as a crew chief, and worked on P-40 fighters. Besides being good mechanics, the fellows in the shop were good teachers and by and by I knew nearly as much about the B-25 as I did about the P-40. Sometimes a thorough knowledge of the airplane paid off for a pilot.

If a radio was broken, we would fix or replace it with salvaged parts from wrecked planes. Reclaimed parts were also used to replace wing sections, landing gear and tail sections. Occasionally they had to pull an engine and replace it. One day I was in the shop and heard a shout of surprise from Master Sgt. Harold Lynch. I came over to the bench where he was overhauling an engine and he said, "This is the same engine that I changed out in the states a few years ago." The engine undoubtedly had seen plenty of service since he worked on it and also has plenty of history attached to it. The planes in our squadron had about 200 to 500 hours on them when I arrived. Most of that was in formation flying where pilots were on the throttles continuously which tended to tire out the engines a bit. Despite this, they stood up pretty well. In addition to swinging a wrench when things got busy, I occasionally played chess with the mechanics.

Capt. Stoler, the Maintenance Officer, trusted me to break in new and overhauled airplane engines. I would only use half power on that engine during takeoff and baby it during the flight. I also prided myself on being able to execute smooth low-speed approaches. The B-25 had excellent low-speed flying characteristics as evidenced by its use from an aircraft carrier on the Tokyo raid. With practice, a pilot could touch down just before the airplane reached stall speed. Many pilots would land about fifteen miles an hour faster than necessary which put a strain on the tires, brakes and gear.

Sometimes Capt. Stoler would fly with me. I had a disastrous thing happen while he was riding in the right seat. I landed after putting break-in time on a new engine and there was a mission that was coming in behind my plane. There were eighteen airplanes in that flight. I don't remember if it was a real or practice mission, but they were entering the landing pattern as I touched down.

I followed an airplane that had come in ahead of me onto the narrow taxiway. The pilot suddenly made a 180 degree turn and we were facing each other. He had gone by his hard stand and was attempting to get back to it. We were blocking the only available exit path which the arriving aircraft were using to clear the runway. I felt it was urgent to clear the bottleneck. Turning my plane off the taxiway, we traversed a twenty-four inch strip of gravel and continued to a section where the dirt was hard packed. That gave the first airplane enough room to get by to his hard stand. I hadn't had any trouble crossing the gravel strip. As I reversed course to return to the taxiway, the nose wheel got into the gravel and twisted hard to one side. I didn't realize the nose wheel was twisted. B-25 nose wheels freely swivel and are not steerable. As we entered the gravel, I felt the nose wheel sink a little which was to be expected.

Several ground crewman who were close to my plane watched as I put on some power to get through the gravel. They gave no indication that the wheel was cocked to one side and held by the gravel. The front gear suddenly collapsed, and the airplane slammed down on the nose. I heard the propellers emitted a terrible sound as they struck the ground, and both engines destroyed themselves trying to turn the twisted blades. It was a really disgusting turn of events, especially since Capt. Stoler was with me. The bitterness and frustration of that moment would remain with me forever.

I did not dare hazard a look at the crewmen, who stood gaping at my smoking plane which was canted an angle. As they sometimes say, "If looks could kill." My unblemished flying record was now less than perfect. Those painful moments seemed to last forever as the eighteen planes taxied passed me with eyes right. Of course, there was an investigation and I was charged fifty percent pilot error for the accident. It must've gone in my records, although I never saw it.

We didn't ordinarily have tire problems in combat. We had steel mats at the end of the Pompeii and Corsica runways, but we didn't touchdown on those. The runway was hard packed dirt and it was beneficial for tires. The runway was only 100 yards from shore.

One of the missions to southern France was kind of rough, and my plane was struck by several ack-ack bursts. Everything seemed to be working all right on the return flight. At touchdown, the airplane lurched to the right. A main gear tire had been blown out. We started to angle off the runway, and the copilot got on the controls with me to keep the plane heading straight down the runway. We couldn't taxi, but managed to get clear of the runway so that the other airplanes could land.

Sahara Sue II, the airplane that I flew most frequently, accumulated about 280 holes in it. The mechanics were pretty good at patching battle damage and all the holes were filled in. The thing that I really appreciated about those airplanes was the fuel tank. We almost never had any planes catch on fire from burning fuel tanks. The fuel cells were about three inches thick with rubber on the outside, and fuel resistant rubber inside with foam in between. They were excellent.

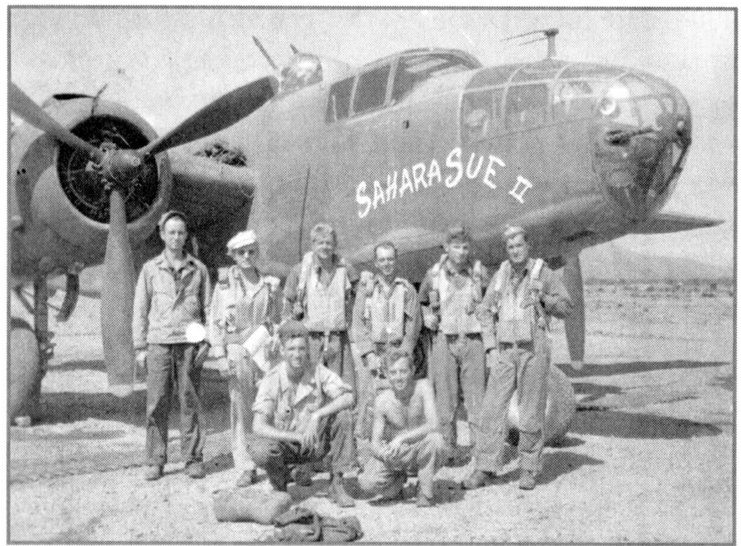


**I am second from the left in the back row**

While taking off on a mission, one of the engines on my ship emitted a loud bang but kept running, albeit with slightly less power. Oil and manifold gauges were in the green, so I opted to continue. I was in the lead airplane, and as such did not have to push very hard. Lead pilots would have their throttle settings a little low so that guys flying on the wings would have no trouble keeping up. Consequently, I wasn't working that engine very hard and flew the four and a half hour mission. After mission debriefing, my copilot and I went over to the maintenance tent and asked one of the mechanics with whom I was familiar to check the engines. He grabbed a ladder and we headed to the airplane. There was a pool of oil on the ground below the offending engine. We removed the engine cowling and found a cylinder head sitting in the bottom of the nacelle! It had blown off the engine on takeoff. The engine had only used about two and one half gallons more oil than normal. That Wright engine worked all right with thirteen cylinders.

On another mission Col. Chapman was riding in the right seat. After takeoff, one of the back crew hollered that we were losing gas. We looked out on the wing and saw that the ground crew had not put the fuel cap on securely and fuel was pouring out. It wasn't a real long mission and I would have elected to continue, however Col. Chapman told me to go back and land.

April 10 Squadron action was over Cretone, Italy today with middling results. There was no A/A, but four ME-109s made a close firing pass. Our gunners fended off the attack with no resulting damage. Whistle blowing for work details started early this morning in preparation for our scheduled move. Capt. Nafe and Capt. Bridges divided their sections so that part would go ahead to Corsica with a party and group of maintenance personnel. Some of the planes will temporarily remain here so that we can stay operational in the transition period. Lieut. Milloway will go ahead and set up headquarters there. Transportation and Operations will also split their staff. Some of the boys are pretty upset because mail service there won't start for at least ten days. The Cairo R&R/resupply plane took off today for a weeks' leave in utopia.

April 11-12 Transition days. There isn't much left to the squadron area other than a single mess tent and the personnel tents. We were instructed to have tents and baggage on trucks by 1500 hrs. and be ready to depart tomorrow at 0530 hrs. When the tents were all down, everyone made a mad scramble for shelter in the few buildings which previously housed the different sections. With the aid of these buildings and the tobacco warehouse, all were out of the elements for the night.

At the appointed hour a convoy was formed on the road adjacent to the squadron and contrary to custom, left about on time. We arrived at the docks in Salerno about 1700 hrs. At that point hurry up and wait became the rule and we did not depart until dawn of the following day. Capt. Bugbee was the only casualty of the day. While directing traffic, his hand was caught between the ship's side and a truck that passed. The injury was painful but not serious.

April 13 Most of the guys were expecting to get on an American ship where they would have a sack to rest their weary bones and showers with hot water. Unfortunately, the British ship was totally lacking in personal comforts and filthy beyond belief. Our personnel threw down their blankets in any bare spot. The ship's mess hall and the open deck assumed the appearance of an East Side flop house. We were tired enough to sleep anywhere. The "luxurious" craft sailed with the tide for Corsica at 0700 hrs. A light British cruiser gave comforting escort in U-boat waters.

April 14 Viterbo airfield was the target for the crews still based at Gaudo and they got pretty good hits on it. We heard that their pattern went well across the dispersal area, destroying at least eight planes. Several other squadrons flew an afternoon mission and they destroyed two planes. Although we were not very comfortable, everyone shipboard enjoyed the picturesque scenery as we passed the Sardinia coast line and approached the rocky islands off Corsica. Our ship docked at Porto Vecchio on the southeast coast at 1300 hrs.

Corsica has wild and jagged mountains towering over deep shadow covered valleys. Long sandy beaches add beauty to this French inhabited island where Napoleon was born. A bivouac was set up in the cork and oak groves just outside the port city.

The woodland, pastures, and flowers were a pleasant change from the drab landscapes at Gaudo.

## Air Medal, First Cluster Awarded

Camille G. Vezine, 079-9512, First Lieut., for meritorious achievement while participating in an aerial flight as pilot of a B-25 type aircraft in an attack upon an enemy aerodrome near Viterbo, Italy on 14 April 1944. Bronx, N. Y.

April 15 Two squadrons from our Gaudo field sent twelve bombers to the railroad bridge at Marciano. They destroyed the track 200 feet south of the bridge. The squadron compound in Italy is nearly deserted. The only occupied buildings are the houses on Officers Row and a house for enlisted men. That structure supposedly belongs to Mussolini.

Our group on Corsica had a night of music by the "Kitchen Gang" an impromptu band who members are Lieuts. Walters and Bissette accompanied by the black truck drivers. At 0800 we set out for our new base. It's a pretty country, but the going is tough because the Germans blew up all the bridges. We arrived at our evening camp and found it to be a good spot. Lieut. Milloway and First Sgt. Dilbeck were on hand to show us the area and we were well set up by sundown.

April 16-17 Both days the target was the railroad bridge north of Toti. The Gaudo based crews got good hits on the tracks and the bombs struck the northwest corner of the approach to the bridge.

An early breakfast preceded the final trek of our 210 mile move. Our convoy reached Alesan airfield at 1230 hrs. As usual, the area resembles a surplus store dumped in somebody's backyard, but this one was surprisingly green and pleasant looking. The location is at the foot of the small hill. New radar sits at the top of the hill. Bamboo grows to twenty feet and higher around the marshy sections, and there are several small streams which may have fish in them. We have heard that there are wild boars which may be hunted in the surrounding hills. The ground was hard as rock, and it was difficult to pound tent stakes. By nightfall things were shaping up and the area was beginning to resemble a military reservation. A shortage of tents meant that living quarters were very crowded for the time being. Some of the fellows began digging slit trenches as a precaution against air attack.

April 18 Spring storms over Italy had plenty of clouds and rain. The planes circled the target with the hope that visibility would improve. This gave the enemy gun positions time to zero in. Lieut. Lewis's ship was holed with small arms fire which pierced his bomb bay and exited through the top turret. The bombardiers used this fire as an aiming point and cratered the bridge.

Six more ships relocated to Corsica with Maj. Hackney leading the way. The barbershop is operational there, and the kitchen is turning out good meals with plenty of chow for everyone. The hard packed ground is causing problems for the kitchen crew. The guys have been trying to dig an eight foot deep grease pit. The ground is so unyielding that they only managed to dig down three feet so far. Ordinance supplied the digging detail three land mines, but even those mighty blasts did not dislodge the boulders stuck in the hard clay. One of the blasts destroyed two tents when showering debris hit them. Sgt. De Lorge was one of the unfortunate ones who had their tents pierced and he insisted on getting a replacement tent and some help to erect it.

Fishing promises to be one of the favorite forms of relaxation while we are stationed here. We hear that action is not too bad in the nearby streams. Capt. Bugbee and Greg Moore were observed this evening digging for worms. We even heard about a proposed fish fry.

April 19 First mission from Corsica! I lead our flight of six planes to Port Piombino and five planes hit the target while one returned with engine trouble. The docks and auxiliary installations were properly plastered by eighteen 340th planes as well as those of the 310th Group. In addition, our bombs made direct hits on two large ships which blew up and sank.

The men at Gaudo were up early packing what remained into our planes. With no thought for balanced loading, they filled planes from the bombardier's compartment back to the tail gunner's position. Several pilots wisely insisted that the loads be adjusted. A ninety minute flight brought them to their new home. Other 340th members came across on the last LST voyage, and there was a little excitement when a suspected German submarine was spotted. The destroyer escort dropped depth charges, and the little convoy started making weaving turns to make their course less predictable. By evening the whole unit was again together.

April 20 Weather conditions in Corsica don't seem to be too favorable for flying. Squadron members were given the day to get tents erected and dig foxholes. A detail of twelve enlisted men flew to Naples. Their assignment was to pick up six Jeeps and bring them back. Shortly after their departure, word came that the Jeeps had instead arrived in Corsica at Porto Vecchio and were awaiting drivers to deliver them. Equipment for playing horse shoes arrived and the game is under full swing.

The PX opened, and all of our liras are being exchange for francs. What a headache that is for our finance officer, Lieut. Thomas Meyer. A number of new flight crews have joined us bringing new B-25Js with them. They replace the four crews that left for the states. Orders on the bulletin board state that each tent must have a slit trench for air raids and mosquito nets must be draped over each bed. Thus far we have had no use for a slit trench although the more pessimistic squadron members expect an air raid soon.

We lost all the tents and many other camp supplies when Vesuvius erupted. Many other supplies were left behind in Africa and Sicily. Consequently, no two tents were alike in our Corsica squadron area. I was with some guys that had a regular six man tent. It was square and had four foot high sides that could be rolled up and tied. It had a single center support pole and the smokestack from our little stove vented through a hole by the pole. Our tent sat on the bare ground. The fellows scrounged wood from cases that the frag bombs came in and made a wooden floor inside. This was a real luxury, and most of the tents were not improved in that way. It was fairly warm in Corsica during the summer, and the fellows got a hold of a light weight British desert tent which they put over the top of our tent. The shade that this provided kept us much more comfortable.

We decided that we wanted more outside light than was available with the single front opening. After rolling up the tent sides, sandbags were stacked three feet high around the perimeter. We used some of the British aircraft surveillance film as makeshift windows. After washing the emulsion off the ten inch film, we inserted double wide sections into wooden frames. These homemade windows went between the sandbags and the tent and gave us ample daytime light around two sections. We got hold of a boudoir lamp from Naples and had a desk positioned near the windows. All in all we had a pretty good place to live there.

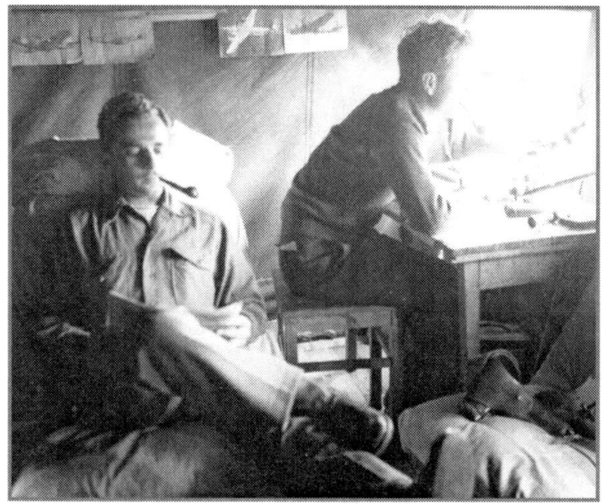

Our stove was a standard GI issue unit which was about the size of a bushel barrel. It was usually fueled with either coal or wood. It could be split into two pieces which nested together for transportation. I rigged up a blue flame burner in the stove which operated on 100 octane aviation gas. The gas burner would nicely go inside one of these stoves. When we moved, we would bring the burner with us and leave the stove behind. GI stoves were plentiful and we could find one at our new place of residence.

To fire up the stove, one of us would open the lower door and throw about a half cup of gasoline on top of the burner. The door of the stove faced toward the tent opening. Tossing a lit match into the stove produced a hearty Kavoom! The flame would sometimes go right out the door of the tent. That fire would heat up the tubing, and all that was required after that was to open the valve to the tank. No pumping was necessary, and the nice clean blue flame was very similar to the flame from a Coleman stove. Outside the tent sat a fifty gallon tank on saw horses, and gravity kept the fuel flowing to the stove. With this rig we did not have to search for coal or wood. Our tent was much cleaner and warmer than our compatriots. I suppose that gas tank could have proved fatal if we were caught inside during an air raid.

April 21 Old Man Weather owned the skies again today. Plans are being made for another trip to Cairo. Capt. Nafe also mentioned that several planes need to be flown to Foggia for modification. It's possible a little pleasure with business may be combined.

April 22 Six squadron planes led the mission today to a railroad bridge near Ficulle. The combined flights struck the rails leading up to the bridge, and one bomb hit the bridge.

The waylaid motor pool vehicles finally arrived. There are two new Jeeps and one which has been reconditioned. We also have a new deuce and a half. Three Harley- Davidson motorcycles are supposed to be official vehicles, but they are more often used for joyriding.

*April 22, 1944*

*Dear Eleanor,*

*I am sitting here in my tent with the warm sunlight streaming in the open door. It is quiet for once. All my tent roommates are on this morning's mission while I take a much-needed rest. A curious lizard lies in the sun watching me, and scuttles around the corner whenever I look up. Napoleon, our pup, is behind one of the beds chewing a slipper or some other item which will soon be beyond recognition if I don't rescue it. He is black and white with pink and black nose. Somehow he always keeps himself clean. A cute mutt.*

*I have been checked out as flight leader after only two practice missions with some special equipment. We are trying hard, my bombardier and me. We are out training on the days that we are not flying missions.*

*Of course you have read about the explosion of Mount Vesuvius. I was fortunate to be on R&R on Capri when it blew up and I could see a lot of the eruption from there. I will describe it to you when I come home. That last sentence sounds really good to me. Hopefully it won't be a terribly long time now. Hurry up and finish your nurses training. I don't want to have a chaperone when I see you. That would definitely try my patience!*

*All my love, Dale*

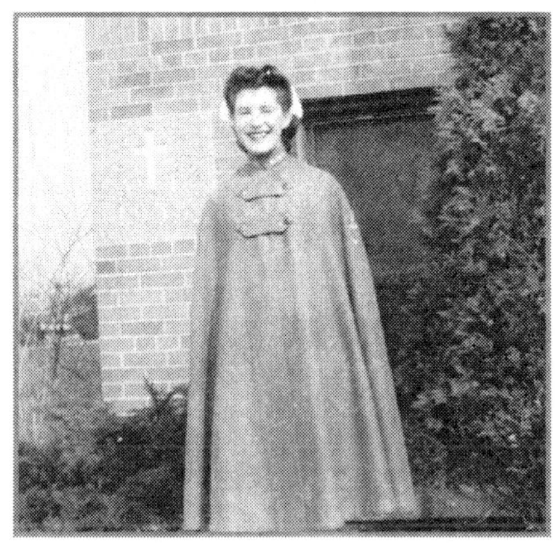

**April 23** **We seem to be getting better at targeting.** Photos from yesterday's mission show that we hit the railroad bridge and cut the tracks at Ficulle. Maj. Hackney and Capt. Shealy went to the quartermaster and they came back with shoes, fatigues, field jackets, OD pants and shirts. They were also successful in obtaining lumber for the mess hall.

April 24 Returning pilots reported a good afternoon mission to the railroad bridge of Orvieto. The 486th bomb pattern went across the bridge with direct hits. Ack-ack was moderate and accurate, holing three of our ships. Some of the guys are wearing little or nothing on the beach and their tans prove it. The weather has been beautiful and conducive to beach play.

There was an evening squadron meeting, and Maj. Hackney spoke on several things including the necessity of caring for personal equipment and a ban on off-road motorcycle riding. He also asked us not to buzz the beach. The Major ended his comments by complementing us on the effort we made in our last relocations. Lieut. Meyer, the Adjutant, asked us to maintain squadron vehicles in better condition. He also discouraged the use of vehicles to visit out-of-bounds towns. Some locations require a pass. He went on to say that misappropriation of mess hall supplies was getting out of hand. Lastly, cautioned the crews to make sure that gas caps on our planes were securely tightened before flight. The Group Intelligence Officer briefed us on the war situation in all parts of the world. He wouldn't say or didn't know the date of the France invasion, but wouldn't be surprised if it occurred within the next month.

April 25 Ack-ack was really tough today. We went back to Ficulle with each squadron furnishing nine planes. Three planes in our formation were holed. In 6H, Sgt. Bills was wounded, and we counted eighteen holes in the plane. Much more serious damage was inflicted on 6F flown by officers Sellers, Hartsock, and Olson, with Sergeants Burnett, McDonald, and Damaini. A/A zeroed in on them with a sustained burst which put 195 large holes in the wings and fuselage! The right engine got knocked out and they feathered the prop. Amazingly, all of them arrived back here at Alesan safely. This was a comforting example of how much damage our planes could absorb and remain airborne.

Plane 6Y was also holed, but not as badly as 6H and 6F. The other misfortune of this eventful day was an overturned Jeep which injured Lieut. McMillan. Fortunately he was only badly bruised.

April 26/27 Both days the wind blew hard, with a good deal of thunder and lightning. The mess tent and the barber's tent blew down and heavy rain turned the area into a muddy mess. The line personnel are glad for the break because it gives them an opportunity to get the armor plating installed in the newly arrived B-25J models. The mechanics don't understand why planes are arriving from the states without this essential protection, and they loudly complain. It's a real headache to try to get armor installed with all the equipment in the ships.

Tonight we have more wind and rain. Despite this, the guys made a volleyball court and played five games. The energy level was high on both sides of the net. One of the mascots is named GI, a small puppy of various breeds. Like most of our pets, GI is allowed to run free and he was injured by a truck near the operations trailer. An emergency operation was performed on GI by Sgt. Rounis and several other first aiders. GI is now doing nicely and will probably be on his feet shortly.

April 28 The first bright clear morning in three days created an opportunity for several routine missions. An unusual low altitude mission was also flown, and was a first for our squadron. This special mission combined four B-25s with twenty Spitfires. Our bombers carried three 1000 pound bombs, and the combined force arrived over the Italian coast at 8000 feet. They quickly descended to 400 feet and destroyed one of the two bridges at Montepulciano. Together with the fighters, they then strafed everything in sight. This mission may be the forerunner to similar attacks. Crew members that I spoke to said that they enjoyed it and actually had a good time.

The mail situation hasn't been too good and squadron morale is suffering for it. Wagering about the invasion date is going on at a fast and furious pace, and some of the pots are quite large. We are all in great hopes that it will be soon.

April 29 We took off early today and the target was Terni viaduct. The first element's bombs straddled the tracks leading up to the viaduct. The second element destroyed a bridge across the canal about 100 yards to the left of the first target. The campaign in Italy is pitting our bomb dropping skills against the German engineers. We hit a bridge, and very quickly they have it replaced.

We were happy to get a truck full of laundry back. A lot of guys turned up at the Officers Club this afternoon wearing khaki. Capt. Dozier, Lieut. "Chief" Glade, S/Sgt. Brown and T/Sgt. Moxon departed today for a thirty day furlough in the USA. They will return to us afterward. This newly implemented leave policy has its pros and cons, but as a whole most of the guys are more than willing to spend a month at home with a prayer that the war will be winding down before their leave is up.

April 30 An evening mission ended the month, and the squadron target was Marciana Railroad Bridge. I was lead pilot for our flight of airplanes. The first element hit it squarely. The second element bombed the warehouses and observed black smoke rising from them at a point immediately south of the bridge.

May 1 Two missions were flown today, and all available crews were in the air. Oviedo was a major transportation point with several rail lines. We returned there today with an escort of twelve Spitfires to bomb the north railroad bridge, but it was obscured by clouds. There were good hits on both sides of the approach to the railroad bridge at Albinin, the alternate target.

Three ships were holed by moderate and accurate antiaircraft. S/Sgt. Kellereski, a gunner on a 489th ship was seriously wounded. Late in the afternoon a low level attack formation left with a Spitfighter escort. The returning pilots told us that the results were favorable, with all ships returning safely.

The beaches off the squadron area have been de-mined and are now open for swimming. However, it will have to warm up a little before we try the water. Two more softball games were played this evening, with Engineering losing to Communications and the Bombardiers on the losing end of their game with Armament. "Swing Time Johnny" was the attraction at the movie tonight. Approval of the Andrews Sisters numbers was unanimous. The movies seem to be increasingly well attended. Our improvised screen is a canvas covered wood frame about eight by seven feet is at the bottom of a somewhat weedy and stony hill. Consequently, folding chairs, small metal drums, or wooden barrels comprise our rustic outdoor seating area.

## Air Medal, First Cluster Awarded

Raymond G. Hobson, 066-8240, First Lieut., for meritorious achievement while participating in an aerial flight as pilot of a B-25 type aircraft in an attack upon a railroad bridge at Albinin, Italy on 1 May, 1944. Point Pleasant, NY.

The 340th Group was engaged primarily in "Operation Strangle" during this period. This battle plan was designed to expedite the fall of Rome by starving the enemy of supplies and reinforcements. To that end, we bombed road intersections and bridges. These were small and difficult targets which were often heavily defended, but we knocked many of them out. We also attacked railroad installations in central and north central Italy.

Ultimately, the goal was to move the Gustav line far to the north. Our bombing was the airborne component of the Anzio invasion, which was also connected to the Cassino battle lines.

Fierce opposition by the enemy on the Gustav line, and their determined counterattacks at Anzio caused the "Operation Strangle" to be considerably drawn out. The group flew forty-six missions which totaled 848 sorties; a reasonable performance considering our problems at Pompeii. It was not completed until the end of May. We were also directed to drop ordinance for army support. These were frag missions which bombed troop concentrations.

May 2 Our improving bomb accuracy suffered a disappointing reversal today. Six 486th planes went to the north rail bridge at Oviedo, but none of the bombs hit the target area. The other squadrons did have hits on the north approach of the bridge.

The mail situation is starting to perk up a bit, and it sure has an excellent effect on morale. Contributing to that was the official word that ground crews would be included in the rotation of personnel to the states. This was very welcome news as many them have been away from the U.S. from fourteen to sixteen months. Unfortunately, the rotation rate is only .5 percent per month which means it will take about 16.5 years to get the original members home! 500 francs is the pool bet on the invasion date. This afternoon the Clerks defeated our Pilots baseball team nine to seven in a hotly contested contest.

May 3 Bombing results were much better today. Our target was the road bridge five miles north of Todi. Bubbles and I led the first element which laid a pattern across the south approach. The second element bombed the north approach and middle of the bridge, with a direct hit on the middle section. Mission photos show massive damage.

Many airmen are awaiting orders to rotate back to the States. A fair number of them have developed "ailments" of all kinds. While not exactly goldbricking, they are attempting to exempt themselves from flying status. Capt. Nathan was forced to issue orders that those with rotation fever should refrain from going to the dispensary unless it is an emergency.

Visiting Ajaccio is a pleasant day off activity. The birthplace of Napoleon is located on the west coast of Corsica. Trips to the west coast usually depart at dawn because the 110 mile trip by Jeep takes five hours. The scenery is postcard beautiful. While the sun shines, the snow glistens from the mountain tops. The entire journey is one continuous series of S turns on narrow mountain roads. Any driver carelessness can result in a drop of hundreds of feet over a precipice. Along the road, small streams flow from here and there with miniature waterfalls. Beautiful unused beaches line the west side of the island.

Every morning a P-47 buzzes the squadron area at an almost death-defying altitude. The pilot is believed to be Lieut. Schooley, who completed his missions with the 340th last month. He may be carrying out a stated goal of flying P-47s pending orders to go home.

May 4 The mess hall had to stay open late this evening because the mission to the railroad bridge south of Arezzo didn't finish up until 1930 hrs. The 486th pattern hit the approach, but did not collapse the bridge. We also hit a road junction in that area. Earlier, Peggy from the Red Cross Unit passed out donuts and coffee to the fellows in the squadron area. I watched with amusement as Tom Wheeler waited patiently until Peggy turned her back to the donut container, whereupon he made a haul.

May 5 Thunder shook us awake, and mission plans were scuttled. Before we relocated from Pompeii, airmen would take off on stand down days to the nearest town where wine, women and song were abundant. However, many of us are now playing ball, reading, writing letters, sleeping or washing clothes. Laundry is getting to be quite a problem over here. Our quartermaster will only accept six items per week because the laundry can't handle any more due to the local labor shortage.

Lieut. Lemaster, the PX officer, really has been taking care of us. Every fifth day there is a ration of candy, coke and smokes (pipes, tobacco, cigarettes and cigars) for everyone. Sgt. Greg Moore gave a negative of his girlfriend to the photographic crew so that they could print a picture for him. Greg's bathing beauty negative was reproduced enough times to adorn every bulletin board in the squadron, plus every other place in public view! She now has an unlimited number of admirers.

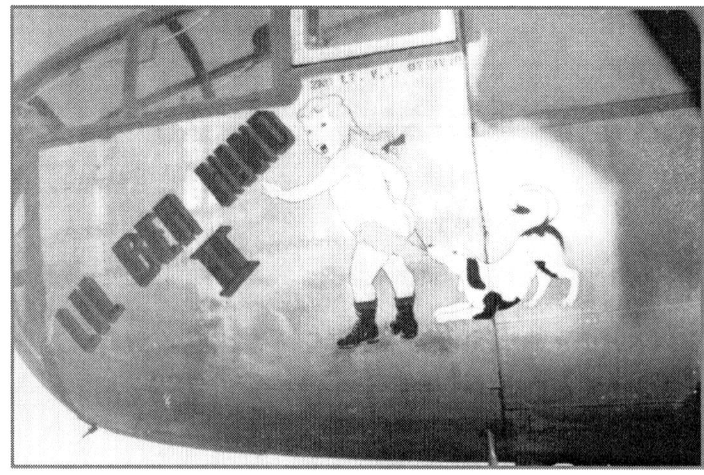

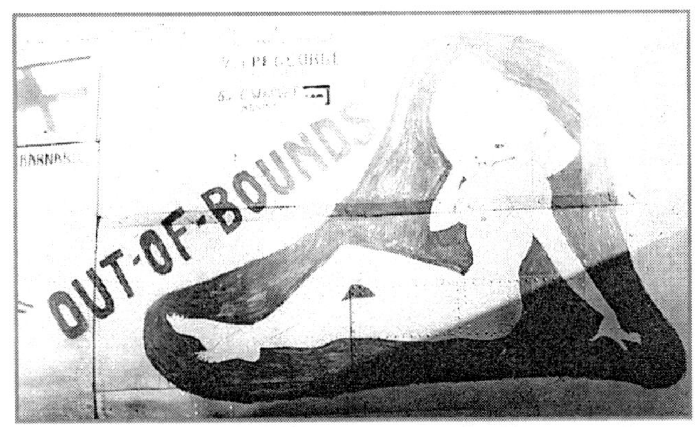
OUT-OF-BOUNDS

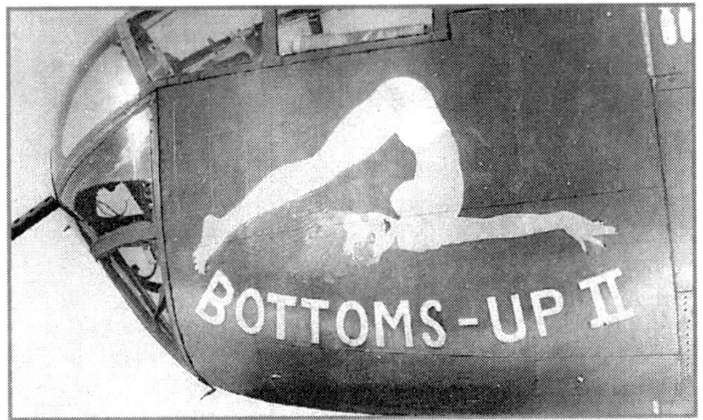
BOTTOMS-UP II

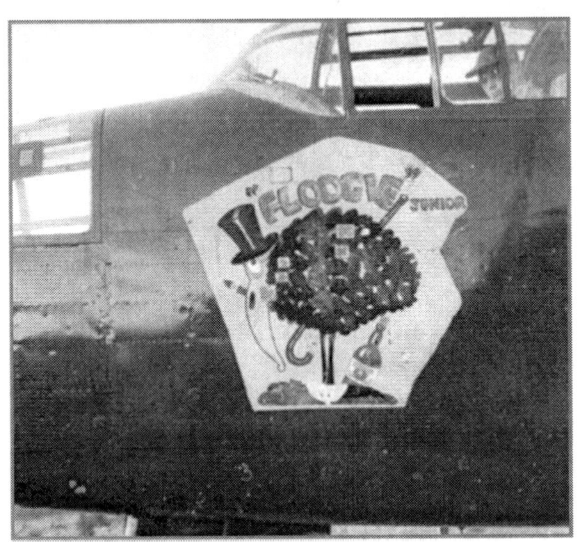
JUNIOR

By the time we moved to Corsica, we had learned the ropes on how to get fresh food from Sardinia to augment our regular rations. Sardinia was about an hour away from our base. Our fellows would take an airplane down there with a crate in the bomb bay and get a load of vegetables. One day I was up on a practice mission and turned the plane on final approach to Alesan field. Another B-25 was touching down ahead of me. He slammed onto the runway very hard. The bomb bay doors flew open, and a crate with 500 pounds of vegetables hit the runway! The crate careened down several hundred feet spilling its contents.

Going down to Sardinia for vegetables became a twice monthly run. We got cucumbers, a leafy vegetable that had a sort of anise flavor, some tomatoes and of course olives. We flew down to Cyprus for liquor. Cypriot liquor came with various kinds of labels on the bottles, but it all tasted the same to me and was most often flavored by orange peels. The alcoholic content was reasonably high and at times it was all we had in the officers clubs.

The Army decided to set up an in-house brewery and assigned a master sergeant who knew something about making beer as a brew master. He constructed a brewery in Naples. The beer that he was making was pretty decent, and came to us in glass bottles. Refrigeration was not available, and we looked for alternate ways of cooling the beer. We found out that you could take a bug bomb which was pressurized with Freon and bury it and the beer a little ways in the sand. When the Freon canister was discharged it would cool the beer down a little, but it was not very effective. After several months this source of beer ended. We started getting beer brewed in New York which was not very good.

May 6-9 Thunderstorms darkened the skies over Italy. The larger cells reportedly produced some golf ball sized hail. That didn't keep some of our personnel from getting killed. Two officers and an enlisted man in the 488th died when their low-flying B-25 piled into the hills near Cervione, just northwest of Alesan field. No one sits around on these days, and crews take advantage of the time to clean airplanes and guns. Twelve newly arrived airmen have joined the armament section which has been understaffed. Lately, some of those fellows have had to do the work of two men. Two planes from the 489th departed for the States today with planes that will be overhauled and modified.

Sgt. Stan Hickey, Group Public Relations man, is getting a lot of cooperation with a new project. Soldiers in our unit who reside in the same state are being photographed as a group. Every day, several states are selected in alphabetical sequence. These pictures will be distributed to the news agencies and picture pools throughout America for release in local papers. My friends from the Michigan/Illinois area went with me to the camera shoot.

May 10 Clouds still prevent a clear view over Italian targets, but the squadron departed early to the Terni Viaduct. We bombed the nearby marshaling yards and hit it just short of the chokepoint. It is rumored that the 340th Bomb Group will receive a Presidential Unit Citation for the excellent job that they did in the Tunisian and Sicilian campaigns.

A dance is planned soon for the enlisted men, and they are very enthusiastic about this. There is a baseball game every night and everyone plays. So much enthusiasm has been shown in the nightly softball games that individuals are keeping the equipment in their own tents. They want to be certain of having it on hand at game time. Lieut. Jim Shinwell took the situation in hand and collected all the baseball gloves so that none of them are in lockers at game time. When they're not playing baseball, many of those guys can be found in a tent playing bingo. Towns in Corsica are still out of bounds to members of our Group.

May 11 Portferraio harbor was visited by six squadron aircraft today. The results were excellent. Bombs knocked out the power station, blast furnaces and buildings. All combat crew members were called to a meeting at the Group operations by Col. Chapman. He told us that the Group is to play a part in a coordinated attack against Cassino tomorrow. We will saturate the area with bombs to pave the way for an infantry assault. Col. Chapman said that the French invasion is not far off.

## Air Medal, Second Cluster Awarded

William P. Laney, 074-7828, First Lieut., for meritorious achievement while participating in an aerial flight as pilot of a B-25 type aircraft in an attack upon Portferraio harbor, Elba, on 11 May 1944. Munroe, NC.

May 12 Anything might happen from here on in. New orders are for us to put up twenty planes from each squadron on each mission! We sent twenty-four ships today to attack the Cassino area; the ships were split into flights of twelve. A total of sixty bombers formed up from the 340th. The attack was divided into morning and afternoon missions. I flew on both of these three-hour flights. In addition to our planes, we saw many flights of B-24s and B-26s dropping bombs on the target. Officers Gartner, Powers and Rogers with Sergeants Bradley, Schmidt and Delucca were lost today in ship 8Y. It was Delucca's first mission, and the other men aboard the plane were also rather new. We saw their ship turn on its back and fall into a vertical dive.

There was quite a bit of excitement tonight when our antiaircraft guns opened up against some German night raiders. The sky was lit up by flares, and it sounded like all hell broke loose.

We will probably hear a report from the gun crews tomorrow. We all hope that is as close as we'll ever get.

### Soldiers Medal Awarded

Fred Sedach, 074-3904, First Lieut., 486th Bomb Sq., 340th Bomb Group, for heroism while participating in an aerial flight as bombardier of a B-25 type aircraft. Upon completion of the bomb run over Itri, Italy, on 12 May 1844, it was discovered that one fragmentation cluster had failed to release over the target and was protruding from the open bomb bay hanging by the arming wire. Realizing the danger of the hanging bomb, Lieut. Sedach removed his parachute and climbed headfirst into the bomb bay. Balancing himself in this precarious position for several minutes, he jettisoned the bomb harmlessly into the water. His selfless devotion to duty in the face of grave danger reflects highest credit upon himself and the Armed Forces of the United States. Rumford, RI.

### Air Medal Awarded

Edward H. Zoolalian, 335-85059, Sgt., for meritorious achievement while participating in an aerial flight as tail gunner of a B-25 type aircraft in an attack upon enemy communication lines near Itri, Italy on 12 May 1944. Philadelphia, PA.

Maurice B. Wynn, Jr., 141-51992, Sgt., for meritorious achievement while participating in an aerial flight as tail gunner of a B-25 type aircraft in an attack upon enemy communication lines near Itri, Italy, on 12 May 1944. Macon, GA.

## Air Medal, Second Cluster Awarded

Edward F. Murray, 074-4400, First Lieut., for meritorious achievement while participating in an aerial flight as bombardier of a B-25 type aircraft in an attack upon any communication lines near Itri, Italy on 12 May 1944. New York, NY.

One of our missions attacked a German bivouac area which was used for R&R. The bivouac area was some distance from the front, and the soldiers at the encampment were on rest status. Bombs from my flight scored many direct hits and multiple building fires were visible. We were armed with fragmentation bombs which as earlier noted were used as anti-personnel weapons. My opinion about this targeting decision was not expressed in public.

A fragmentation bomb attack was interesting. The individual bombs weighed thirty pounds and they were clustered in groups of six nose to nose. A piece of black pipe went down the middle of the cluster, and wires went from the bomb triggers into the black pipe. At the end of the black pipe there was a forty-five caliber cartridge and a firing pin. When the cluster of bombs was dropped, a safety wire pulled out and the cartridge fired which went down the pipe and cut all wires. This allowed the bombs to scatter and arm as they came down. We usually carried twenty-two clusters on each plane. Since there weren't enough bomb racks in the plane, some of the clusters were wired together. Each plane would drop 132 of these bombs.

We couldn't drop the cluster bombs in a normal six plane formation. The planes could not fly safely through all the discharged pipes and wires. We bombed in echelon on these missions. The planes were positioned successively to the left or right to form an oblique or step-like line. We had an incident where one echelon of six planes followed another, and they were supposed to be 200 feet higher than the one in front. They came in 200 feet lower. I don't know how that screw up happened, but one of those frag bombs came smashing through the window of a plane in the second group. It landed between the pilot and copilot, but miraculously did not injure either one.

It was the copilot's first combat mission. He pushed his seat back, went back and pulled the hatch handle and jumped out! The pilot picked up the bomb and tossed it out the hatch behind him. He closed the hatch and managed to get the airplane back to base. The bombs did have a propeller on them which armed the bombs by spinning. They had to a fall a certain number of feet before they were armed. That bomb obviously had not fallen far enough to become armed before hitting the plane.

May 13 The Luftwaffe made two major nighttime attacks on Corsica airfields. Rumors circulated afterword that the raids were partially in reprisal for our mission to the German bivouac camp. The first attack which began at 2230 hrs. struck a British Spitfighter base called Borgo Poretta. It was located about twenty miles north of us. I saw some of this action going on while standing with several friends. One of them expressed an opinion that we could be next. The wisdom of disabling the fighter base before our attack became apparent later.

The Alesan field attack began at 0335 hrs. and caused many casualties as well as extensive damage to our planes and other equipment. The raid was initiated when a British Beaufighter flew over the field dropping flares, which brightly illuminated the area. It also dropped anti-personnel bombs. The twin engine fighter-bomber was presumably captured by the enemy and later employed for Pathfinder use. Those of us who had slit trenches jumped into them while the antiaircraft batteries opened up. Then we saw JU-88s passing overhead on a bomb run. FW-190s with ME-109s approached at low altitude while strafing our ack-ack positions. One of the first bombs hit the 90 mm antiaircraft gun, knocking it out. After that our ability to return fire was limited.

Our planes had been prepared for the next day's mission, and many of them were full of bombs and fuel. Bombs started hitting these loaded planes and the fuel dump. They also fell on the radio station trailer west of the field and struck the Operations building. The Luftwaffe also dropped fragmentation bombs which were intended for the Headquarters tent. While some those bomb clusters found their target, most of them fortunately fell a few hundred yards offshore into the sea. They also attacked the 489th squadron about a mile away.

Of the parked aircraft, twenty-three were totally destroyed and roughly ninety were damaged. It was hell, with fires burning everywhere. Some of the B-25 explosions were so violent that engines were found blocks away from where the airplane had been parked. In some cases a large crater was all that remained. We found out later that there were nearly ninety JU-88s involved. The attack lasted about an hour and fifteen minutes. The JU-88s came over on bomb runs at about 3000 feet. After the antiaircraft cannon was out a commission, they dove down with the fighters on strafing runs as low as fifty feet.

Many of the personnel made it into foxholes and slit trenches, but casualties were still high from the bombing and strafing as well as our planes blowing up with full bomb loads. Some men did not wake up in time. Others ignored the warning sirens thinking that it was just another nuisance raid. For many of them that meant sudden death or painful injuries. On several prior evenings what appeared to be a stray bomber overhead initiated a full air raid response. Our half-dressed guys would stumble out into their slit trenches carrying their gas masks.

Many airmen were too terrified to run to the nearest foxhole once the bombs began to explode. Making it into a trench was no guarantee of safety. Frag bombs and heavy strafing took a toll on the soldiers in the foxholes. Fire engine personnel bravely began putting out fires before the attack was over and most of those men were injured.

The 489th area was hardest hit of all four squadrons and suffered the greatest damage and casualties. They hadn't dug many of their slit trenches yet, and men who might otherwise have protected themselves were killed or seriously injured. In truth, many 340th pilots had been very careless about "digging in." Any talk of wearing helmets and digging slit trenches was considered almost cowardly. One pilot jumped into a slit trench and landed on top of two others. He was killed instantly by a piece of shrapnel, and the two soldiers below him were severely wounded. None of them were completely below ground level. The enemy's saturation of their area with frag bombs caused many other casualties. Each of the German frag bombs weighed only three pounds and a JU-88s could carry 1000 of them.

Of course, our medical people rushed in and worked all day. The overtaxed hospitals sent the most seriously wounded to the 35th Station Hospital which was about four miles north of the airfield. That hospital was already busy treating wounded from the Borgo Poretta airfield. Total casualties for the 340th were twenty-five dead and over 100 wounded. I had mentioned before that Capt. Charles Nathan was a good officer and an excellent physician with surgical skills. In the middle of the attack he brought a Jeep close to the flight line and did emergency trauma care on the back of the Jeep. He had no protection from the ongoing attack and his courageous actions undoubtedly saved lives. Capt. Nathan received the Bronze Star for his brave work and we had immense respect for him.

Numerous vehicles of various types were so badly damaged that they couldn't be salvaged. Scores of tents on the field were badly shot up and some leveled to the ground. Many of the destroyed B-25s were brand-new. Most of our guys had their tents on the airfield. Pictures show some of that damage. We lost all the operations and intelligence records as well as the historical files of the organization. Very useful maps and aeronautical charts were also destroyed. The control tower was also damaged. Most of our fuel supplies burned. We were amazed how long the attack went on. If you compare their time over target to the amount of time we spent on bomb runs, the conclusion must be that they were determined to make a good job of it.

Of course, putting this event into words does not convey the emotions that I still feel when I think about the attack. I woke to the drone of airplane engines overhead and instantly realized that they could not be ours. After shaking my roommates awake, we bolted out of our tent just as the antiaircraft guns opened up. Our slit trench was about thirty feet from our tent and we made a beeline for it. Peering out, we looked at the flight line and saw one of our planes lift up as if it were levitating. It smashed on top of another one, and both planes exploded with the force of 1200 gallons of aviation gas combined with 6000 pounds of bombs. That explosion set several nearby planes on fire, and moments later they also blew up with equally fearsome concussions. It was nothing less than a holocaust. I felt a sudden impact as other men jumped into our slit trench partially covering me.

Fighters whizzed by at low level, firing their machine guns and cannon. With my view partially blocked, my other senses told me what was going on. I could feel the heat emanating from burning tents, vehicles and airplanes. I heard sporadic small arms fire from nearby trenches. Our defense seemed so puny compared to the firepower overhead. Our three-foot deep slit trench was filled to the surface with men and I felt the crush of bodies on and next to me. Mercifully, we escaped a direct blast from the enemy. When the raid finally ended, we stood up and surveyed the burning flight line and our riddled tents. We went from trench to trench checking for the wounded, and carrying the ones who could be moved to a makeshift trauma center set up in the mess tent.

The Borgo Poretta raid destroyed twenty-five Spitfighters and killed a number of men. Intelligence later reported that there were no German planes brought down in either attack. One of the Spitfighters trailed the raiders to their base. That information was passed to a P-47 squadron which went over and cleaned them up. From a German standpoint, it was a very successful raid.

### Killed due to enemy action in our squadron:

Sgt. Walter J. Labe, 130-79817; Sgt. James B. Saunders, 363-35395; Sgt. John Koban, 311-44496

### Wounded seriously due to enemy action:

T/Sgt. Donald G. Neumeyer, 350-39801; S/Sgt. John Kerr, 120-78298; Cpl. Edward E. Hildebrand, 384-64926; Cpl. Walter C. Hafer, 336-18441; Pfc. Sol Hartenstein, 328-60942; Pfc. Leo H. Hoeschele, 326-69131.

In the 489th, my friends, Lieutenants Connolly and Friedman were dead. They were a lead pilot-bombardier team who had trained with me in Group meetings. Their excellent flying had been observed by many in the Group. Friedman was killed after being wounded while lying in bed. As he ran from his tent, a frag bomb exploded nearby. All of the lead pilot/bombardier crews from the 489th suffered casualties which affected their operations for several weeks. The tents on that side of the field looked like sieves with many holes shot through them.

This was one of the last large, effective German air attacks of the war. Second German Air Force Chief Gen. Field Marshal von Richthofen, after much effort, received permission from Hitler to attack airbases on Corsica.

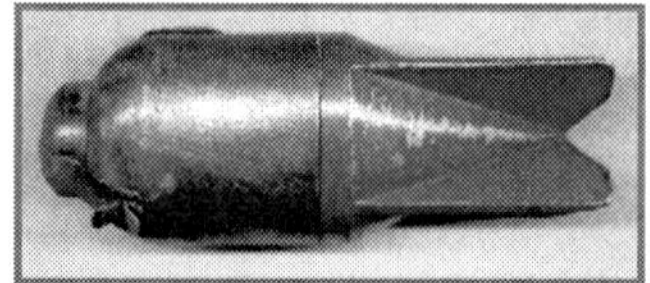

**German Frag Bomb**

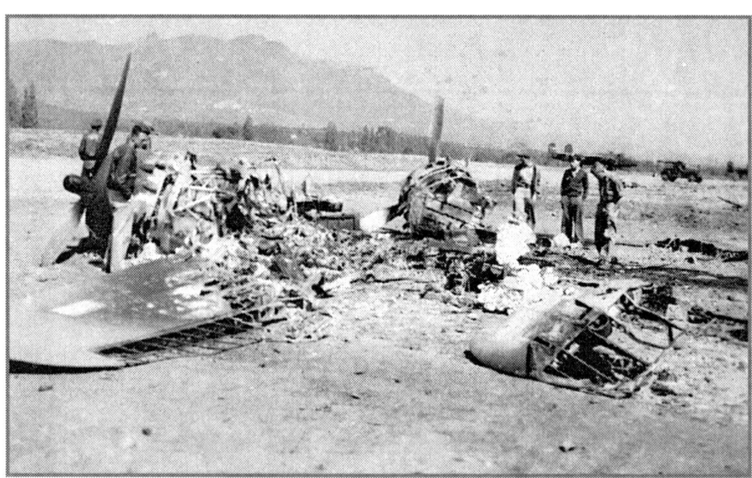

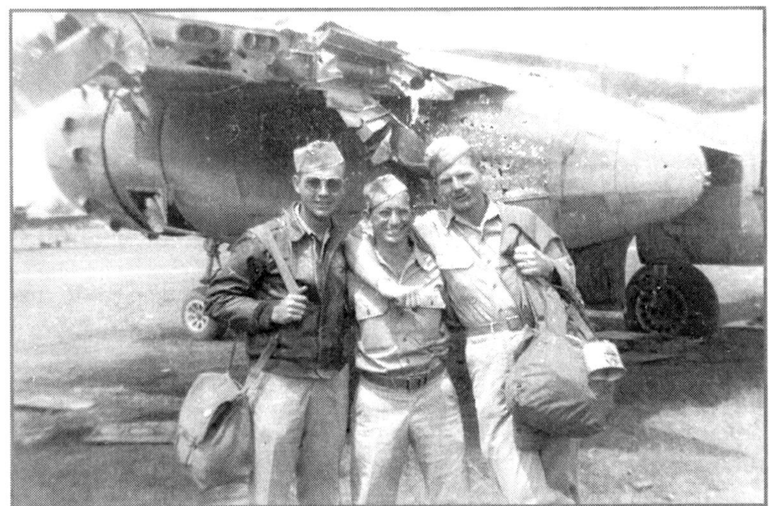

**Hymie Setzer is in the center**
(photo courtesy Daniel Setzer)

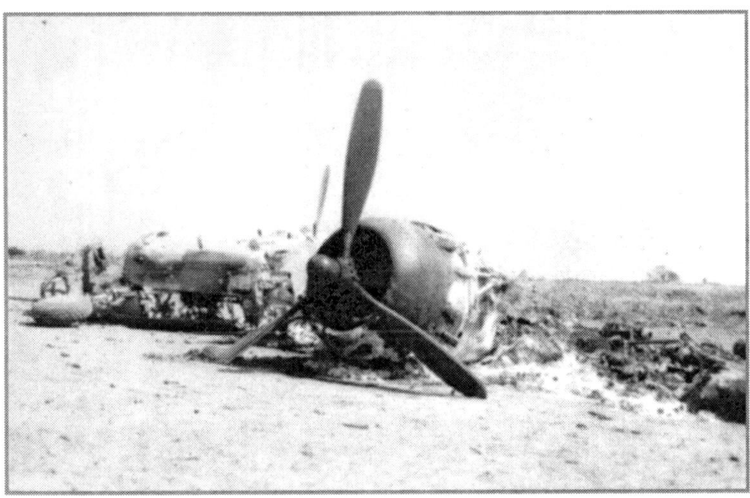

Despite the great damage and loss of life, we flew a mission that day. The reasoning was that we needed to show the Germans that they hadn't succeeded in wiping us out. The engineers worked really hard clearing the runway. Col. Chapman had us walk the length of the runway shoulder to shoulder picking up smaller fragments that could flatten tires. Many of the flyable airplanes had flat tires from all the shrapnel and the mechanics had to do some swapping to get the mission up. Immediately after breakfast there was a rush for shovels and pick axes. Some weird designs of bomb shelters built over foxholes blossomed all over the place. At the first sound of a jeep backfiring, men dove into the half-finished trenches.

As we were preparing for the mission, some damn fool in an A-20 flew low over the field while firing his guns and everyone dove for cover. I led six 486th ships to bomb the mouth of the tunnel about a mile south of Itri. The ack-ack was heavy, intense and accurate. One ship, 6M, left the formation off Gaeta point and went to Naples and did a superior job making a belly landing. Lieut. Jacobson, the copilot, was seriously wounded in both legs and Lieut. Bernard the bombardier, had a piece of flak go through his hand. Despite this, Lieut. Bernard administered first aid to Lieut. Jacobson all the way there. The airplane was badly shot up, but the whole crew remained cool and collected. This was the third belly landing for Lieut. Leggett, the pilot.

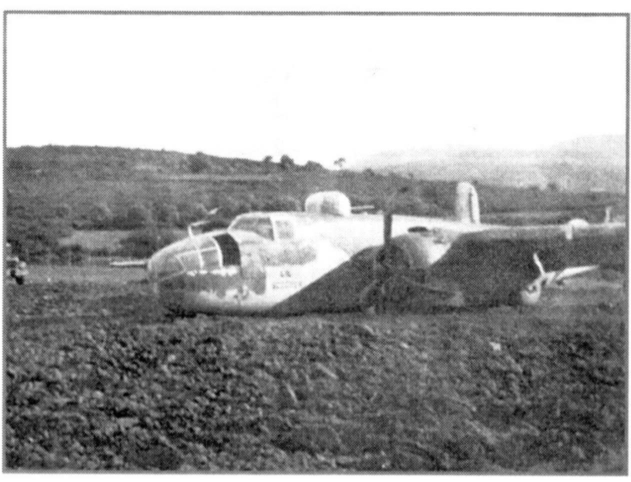

(Courtesy 57th Bomb Wing)

**May 14** **After one of the most eventful days since I** arrived here, 486th squadron sent six airplanes to the railroad bridge at Arezzo. Our bombs went to the right of the bridge, but cut the tracks.

New foxholes dug into the hard packed dirt rival the size of the buildings overhead. The 845th Aviation Engineers did an excellent job of restoring the field to operational status. Before sunrise, their men were filling in bomb craters near the edge of the runway. Soon a bulldozer was scraping away the still burning remains of Group Headquarters and construction began on a new building. Nerves were at a high tension throughout the day, and probably shall remain so for some time. My ears rang for several days from the shattering explosions.

An air of solitude permeated the squadron. To shake this off, Major Hackney organized a blood drive and all able-bodied men went to the hospital and donated blood. Funeral services for our comrades were held this afternoon in Bastia. Guards of honor from all squadrons in the Group attended this inspiring but depressing ceremony.

## Air Medal, Third Cluster Awarded

Joseph F. Podvojsky, 079-5822, First Lieut., for the meritorious achievement while participating in an aerial flight as pilot of a B-25 type aircraft in an attack upon a railroad bridge near Arezzo, Italy, on 14 May 1944. Homestead, PA.

May 15 Cloud coverage obscured the Ficulle railroad bridge and our formation of six planes proceeded onto the alternate, Piombino Harbor. They saw several hits on the south jetty. Ack-ack was inaccurate, with no damage done to the formation.

May 16 Todays mission was a mirror of yesterdays. I was in on this one. We diverted our attention to the alternate target, Piombino Harbor. Four jetties were set ablaze which engulfed the cargo cranes. Flak was fairly intense with three ships holed. Sgt. Jeff Hawkins passed away last night, another victim of the air raid. Many of us attended his funeral the next day.

## Air Medal, Fourth Cluster Awarded

Dale J. Satterthwaite, 080-4516, First Lieut., for meritorious achievement while participating in an aerial flight as pilot of a B-25 type aircraft in an attack upon Piombino Harbor, Italy, on 16 May 1944. Oaklawn, Ill.

## Air Medal, Fifth Cluster Awarded

Vincent Myers, 066-3652, Capt., for the meritorious achievement while participating in an aerial flight as bombardier of a B-25 type aircraft in an attack upon Piombino Harbor, Italy, on 16 May 1944. Apache, OK.

May 17 Poggiobonsi Railroad Bridge was the first of two targets for the day. Six planes covered the bridge with bomb craters. The ack-ack was heavy, but fortunately inaccurate and all our crews safely returned. Crews on the second mission, which was Frosinone, reported that their bombs fell about 100 feet from the railroad crossing. Again, all ships returned safely. "Whistling in Brooklyn" with Red Skelton provided some good entertainment at the movies tonight.

May 18 48,000 pounds of bombs were directed at the railroad bridge at Via Reggio today with fairly good results. The bomb bursts started at the railroad tracks, and extended into an industrial plant. The second formation dropped their bombs on the tracks between the bridge and the marshaling yard. There was no defensive fire and we all returned safely.

Lenny Tetreault, one of my tent mates, speaks French like a local. He returned from an unauthorized sojourn with a big smile on his face. Lenny spent the afternoon in the hills putting his excellent command of the French language into play. He tells us that the Corsicans have some very good wine which remains in its hiding place until some extra special visitor comes along.

May 19 We carried the same weight of bombs as on yesterday's mission to Pontassieve Railroad Bridge and scored hits on the tracks leading to the bridge. No direct strikes were observed on the target itself. 486th ships were the third formation over the target, and the antiaircraft had time to zero in. Our lead ship received serious damage and returned to Alesan airfield on one engine.

After the German air raid, the number of 40 mm defensive guns at Alesan airfield was doubled. Barbed wire was placed along the beach, and anti-personnel mine fields were planted there as well. Col. Thomas of the 12th Air Force Command let us know that the 340th has priority over other units for food and supplies. This acknowledgment of our need for resupply was very welcome. There is a continuous dialogue in the squadron about the invasion date, and particularly when Rome will be liberated. The Italian campaign is leading the charge and taking the brunt of the flight for the Allies. We will be happy when the Germans have other fronts to contend with.

My friends have prevailed upon Lenny Tetreault to show them where a drink might be had. They returned with several bottles of wine, which we all agree is wretched. It was delegated to cleaning fluid duty. Perhaps Lenny received some consideration because he is conversant in French.

## Distinguished Flying Cross Awarded

James L. Williams, 068-1848, First Lieut., 487th Bomb Sq., 340th Bomb Group for extraordinary achievement while participating in an aerial flight as a bombardier of a B-25 type aircraft serving as lead bombardier on many combat missions. Lieut. Williams has distinguished himself through his outstanding leadership and superior tactical skill. On 19 May 1944, Lieutenant Williams was lead bombardier on an eighteen ship formation attacking the vital enemy marshaling yards at Pontassieve, Italy. As the formation started the bomb run, an intense and accurate barrage of antiaircraft fire riddled his ship. Lieut. Williams remained cool and calm as he directed the pilot on the bomb run. In spite of the heavy ground haze which partially obscured the target, Lieut. Williams dropped his bombs with unerring accuracy into the target area, thereby severing the enemy's main rail supply route. This proficiency, judgment and devotion to duty under fire reflect the highest credit upon himself and the Military Service of the United States. Wilmington, NC.

May 20 Mission plans were wiped out on the 20th by high wind and rain.

I was asked to lead a mission to a bridge which was close to a building with a Red Cross on the roof. Because that building was there, dropping bombs from nine thousand feet was not possible. Upper-level brass decided that we were to go after the bridge at low level. The plan was to skip bombs with delayed timer fuses off the water into the structure. The problem that we faced was how to make the bombs "stick" to the reinforced concrete. It took more than one bomb to take the bridge down. The fuses were set for a thirty second delay. A similarly shaped bridge behind our lines became a practice target. We tried dropping the bombs facing backwards in the bomb bay, and we tried drogue parachutes. These were 1000 pound general-purpose bombs, and for this mission we carried four of them.

No matter how we released the bombs, when they hit the bridge supports they would take off into the next county. We couldn't figure out any way to make them penetrate the concrete before exploding. The brass decided that we would drop our loads into the parapets on either side of the bridge. We practiced many low-level formation approaches over water, and we were low enough for the props to kick up spray. Before the lead aircraft started a turn, the pilot would give a signal to the other aircraft. The plane on the outside of turn would have no problem, but the plane on the inside would have to drop way back while trying to keep the lead ship in sight. It was in truth a lot of fun to practice that. The skip bombing technique was not easy to master.

May 21 I led the four plane mission described above on an afternoon raid and we launched our bombs at low level into the bridge. The bombs slammed into the masonry accurately, but deflected and detonated several seconds later which left the bridge standing. At the debriefing the major told us that these missions will end soon with fighter-bombers becoming the plane of choice.

Sgt. Gerald Powers and all the ground members of his new ship posed in front of the plane today. It was partially paid for by generous donations from Muncie Indiana high school children. The new B-25J bears the name Muncie for the kids who supported the school drive. A note from the children asked for a detailed account of its first mission and Public Relations is endeavoring to give it to them through the newspaper.

*May 21, 1944*

*Dear Eleanor*

*Tomorrow, weather permitting; I will go on my 45th mission. Most of the fellows have stopped flying missions when they get to their 50th, but I expect to go a few more than that. It hasn't seemed to bother me so far. Leading a flight is more of a strain than flying as a wingman because I feel responsible for the fate of nearly 150 men. If my lead airplane drops its bombs accurately, then all the other squadron aircraft will hit their targets. I rather enjoy it though because I am more independent and am able to see what's going on instead of holding my eyes glued to the lead ship.*

*Our accuracy has been fairly good lately. If Bubbles and I improve a little more, we will be the best bombardier/pilot team in the squadron. Bubbles got his nickname from the bubbles in the bomb sight. My nickname is "Satchel." This alias stems from the large camera case that I usually have with me. Some of the other fellows are known as "The Face," "Harry the Horse," "Trigger," "Luigi," "Cedric," "Buck," "Bone Face," "Groucho," "Sad Sam," etc. They are a swell bunch of fellows.*

*We are building a clubhouse in our squadron area which will house a mess hall and bar. The construction takes a great deal of work of course, but we will be able to have our own cooks. It will be a big improvement over the food that we are getting in the mess hall. We are also setting up a rest camp for the squadron at a lake a few miles from here. Fish are plentiful in the lake and the hills above it can be hunted for wild boar. I put together a powered motorboat, and we will run it down there for the boys on vacation.*

*I am going to Cairo soon. I have wanted to visit that place ever since I came over. It will be a business trip, but I will also probably have a chance to go to Palestine and all the holy places.*

*I was intending to go to church this morning. Our chapel is just a little ways from my tent. I went down there but couldn't get close enough to hear the sermon, so I came back to write this letter. I can hear the hymns from here anyway, and they sound good. Church attendance has gone up considerably since a certain censored occurrence. It occurs to me that I will just about be on my bomb run this afternoon at the time you will be in church. There is about six hour's difference in our time you know.*

*It is a beautiful morning - the mountains are sharp and clear and the ocean blue along our beautiful beach. I am going to get this off today so I will say you are always in my heart.*

*Love, Dale*

**"Harry the Horse" paid for his education at the Colorado** School of Mines by raising and selling quarter horses. He located a mare on Corsica that the owner was willing to let him ride. He tied her up outside the Officers Club several times, much to the amusement of the patrons. "Trigger" had an amazing collection of guns. Some of them were antiques that he collected around the countryside. He constantly bartered for guns, and had in his collection a German machine pistol, a Thompson submachine gun and several pearl handled revolvers. "Bone Face" was a fellow who was nearly albino. On several occasions his white complexion blistered and turned red from sun exposure. "Groucho" resembled his namesake and was one of the best gamblers in the crowd. I was never foolish enough to enter a game with him.

May 22 Today's early morning mission was canceled just as crews were heading for their ships. We were told to remain on standby. At 1430 hrs. Bubbles and I lead an eighteen plane force to our target near Cadore, Italy. The 48 x 1000 pound bomb load was dropped from 12,200 feet and struck the road in the target area. Just as we finished the bomb run, ship 7C with Lieuts. Casey, Donvrovoid and George and Sgts. Koplan, Wilkerson and Obrovata was hit by flak. We saw that their plane was on fire before it exploded upon impact with the ground. Only one parachute was seen. The formation ran low on gas as this was a very long flight. Some made very hasty landings after dropping red flares. One plane had less than 20 gallons of fuel remaining. In theory that is enough to remain airborne for ten minutes, but often the last few gallons of fuel can't be pumped to the engines. Following this rough mission, we talked amongst ourselves for hours afterword.

Lieuts. Doyle, Narussewicz and Sgt. Robinson came back after being marooned on Capri for two weeks. The Germans mined the harbor which prevented any ship traffic to and from the island for a week. The dangerous work of clearing the mines is complete, and Capri is again functioning.

May 23th Italian targets received a one-day reprieve because they were clouded over. The weather here is sunny. Sunbathing on the beach was today's main activity. Beach goers were guided by maps showing the location of planted mines.

My friend Ted Wheeler held an open house for the squadron in his newly constructed two room house. It had such luxuries as shutters that operated from inside and even handmade ashtrays. Ted put his professional carpentry to work with wood scavenged from bomb boxes. The fellows nicknamed him "Buck" for his Jack-of-all trades skills. It was not long before the C/O and X/O put pressure on him to relinquish the house to them. Eventually, Ted did vacate the house in their favor. After occupying the house for four months, they returned it to him and moved into a sort of prefab home that the Army gave them.

May 24 The North Orvieto Road Bridge was demolished on an afternoon mission by my flight of six 486th planes combined with twelve others from the Group. Large fires destroyed several buildings on the south side of the bridge. Ack-ack was heavy but inaccurate, with no damage. "Standing Room Only" with Paulette Goddard and Fred McMurray was the flicker at the movie tonight.

May 25 A stand down was in effect until 1600 hrs. when twelve of our ships and crews prepared for a mission over the South Ficulle Bridge. The first formation of the planes dropped their loads a little short of the target. The second formation scored a direct hit. Enemy opposition brought down 9W, a plane from the 489th. Five parachutes were observed and the plane appeared to flare out as it hit the ground, so someone may have landed it.

Peggy was on hand prior to the mission with hot coffee and donuts for all the men in the squadron area. Apparently she has a soft spot in her heart for the 486th, or at least some of its members. Her visits are becoming more frequent.

May 26 Our string of late afternoon missions continued today with a twelve plane attack on Cortona South Bridge. The formation was over the bridge at 1800 hrs. and we dropped our bombs from 9400 feet. In the waning light, we saw a neat pattern of bombs hit the tracks on the north end of the bridge and damage the approach. The patterns of the second formation had direct hits on the southern approach. There was no opposition, and all returned safely. We have heard that the Anzio beachhead forces joined up with Cassino units today, which is a real victory and raises our morale.

May 27 An earlier mission departure was a welcome change. Our target was the railroad bridge at Bucine North Viaduct with forty-seven planes. For several weeks previously, B-26 bombers had attacked the target without creating any significant damage. Bombs from my six planes hit the center of the viaduct, with three center spans knocked down. The second box of planes was some distance behind us and did not see the target on their initial pass. They circled back and approached the IP from the opposite direction. Their bombs missed the target.

The flight crews that arrived with me around January are quickly approaching their fifty mission mark and some of them are sweating out their orders to go home. This is due to the double mission days that have been in effect for a while. Rightfully, the ground personnel are rather annoyed seeing flight crews return to the states when there is no chance that they will do the same. Some of the ground crew regret that they did not volunteer for combat. Many of them would have the requisite number of missions to go home. A few practice shots from the antiaircraft guns on our field had everyone making a beeline for their slit trenches the other night.

May 28 Today was a non-combat day for Bubbles and me. I got caught up on my maintenance reports and test flew several planes released from the shop. An early mission to a railroad bridge northwest of Pisa was not successful. The first bombs fell just beyond the target and landed in the river. Bombs from the other six planes landed short of the tracks. We were disappointed to learn that Rome is not as close to liberation as we hoped. Our coming missions will probably be further south in support of that effort.

May 29 The morning gang had a twelve plane mission to Castiglione Fiorentino Railroad Bridge. They reported back that they destroyed the tracks for 500 feet, but missed the bridge. No opposition was encountered. My afternoon mission left with twenty-four planes. We split up the flights as we approached Italy and hit both the primary and secondary targets. My group hit a road and railroad bridge at Necropoli. Bombs hit the road bridge and scored probable hits on the rail approach. The secondary target NW of Pisa had hits across the track south of the bridge. Ack-ack was moderate and accurate, causing slight damage to three of our ships.

Three soldiers from our unit found themselves defendants at a court martial today after being detained for stealing some aviation fuel and selling it to the locals. Punishments were as follows: Private A. Rice - 30 days hard labor and $25 fine; Private H. Smith - four months hard labor, no fine; Private T. Wright - four months hard labor and a $60 fine. They should have sought the tutelage of Sgt. ____cciolo before embarking on black market business.

## Air Medal, Fifth Cluster Awarded

Everett C. Tippett, 341-46936, S/Sgt., for the meritorious achievement while participating in an aerial flight as gunner of a B-25 type aircraft in an attack upon a road bridge near Pisa, Italy, on 29 May 1944. Lynnwood, CA.

May 30 Following an unsuccessful mission today, Col. Chapman deemed it necessary to call a meeting of all combat crews. He told them that it would be necessary to fly at a lower altitude. He further stated that there will be no stand downs declared early in the day until our push to Rome is over. In other words, the meeting consisted of a general trip to the woodshed. I did not take these remarks as a personal criticism. Bubbles and I had become a consistent and reliable team.

Our first dance since Pompeii was held tonight in Cervione, a small village about five miles from the base. No one anticipated very much and they were not disappointed. There were at least two hundred GIs stuffed in an unattractive hall. Also present were approximately twenty French girls and Peggy of the Red Cross brigade who sponsored the affair. A fine black band made up for a lot. All of the girls had quite a time trying to keep up with the All-American jitterbugs. They were mainly there for the spam sandwiches and coffee served after the dance. At midnight the girls departed with their mothers.

May 31 Apparently last night's lecture from Col. Chapman had a good affect. Large fires and explosions were the evidence of our bomb run at the Grottaferrata Road Block which is a few miles from Rome. Three of our planes received moderate damage, and one of them went off the end of the runway when it returned. A late night blast of antiaircraft cannon fire once more chased us into our slit trenches, but no enemy planes appeared. This definitely contributes to the fatigue factor.

Recently, we did an exchange of five flight crewmen with five soldiers from the 5th Army. The idea was to educate both Army forces about the goings-on on each side. Our airmen returned from the 5th Army front today with many hair-raising stories. They spent the entire week in foxholes 300 yards from the front fighting lines and made several combat patrols with the troops which included firefights and grenade exchanges. Heatstroke was a major problem for the soldiers.

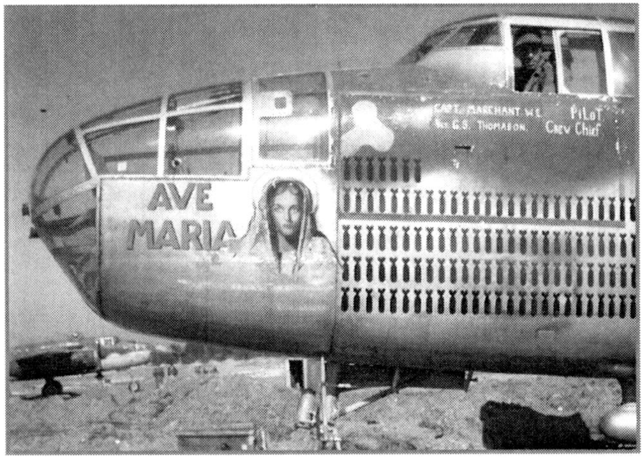


(Courtesy Bing Images)

When I first arrived in Italy, no specific fighter cover was assigned to our missions. Fighters did patrol over the Anzio beachhead, but our missions were typically short and so no escort was needed. As we began flying missions into northern Italy, Fighter Command assigned P-40s for our cover. Unfortunately, we were disappointed to find that the performance of the P-40s did not match our B-25s.

Usually the P-40s were not able to keep pace while we climbed, even though we carried heavy bomb loads. The chatter coming from the fighters usually took on a familiar pattern, "I can't quite keep up." Another fighter pilot said "Close your cowl flaps a little." The pilot answered back, "I'm up against the red line now." We would go ahead toward our target with the fighters eventually getting above us a little. Fortunately, we never got serious attacks by ME-109s in those months. It was useless exercise to send those P-40s.

In early spring the fighter squadrons were outfitted with Spitfires. It was no problem for these Spits to climb and stay above us. If we were assigned a four hour mission however, the Spitfires did not have enough range to complete the missions to France and northern Italy. They would escort us as far as their fuel allowed and then turn back. So again we had no fighter cover over the target. They quit sending the Spitfires and for several months there was no fighter cover.

In September, escort coverage was resumed with P-47s which carried belly tanks. We didn't worry about fighters unless we saw those belly tanks drop. The P-47s were in some dogfights near us, and we seldom had to fight fighters ourselves. Occasionally, we did have some attacks by ME-109s and FW-190s, and our gunners were successful in knocking some of them down. During the entire year I was there, the 340th never lost a plane to fighters. Our strategy while flying on unescorted missions was to get down low when enemy fighters were in the area. That prevented them from mounting an attack from underneath us. Of course, we would pick up speed in a dive. The fighters didn't have enough power advantage to make more than one or two passes before we got back over our own lines.

One day I was leading eighteen planes to a target east of Pisa. We were five hundred feet below broken cumulus clouds. We hadn't seen any enemy fighters recently and that may have lulled us into letting our guard down a little. An ME-109 was trailing us and using the cloud cover to shield his presence. The enemy pilot flew parallel to our course and used his superior speed to circle in front of us. He flew through the clouds and dove toward us.

The fighter burst out of the cloud cover less than half a mile away directly in front of us. An ME-109 had a top speed of nearly 370 MPH straight and level. In this instance the plane was moving at least that fast in a dive. The formation was flying at 230 MPH, so the combined closing speed was about 600 MPH. In about one second the fighter completely filled the forward view. It leveled out and came directly towards us at our altitude. The plane on my right was very close, and the fighter streaked between us. There was no time to pray he would not hit one of us, and turning was out of the question. I didn't think there was enough room to avoid a collision. Somehow the fighter passed cleanly through.

No fire came from the enemy's cannon and machine guns. We had no time to react with our guns. The entire incident took less than three seconds. His plan may have been to separate the planes and thereby have individual targets. Possible he hoped our lumbering planes would have a mid-air as we tried to avoid hitting him. We had heard rumors about fighters crashing into bombers to bring them down. If one of the front planes had been struck, then other formation planes would collide with the debris. Bubbles left his position in the glass nose and moved into the cockpit behind our seats. The three of us looked at each other. Color had drained from their faces and they had wide eyes with shocked expressions. I am sure that I looked the same way. No one said anything. The fighter would not have missed us if the guns had fired.

Elba was visible from our base in Corsica, and there was a Luftwaffe fighter base there. Curiously, we were never sent there on a mission, but we were advised to make a dogleg south to avoid that base if we flew toward Rome. Not long after we arrived on Corsica one of our planes flew to Naples with some Italian guys and GIs on board. One of the fellows was an engineer/gunner. The pilots saw two ME-109s coming towards them from a long way off. They told the engineer/gunner to man a waist gun. One of the other fellows got up in the overhead turret. Both of them had just gotten nicely situated when the fighters made a pass from astern. Our gunners fired off a burst, and the lead attacker abruptly headed toward the water while the other fighter broke off the attack. The Italians onboard confirmed that the damaged one hit the water, but the gunner did not get credit for the kill because the Italians were not considered credible witnesses!

About two months after our arrival the Allies shelled that airbase to neutralize it and the troops that went in there were from French Morocco. The common slang name for these troops was "Goums." They made an amphibious landing and captured a number of Germans. The prisoners were supposed to be transported to Corsica. The rumor was that more prisoners left Elba than arrived in Corsica. There were a number of French Moroccan soldiers on Corsica. We saw them riding on the back haunches of burros with their belongings nested in front of them. They seem to be independent and unattached. We never saw a troop of them together.

June 1 Mission performance is on the upswing. A total of forty-five ships attacked the marshaling yards at Fornato with devastating effects. Several trains in the yard were set on fire, and one fell over on its side. Flak was nil and all ships returned safely. A mountain of packages and mail came in today much to the delight of the recipients.

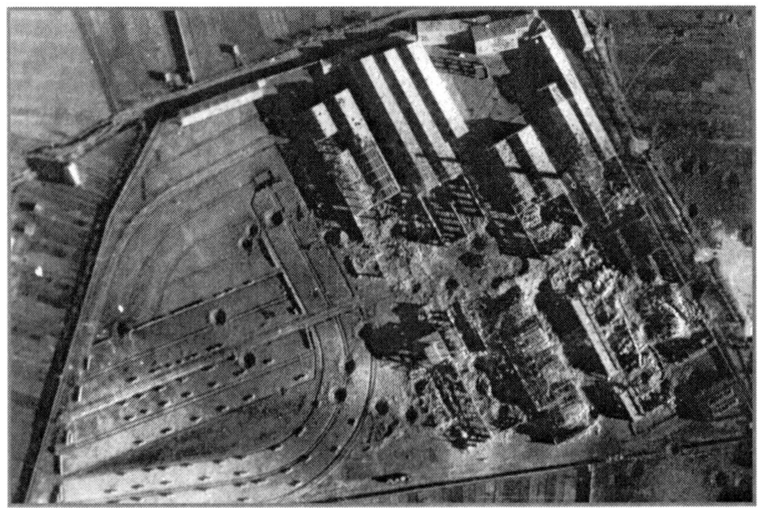

(Courtesy Daniel Setzer)

## Air Metal, First Cluster Awarded

Jefferson H. Pettyjohn, 384-45280, Tech Sgt., for the meritorious achievement while participating in an aerial flight as a radio/gunner of a B-25 type aircraft in an attack upon the marshaling yards at Fornato, Italy on to 1 June 1944. Ft. Smith, AK.

Bubbles wanted to learn to fly, and under my tutelage he accumulated a number of unofficial hours while flying practice missions. He was a capable pilot. In return, I wanted to become proficient with the Norden bomb sight and he quickly had me up to speed with it. We usually didn't carry gunner crews on these flights. On a number of these I acted as bombardier and pickled off the "blue" practice bombs while Bubbles flew the plane. The copilot ensured that nothing untoward happened. In those reverse roles we both did well.

Col. Chapman addressed the pilots and bombardiers one morning, and a collective groan issued from the crowd. He announced that pilot/bombardier teams would henceforth be required to practice on the bomb run simulator. Later youngsters might actually pay to play on this device which was set up in an outdoor square. We would've paid large amounts of money to skip the training. A large wooden machine on wheels had front and back seats which were positioned seven feet in the air. Underneath, electric motors independently powered each wheel. Steering was controlled from the backseat where the pilot sat. The front bombardier position was equipped with a device which simulated the Norden bombsight.

To initiate a practice, a ground operator released a motorized target about thirty feet in front of us that looked like a large turtle. It made a path roughly at right angles to the direction of the simulator. The target's speed and direction could be changed to simulate different conditions. The practice team would try to drive the simulator on top of the target. The whole point of the device was to give crews practice making bomb runs in a cross wind. Using the "turtle" as a target, the bombardier would feed corrections to the sight. A PDI gauge showed these corrections to the pilot who was supposed to aim the contraption at the intercept point. We found the exercise both boring and fatiguing. Most of us had used it for many hours in the states and didn't expect to see it again.

## Distinguished Flying Cross Awarded

Charles R. Ross, 067-6654, Second Lieut., 486th Bomb Squadron, 340th Bomb Group, for extraordinary achievement while participating in an aerial flight as pilot of a B-25 type aircraft. On June 3, 1944 Lieut. Ross flew number two position in an attack upon a supply and communication lines near Legaro Italy. Intense and accurate antiaircraft fire damaged his bomber on the approach to the target and injured Lieut. Ross and his copilot painfully. Despite this, Lieut. Ross held his bomber in level flight throughout the bomb run enabling his bombardier to drop his bombs which scored hits upon the objective. They then feathered the propeller on the right engine.

Lieut. Ross's injuries included a compound fracture of his right leg, multiple lacerations of his face, and his left leg. The copilot's left leg and hand were severely wounded. Lieut. Ross held formation as best he could. Unable to keep in formation with just one engine, they dropped back and three Spitfires escorted the plane home.

The pilot with his broken right leg, and the copilot with his injured left leg, coordinated the use of their good legs to maintain rudder control on the crippled aircraft. They made a successful emergency landing. It was not until after the ship landed that the crew learned about both pilots' severe leg injuries. His steadfast devotion to duty and outstanding proficiency as a combat pilot reflect great credit upon himself and the Armed Forces of the United States. Montrose, CO.

Since we were near the water with a protected bay, I thought it would be nice to have a boat. I took a Jeep and went up to the town of Bastia which was about twenty miles north of us. There was a harbor there, and I strolled around the harbor and came upon a thirty foot air-sea rescue boat. A soldier was guarding the rescue boat and I told him why I was there. He said, "You see that boat that's about seventy feet up the dock? It's been sitting there for weeks, and I don't think the owner is around. Why don't you bring a truck down and take it away." It was a big double ended open boat with large beams where the motor used to sit.

This harbor was under the cognizance of the Navy. They had a squadron of PT boats there. Access to the harbor was through a single gate. I returned a few days later with a deuce and a half truck and several friends. At the gate there was an ensign in charge and I explained to them that I had permission to pick up a boat. He waved us on through. The boat was longer than the truck bed by six feet and must have weighed more than 600 pounds. We used some empty bomb casings, two winches and ninety minutes of elbow grease to get it on the truck bed.

We dropped the boat off at our base next to my tent. I was in search of an engine. Near the base was a pool of abandoned German vehicles that the Corsicans had gathered together in a wrecking yard. Rummaging around the yard, I found a VW engine that had been pulled out of a "Thing" type vehicle, and it was light enough to put in the back of my Jeep. I signed some kind of paper for the wrecking yard owners, but didn't pay for the engine.

Since I was the Assistant Maintenance Officer, there was no problem to get the shop to fabricate some engine mounts. I also needed a propeller shaft and a propeller. I had a battery, but there was no acid for it. An abandoned glove factory sat five miles from Alesan airfield. I climbed through the window and found machinery that could be disassembled and made into a serviceable propeller shaft.

Some of my old Orlando, Florida crew chief friends were assigned to B-26 Marauders at Trunconi airfield on Sardinia. I volunteered for one of the vegetable supply flights and had a joyous reunion with my buddies. We had some amusing conversations about my liberated boat project. They took me down to a harbor where our forces kept air rescue seaplanes. Inside the marina were a number of boats and we found a suitable propeller in the shop area. They also gave me some acid for my battery. The maintenance shop back at Alesan field turned the shaft on a lathe until it fit the propeller. Fortunately, it fit right into the packing bearings on the boat. A strong piece of leather bolted from the engine flywheel to the flange on the propeller shaft completed the engine transformation. We were ready to go boating.

We reloaded the boat on the truck and took it up to a lake about fifteen miles away. The squadron had acquired a ten room house there which was used for R&R. This salty lake was actually ocean water that had become enclosed by dunes at the mouth of the bay. There were some large fish in the water. Most of the flight crews were allowed a week at this house where they would swim and loll around. The supply sergeants would give them some rations to take up there for meals. It was a pretty good deal.

We found some oars for the boat and used one of them as a rudder. The motor cranked right up and the boat worked perfectly. I removed the motor and told the fellows that they could use the boat, but they would have to row it until I returned from my R&R trip. I was afraid that they would wipe out the engine.

By the middle of May I had flown about fifty missions, enough to put my name up for consideration for a Cairo Cossacks R&R flight. Several weeks afterward I received the happy news that I was leaving next week with Lieut. Buchannan flying as copilot. Usually there were eight other fellow travelers. When a trip to the Middle East was laid on, flight crews would broadcast the news around so that soldiers in nearby army units could sign up to go. They told me that I be flying a B-25G. The G model had the 75 mm cannon. We were also authorized to visit Alexandria, Egypt and Tel Aviv, Palestine.

The adjutant signed over $2000 which would be used to purchase supplies for the Group. My specific quartermaster duties were to buy eggs and liquor for the Officers Club. We always purchased supplies at the same stores in Cairo. Nevertheless, we negotiated carefully and made sure the quantity of supplies was correct.

Sgt. ____cciolo approached me and asked if I would buy a big quantity of shoes when I got to Cairo. He said his connections could make good money selling them to civilians. I politely declined his offer. Later on some of the fellows did bring bags of shoes back from Cairo for him. Most of the soap from our squadron wound up marketed on the black market through his wheeling dealings. Soap was a very rare commodity. I think he had enough money to retire when he returned to the states.

I was in the Officers Club the night before the Cairo trip began, and there was a chaplain there. This fellow was a Lieut. Colonel, which was a high rank for a chaplain. He was at the craps table playing and he was making side bets. That kind of intrigued me. I watched him for a while and learned that he was going to go with us to Alexandria. There were ten of us making the trip.

June 2 Lieut. Buchanan had completed the preflight when I got to the flight line at 0630 hrs. All the attendees had been there for an hour, and there were plenty of smiles and good-natured ribbing. As they boarded, I checked off the passenger list to make sure no uninvited guests were aboard. In addition to the chaplain and Bubbles, I checked off Lieuts. Phelps and Podvogaski and Sgts. Stahl, Baker, Engle and Cpl. Kalapanidas. We couldn't make it to Cairo on a single hop, and landed in Benghazi for fuel. From Corsica to Cairo is 1700 miles, as the crow flies. On the flight from Benghazi to Cairo we were flying over El Alamein, and I was just flabbergasted at the number of vehicles that had been destroyed or abandoned. Buchanan took over while I went back and excitedly pointed out this massive field of destruction to the others. Wreckage was spread from one horizon to the other.

Bubbles took the opportunity to practice shooting the sun with his sextant. After working up a sweat to fix our position, he proudly displayed our location on his chart to our passengers. Sgt. Stall twisted his fists while yawning and said that if we still had so far to fly, he might as well go back to sleep. I was happy that he made the effort because radio fixes were few and far between out there.

Payne Field in Cairo was equipped with long runways and large hangars. As soon as we arrived, we headed for the restaurant and had hamburgers and sodas. This repast alone was worth the 1700 mile trip. We stayed in Cairo for three days and then flew on to Alexandria and Tel Aviv. When the "chaplain" got off the plane in Cairo, he had removed the insignia that identified him as a clergyman and replaced them with epaulets that indicated he was with an armored division. Our new tank officer held that disguise for the rest of the trip and we marveled at his appetite for the nightlife. There was good beer to be had in Cairo since the Germans had set up several breweries which were still in operation.

Cairo offered a number of things to do and see. The bazaar was interesting and Bubbles bartered for carved ivory at a shop. Three of us shared a large eighth floor room at a nice hotel. I don't remember how they came to be in my possession, but a squadron pilot who was returning to the States left a box full of condoms and I brought them along. We entertained ourselves in the room by filling up condoms with water and lobbing them down into the street where there were some horse drawn carriages. When our "water balloons" hit the street, those horses would try to lift up all four hooves at the same time! The puzzled horse hostler's would run outside to tame their beasts. We all got a good laugh out of that. The next day we visited the pyramids and Sphinx and had our group picture taken while we were aboard camels.

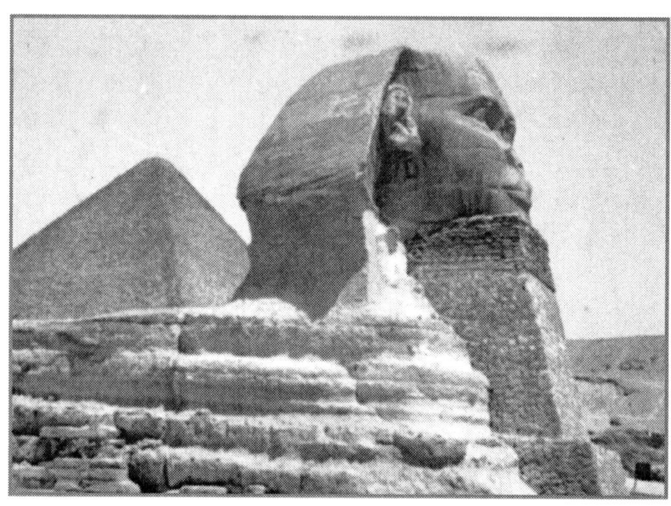

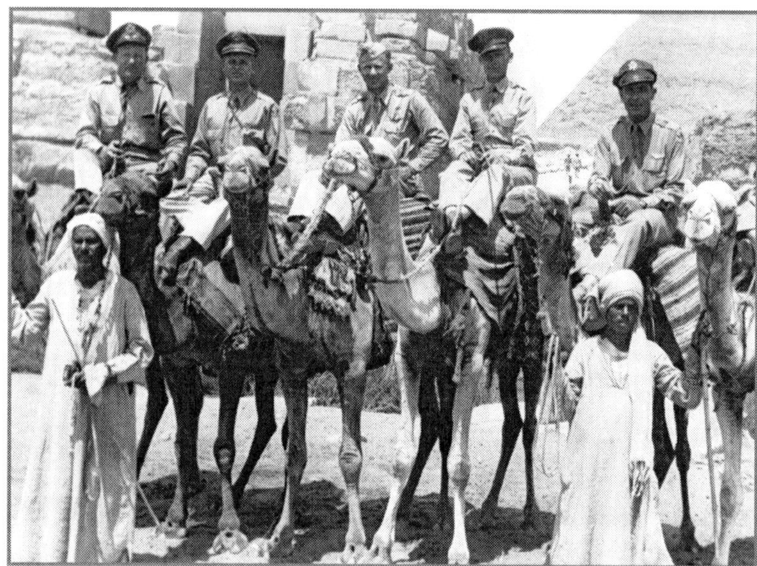

Some female officers at the airbase wanted a ride to Alexandria and we took them there. We had a great time in beautiful, cosmopolitan Alexandria. The beaches were famous as a tourist destination, and the people were very friendly. We spent our evenings at a big rambling bar called simply The American Bar which was packed every night. Alexandria definitely had the best nightlife.

The fellows who preceded us had made the acquaintance of several young ladies, and we had their phone numbers. We went to several nightclubs with our new friends and rode in horse drawn carriages around the town. Some of the girls from Alexandria claimed to be countesses. We learned from our new friends that some are no-acountesses! Several close by restaurants specialized in seafood, and we also enjoyed fresh vegetables and roasted lamb. Many toasts celebrated the liberation of Rome on June 5th. We visited the catacombs where secret burials were made by the Christians in the beginning of the Christian era. They are similar to the ones in Rome. There are reputed to be four and a half miles of these underground passages at varying subterranean levels.

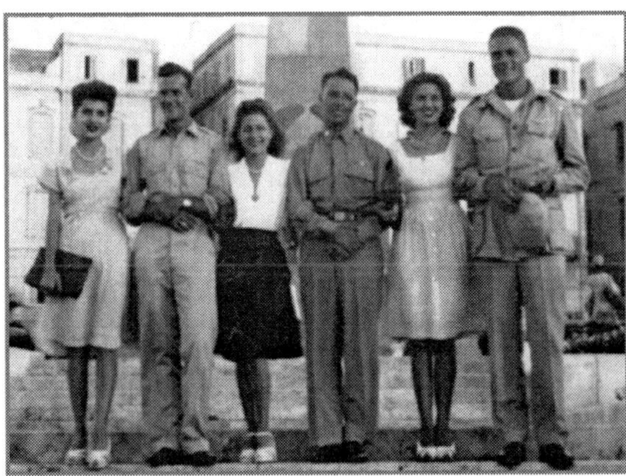

We flew on to Tel Aviv and per the instructions that we had received, made a low pass over the town. Our noisy flyover alerted the staff at the USO club to dispatch a truck to the airfield. I landed the plane on the sod airfield about ten miles from town. There were just a few other airplanes on the field with no hangers or other buildings. We stood under the wing for a while to escape the brilliant sun. Eventually a truck showed up and took us to the USO where a free meal awaited. They told us what accommodations were available in Tel Aviv. We reboarded the truck which deposited us on a downtown corner. The place that I elected to stay was like a YMCA; rather severe in accommodations with clean private rooms. The cost was $3.50 a night. The chaplain/tank officer was with us and he checked in to the King David hotel and was not seen again until we departed.

There were some very nice shops in the bazaars. I purchased some silver filigree, five small sapphires, a star ruby and a man's ring with a large star sapphire at a shop named Pahoomal's. I knew that name from their New York store. My jewelry expenditure was about $600. Total expenses for the trip were about $1100, which was a lot since my monthly pay was about $400. Good news rolled in waves, and we joyously celebrated the June 6th invasion of France.

The next morning, we all gathered and agreed that we would take a cab to Bethlehem and the other holy land villages nearby. Our cab driver turned out to be an interesting guy who was very well educated. While traveling on the dry and dusty road, he related an encounter with a British Colonel. He said the Colonel was a real supercilious type. The man had climbed into his cab, poked him in the back with a swagger stick, and frostily directed him to drive to Bethlehem. The driver said nothing and began the trip. This drive usually took about forty-five minutes. About midway to Bethlehem the cab driver stopped his cab, opened the passenger door and told the Colonel to get out. He drove away and left him there.

We got along well with him. He was a guide as well as a driver. He took us to the Western Wall, the Garden of Gethsemane, and the Mount of Olives as well as several beautiful beach spots. It was my most memorable day of the trip.

The bounty that we returned with included 10,000 eggs, forty cases of beer and fifteen cases of liquor. These were small pullet eggs, and the agreed price was $.10 per egg. The nine guys were on board with all of the stuff that they bought. We also had to factor in the 75 mm cannon which weighed 1200 pounds. This impressive mass outweighed the heaviest bomb load that I ever carried. Our slow climb away from Payne field was made easier by the flat terrain. Cargo and R&R missions were the only assignments that that plane flew. In a timespan of eight days we covered about 5000 miles.

We had been back two days when a fellow came up to me and said "Lieutenant, some MPs came by the R&R lake house, and they were asking questions about the boat." This really astounded me because the lake was well off the beaten path and could only be accessed by a rough dirt road that was two miles long. It was a real surprise that the MPs came to that location.

A week later I got a call to go down to the adjutant's office. Inside the office was a fellow from the Criminal Investigation Division. He said "I understand that you got a boat down at this lake. Where did you get it?" I told him where the boat came from and he said "Well, the owner of that boat saw you guys take it and he's put in a request for $900 payment for it. You'd better take the boat back to him."

I got my guys together and we took the truck up to the lake and picked up the boat. After removing the motor, we returned it to the harbor. My cohorts were disappointed about this turn of events, and they weren't particularly gentle when we placed it on the dock. Not many days later, I was again summoned to the adjutant's office and the CID officer told me that the boat owner had put in a claim for $90 because the boat had a cracked stem and the motor mounts were missing. I told him that we had thrown the old motor mounts away and that we may have cracked the stem when the boat came off the truck at the harbor. He asked me, "How much do you think that is worth?" I told him, "about 1000 francs." At that time, a haircut cost about five francs. He said, "Well, that sounds reasonable to me." I started to reach in my pocket for money and he said, "Oh, you don't have to pay for it, the government will pay him."

I thought that would be the end of the matter, but a few days later I was again summoned to the adjutant's office and he said, "We got a bill from the French for a VW engine." I told him I would handle the matter. The engine that I had ran well. Some of our fellows in the maintenance area used those VW engines for auxiliary power. I brought my engine to one of them and asked them if they had a tired engine that they wanted to trade for it. They were very happy to have my engine. Their worn out engine was returned to the Corsicans. In truth, while I didn't get to use the boat except for that one outing, I had no regrets. It was a worthwhile and entertaining project and allowed me to find an outlet for my off-time.

On the 13th of June six friends and I made an unauthorized trip to Rome. At the time Rome was off-limits to GIs, having been liberated just nine days earlier. A directive had come out barring unauthorized soldiers from entering the city. The squadron had some business to conduct in Sicily. I gathered Bubbles and several willing collaborators and told them that this was the perfect cover. Departing Corsica early, we set a maximum cruise speed and arrived in Sicily about mid-morning. After completing the squadron business, we told a white lie and claimed that urgent missions awaited us as an excuse for a quick departure. Just west of Naples we changed our course and turned north toward Rome.

We were not sure of the location of usable air fields near the city. Luckily, our flight path brought us over a field with Allied airplanes. A radio tower stood hundreds of feet in the air on the downwind leg of the approach and we banked sharply to avoid it. We were uncertain what kind of reception was in store, but the ground crew saluted us as we pulled into the taxi area and motioned us to park next to a Fairchild courier plane. I guess they mistook us for VIPs. We got out and noticed that there were piles of German landmines lining each end of the field that the sappers had dug up.

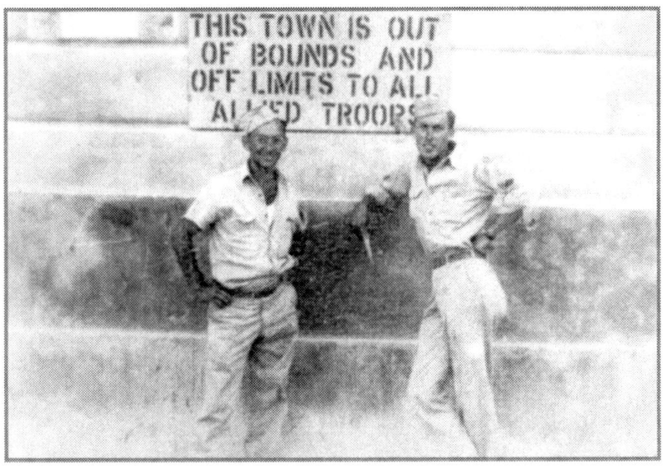


(Courtesy Daniel Setzer)

I figured that we had two days, and as you might imagine we thoroughly enjoyed ourselves. The mood of the Roman populace was still exuberant following the liberation. Several of us were embraced by smiling young ladies as we toured the downtown. We visited the Coliseum and Vatican. I exhausted my film supply taking pictures of the many beautiful buildings. We stayed at the Savola Hotel. That same hotel was the site where someone from the 340th later threw a woman out of a window. Joseph Heller's Catch-22 has an episode that somewhat describes that incident. I don't know the real specifics, but the man who committed the crime was sentenced to twenty years in Leavenworth.

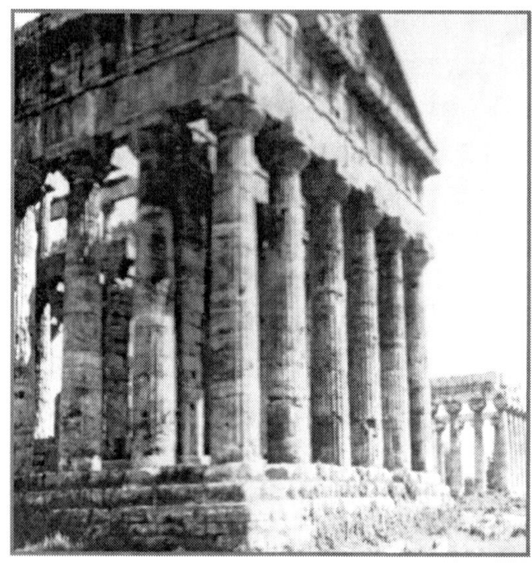

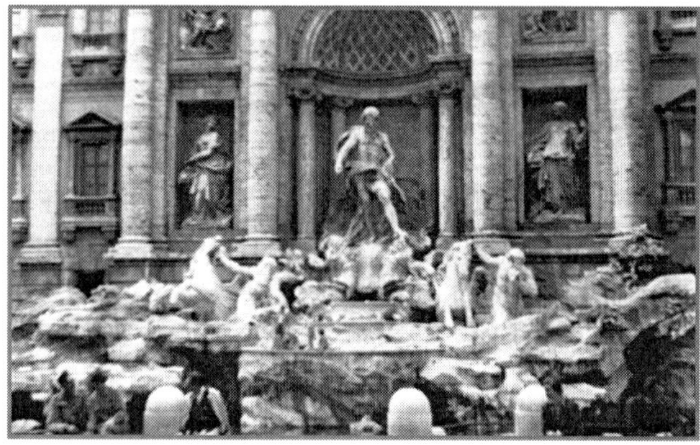

I noticed a camera shop that was open and went in looking for a lens. Not surprisingly, the Germans had taken most of the good equipment before they left. While showing me a lens the owner stared at my unit patch and quietly asked, "Did your Colonel get shot down in March?" I told him that we had lost an officer. He said, "Your Colonel parachuted into my backyard. I came out and talked to him and he was uninjured. Because my neighbors had observed his descent, I explained to him that I had no choice and had to call the German authorities. He said he understood.

I made him a cup of tea and stayed with him until the Germans arrived. He was taken away without fuss or injury."

When we returned to our airplane, the Fairchild courier plane that had been next to us was not there. We flew back to Corsica and after our arrival the crew chief was on the wing servicing the plane. He shouted down, "What happened to the wing?" I climbed up on the wing with him and saw that there was a large, ugly dent. None of us had any idea how it got there. My heart went up in my throat with the immediate supposition that the plane had suffered some sabotage while in Rome.

We knew the plane had departed Corsica without the dent. I walked into Capt. Stoler's office and, with a slight lump in my throat, gave him the short version of our little escapade. He called the Rome airfield where we had been parked. His call got transferred up the chain of command and eventually he was connected to a colonel. Capt. Stoler listened without saying much and hung up after thanking the colonel. He looked quietly at me for several moments. Then he stood and walked over to my chair. To my stunned surprise, he gently rubbed the top of my head in a circular motion. He said, "I am asking the fates to share some of your endless luck with me." He returned to his chair and leaning back, said "The Fairchild parked next to you blew up and tossed shrapnel in every direction. Some of the wreckage must have hit your wing as it fell. When the plane started to taxi, it detonated a buried mine that the sappers failed to unearth. There were no survivors. If your plane had traded parking places with the Fairchild, you might not be here talking to me. At best, you would have come back with far more serious souvenirs."

Despite the truth of our destination being revealed and the damage to the plane, Capt. Stoler very kindly kept this information to himself. One week later the Rome "off limits" rule was reversed. In the next few months nearly everyone who wanted a Roman holiday was granted their wish.

June 16 Today's morning mission to a railroad bridge north of Milan was notable in that we were attacked by six ME-109s. They were unusually persistent, and made four passing attacks. One of our planes was attacked from below. Turret gunner, Staff Sgt. Jim Kelly reports that he saw tracers from his guns hit one of the fighters at about 600 yards out. It peeled off and dove earthward in flames. Other airmen also observed the burning fighter. The remaining fighters beat a retreat.

Just after nightfall the big guns all around Alesan field opened up with a terrific barrage. Everyone hit the trenches in short order. For about fifteen minutes the guns maintained an almost continuous bombardment, which was directed out to sea. When the all clear signal sounded we emerged, relieved that we would not have another overhead bombardment. Some of the guys walked over to the batteries and learned that an unidentified ship out at sea failed to give the proper signals, and thus it was assumed to be an enemy vessel. It probably was.

June 17-20 Solid rain caused the usual result. Our tent areas either had running water or were swimming pools. Some of the fellows suggested that the beaver was an apt logo for the 340th Group these days. Cabin fever grew quickly amongst the aircrews who are trying to accumulate enough missions for rotation to the States. Some of the fellows headed to the beach between the intermittent downpour. The latest returning Cairo Cossacks brought back everything but the kitchen sink. These included baseballs, film, watches, beer, cigarettes, lighters, eggs and a number of other interesting items. The new Officers Club is rapidly nearing completion. Most of the guys are helping with this project after the nightly ball game.

June 21 Partly cloudy skies greeted us today, and twelve of our ships departed with my crew to a railroad bridge north of Casale, Italy. Bubbles told me he saw at least six direct hits. No A/A impeded our progress. Hamburgers and onions for dinner today was just like home - almost.

*June 21, 1944*

*Dear Eleanor*

*Well I'm just getting settled down after another excursion. Last Sunday I flew some fellows to Sicily and then decided to see Rome on the way back. We landed at a field near the town. Bubbles and I thought it was such a nice place that we stayed for two days. We visited as much of the Vatican as we could, St. Peter's Cathedral, the ruins of the Coliseum and the Forum. I took a number of pictures and quite enjoyed the stay. The weather was bad at our base, so the outfit didn't fly and we weren't missed. Our only trouble was that most of our money was in francs and we couldn't use it there. We had to take it easy with only $15 in lira between us.*

*These trips are nice, but they always make me think how really enjoyable they would be if it were peacetime and you were with me. I like to think of returning someday and visiting these places with you at my side. Then that would really mean something.*

*The ladies here on Corsica are much nicer than the ones around Naples. Ladies in Rome are okay, but they don't rate more than a whistle (just kidding). The truth is that I'm dreaming about you all the time. I wish I were there.*

*Love, Dale*

**June 22** **We will be without the friendly personalities of** Lieutenants Sellers, Dombrowski, Tupper and Sergeants Koebeke, Carey and McDonough because they have been shot down. I hope to see them soon after their escape sporting beards and Italian apparel. Our evening beer party was a lively affair and accompanied by Capt. Mayer on the accordion.

June 23 Twelve planes went out on a bridge busting mission near Florence, and the bombardiers said there were at least six direct hits. Col. Chapman announced a new requirement for seventy missions before crews are eligible for rotation. This news was not welcomed with open arms.

We had a housewarming party for the digs constructed by Lieut. Schurr. He made good use of "surplus" material that was left over from our friendly Luftwaffe visit. Some of that material is also getting put to good use building the new Squadron Officers Club.

Cpl. Burton who was supposedly lost on April 6 over Perugia in plane 7T returned to the squadron this evening. He told us that he bailed out just before the plane crashed. Since that time he lived in the hills awaiting the allies. One morning, he heard an exchange of gun fire, and it seemed his chance to escape had finally presented itself. He made his way toward the battle line, but was picked up by the Germans.

A sudden flurry of fire from our forces distracted the guards and he was somehow able to escape and make his way to an American infantry unit. He says it was a hell of a sweat, but he's thanking God that he still alive. Sgts. Benny and Simpson are still hiding out in hills according to Burton, but the rest of the crew is believed dead.

Three airmen from the 489th squadron also returned today. These three went down in 9W on May 25. The fortunate three; King, Vargo and Yocca had this to say - All of the crewmen were able to get out of the plane before it crashed, but not all of them survived the jump. Lieut. Ellen's chute failed to open. Wright was shot and killed by Italian Fascists as he parachuted towards Earth. Scott reached the ground safely and was taken prisoner, as were King, Vargo and Yocca. They managed to escape and eventually reached the safety of friendly territory, but only after many harrowing experiences.

The 486th officers wanted to build a Squadron Mess Hall/Officers Club and we employed some Sardinians to make adobe bricks. Using a cement mixer, they combined the local clay soil with straw and cast the mix into 2 x 6 molds. They were pretty good sized bricks, and the Sardinians made hundreds of them. In the meantime, my friend Ted Wheeler prevailed upon the engineers to bring in a cement truck and pour a 50 x 25 floor for the club. Putting his construction skills to use, he borrowed a small bulldozer and graded the club area before the cement truck came in. The rest of us started laying bricks in earnest. Ted and I took a truck up to a lumber mill in the mountains and brought back "slashings" which were the discarded outer bark peelings. These were thick enough to nail together, so we had a kind of bark roof. We ended up with a pretty good building which had a fireplace and a kitchen. It had enough room to feed fifty people.

We plastered the interior walls. John Sawyer, who painted some of the nose art on our airplanes, agreed to decorate the inside with some of his original art. He provided two beautiful female murals sans clothes. Camouflage netting was hung below the roof as a kind of ceiling.

We had been using the building about a month when a soldier on KP threw some gasoline on the stove which had live embers. The netting caught on fire, and part of the ceiling burned. This happened in the evening and everyone rousted out with buckets of water to quell the flames. We managed to get the fire out before serious damage occurred. Fortunately, John's murals were not damaged. Of the four squadrons, our club was the only good one. We had picnic style tables inside. Alcohol was not served, but it was OK to share our individual stocks of wine and whiskey.

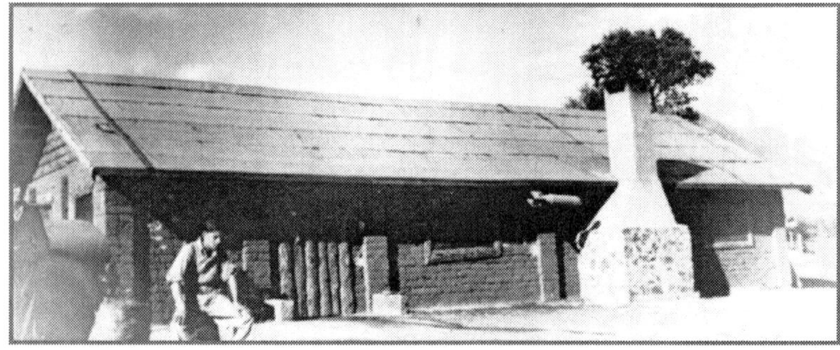

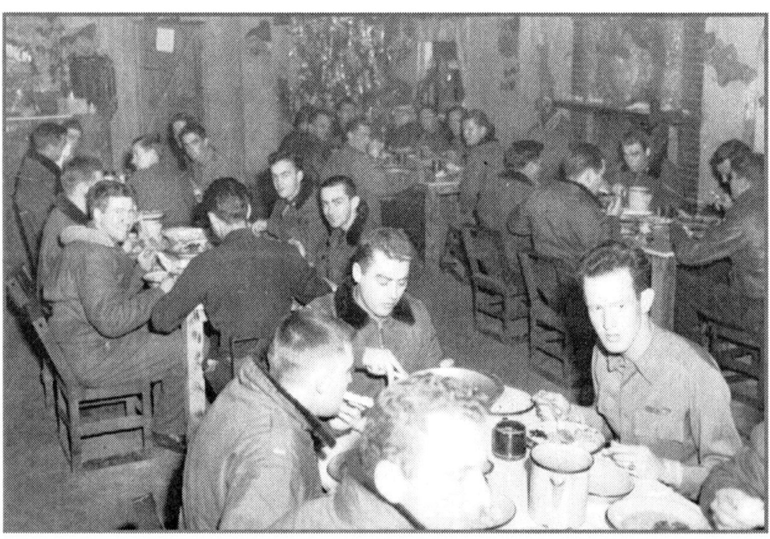

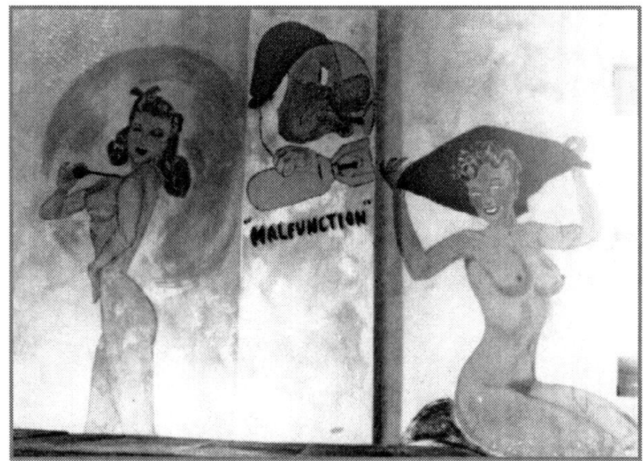


The Group Officers Club on the other side of the base did have a bar which was manned by a bartender. The club had a pool table, and how it came to be there was a mystery. It was mostly used as a dice table. Now and then the headquarters club would have an alternate to the cheap Cypriot whiskey. I brought back Three Feathers whiskey from Cairo which was definitely a step up.

June 24-28 June certainly had its share of stand down days. Lieut. Weil, another long-lost soul who had been missing since March 10, returned today. Although he was the only one to escape, his information was that the others who parachuted from the plane were safe. Weil was in the plane that went down with Col. Jones aboard.

The Squadron Officers Club opened with a party that began at 1900 hrs. on the 25th. Harmonious singing was greatly aided by beer and cocktails. I showed the gang a white silk visored hat which was purchased in Rome on our clandestine visit. The fellows made many jokes about our subterfuge, and wanted to see pictures of the Roman women. They assumed that I had put my camera to good use. Some of them gave me a hard time when I told them my photos were architectural shots.

June 29 88 mm cannon shells came up from gun positions on both sides of the Imperia, Italy rail bridge as we started our bomb run. Flak filled the sky, and several shells whizzed by my windscreen. Bubbles nailed the bridge and the center span collapsed in the water. Three of the eighteen planes were badly damaged and two of them made belly landings at Alesan field. Six men were taken to the hospital, but all will survive. My first DFC was for that mission.

HEADQUARTERS

TWELFTH AIR FORCE

12

# The Distinguished Flying Cross

is awarded

Dale J. Satterthwaite, First Lieutenant, Air Corps

340th Bombardment Group (M)

by direction of the President, under the provisions of Army Regulation 600-45 as amended, and pursuant to authority vested in me by the Commanding General, Mediterranean Theater of Operations.

## Citation

For extraordinary achievement while participating in aerial flight as pilot of a B-25 type aircraft on 29 June 1944. Lieutenant Satterthwaite led an eighteen plane formation in an attack upon a vital railroad bridge near Imperia, Italy. Displaying superior flying ability as he skillfully maneuvered his flight through intense anti-aircraft fire upon the approach to the target, Lieutenant Satterthwaite then led a precision run over the objective. All bombs fell in the target area, with three direct hits on the bridge, effectively blocking this vital link of enemy supply and communication lines. On fifty-two combat missions, Lieutenant Satterthwaite's steadfast devotion to duty and outstanding proficiency have reflected great credit upon himself and the Armed Forces of the United States.

John K. Cannon

JOHN K. CANNON
Major General, USA
Commanding

G. O. No. 116, 31 July 1944

June 30 At 0300 hrs. we had a red alert which everyone takes seriously these days. This follows an alert three nights ago, and has increased our fatigue factor. Mr. Dixon, an Associated Press reporter has been with the Group for several days and went on several missions. He has made friends with a number of fellows in our squadron. Rations were as usual - four candy bars, two cigars and two cokes. The Officers team won their baseball game tonight with the Enlisted Men squad and you could hear the shouts across the hill. Lately, the Enlisted Men have dominated that game. "Up in Arms" was our cinema tonight and most of the viewers found it humorous.

July 1 Ordinance and Armament worked all night to load ships for a morning mission with fragmentation bombs. The mission was cancelled at first light. Then orders came out requiring ships to be loaded with 1000 pounders this afternoon, so all the frags had to be removed. The effort paid off however, with eighteen Group ships taking dead aim on the Fornato railroad bridge. The center span of the bridge was blown to pieces. A late day mission took off to bomb the mouth of the tunnel at Prato, Italy. Tunnel entrances are a very difficult target and the returning crews said that several nearby buildings caught fire, but no bombs entered the tunnel. Six planes were holed and one man was injured by flak.

Our last Cairo Cossacks group stopped at Malta and came back with a restaurant recommendation! They ate at Jim's restaurant where real American fried chicken is served and washed down with beer. Jim is a black American band leader who was waylaid in Malta when the war broke out. He has capitalized on the restaurant business since that time. He told them that Malta has undergone countless air raids in the last few years. General Knapp was escorted around the area today by Captains Shealy and Meyer after they dined in the "luxurious" 486th dining salon.

July 2 We had a chance to bomb something besides a bridge today, and were happy for it. The oil dump at Ostiglia blew up, much to our enjoyment. A/A was heavy and accurate. Three planes were hit, and Sgt. Ryerson was injured with facial wounds. Ryerson later joked about his injuries saying, "She had long fingernails!"

Beer was served at the Officers Club and decidedly raised morale this evening. When Fred Roch prepared to retire last night, he was amazed to find his sack and bed roll well filled with a jackass. He rushed over to the card room in search of the guilty party, but he has not been able to uncover the prankster.

## Air Metal, Forth Cluster Awarded

Joseph F. Podvojsky, 079-5822, Second Lieut., for meritorious achievement while participating in an aerial flight as pilot of a B-25 type aircraft in an attack upon Ostiglia, Italy, on 2 July 1944. Homestead, PA.

July 3 Today's mission to an oil dump near Ferrara was heavily defended. Lieut. Pike's hydraulic brakes failed on his return. His ship barreled off the end of the runway and the landing gear collapsed on the rough ground. They slid to a stop 100 yards off the end of the strip and then the plane crumpled in two. The back twelve feet of the ship completely separated from the rest of the plane. Fortunately, the ship did not burn and the crew injuries were limited to bruises.

Lieut. Martinson was cut by flying Plexiglas and came back on one engine. Capt. Shealy was on board as bombardier. He said that they buzzed a German weather station so close that they could read the weather maps in the shack! Flak hit Sgt. Housken in the shoulder, and Sgts. Slocum and Smits were also hospitalized with moderate injuries.

The formations behind us fared even worse. The 488th squadron had a plane go down. Capt. Crossman, the RAF Liaison Officer went down with the plane. Every one of their planes was holed, and T/Sgt. Hunt, a radio gunner was seriously injured in the leg. Lieut. Mel's ship was said to have cut the "sagebrush" like a lawnmower as they buzzed away from the flak. Their low altitude drew a hail of tracers and small arms fire. One of his gunners fired back and the ground fire ceased. Lieut. Fisher was cut by flak and is in the hospital.

A surprising non-combat related crash happened at Alesan field. Witnesses were amazed to see A P-47 belly land this morning. The pilot, a Major, thought that his landing gear was down. Was he ever surprised! Fortunately he was not injured.

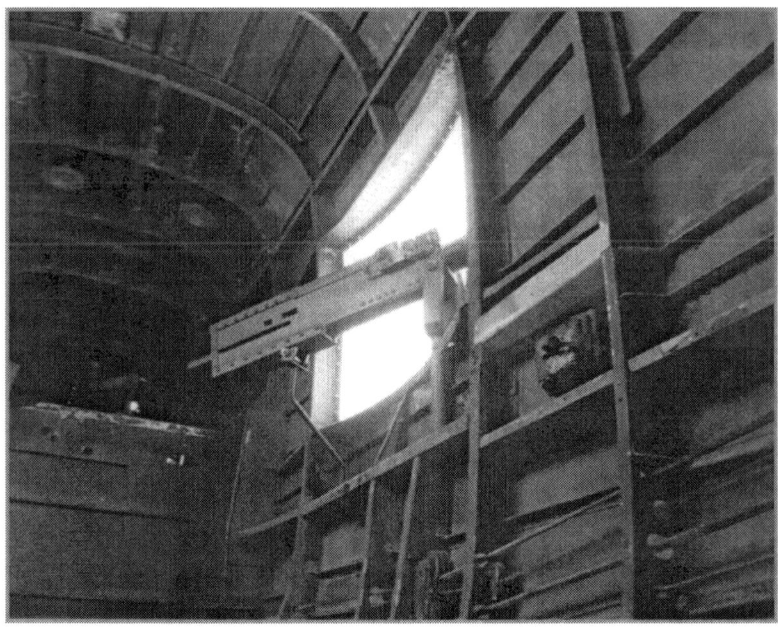

(Courtesy 57th Bomb Wing)

## Distinguished Flying Cross Awarded

Calvert A. Moody, 066-2358, Capt., Headquarters, 340th Bomb Group for extraordinary achievement while participating in an aerial flight as navigator/bombardier of a B-25 type aircraft. On 3, July 1944, while on a mission over fuel dumps at Pontelagoscuro, Italy. Capt. Moody's plane was repeatedly hit by heavy enemy antiaircraft. One shell knocked out the right engine at the beginning of the bomb run. While the pilot struggled to hold the damaged plane on course, Capt. Moody carefully released his bombs, scoring direct hits in the target area.

Forced to break formation because of a loss of power, the mountainous terrain made the choice of bailing out very likely. Capt. Moody helped the pilots select a low level course through the valleys. Despite further damage to the plane from continuing antiaircraft fire, and an attack from enemy fighters, the ship returned to its home base where a successful single engine landing was executed. His extraordinary achievement in combat reflects great credit upon himself and the Armed Forces of the United States. San Luis Obispo, CA.

## Air Metal, Fifth Cluster Awarded

Joseph D. Burnett, 130-44790, S/Sgt., for meritorious achievement while participating in an aerial flight as tail gunner of a B-25 type aircraft in an attack upon an enemy fuel dump near Ferrara, Italy on 3 July 1944. Scranton, PA.

July 4 Fourth of July fireworks were confined to the battlefront this year. After a successful mission to the Borgo Torenzo viaduct, Lieut. Henthorn landed with the nose wheel up. Everyone was okay. Fighters gave us a hot welcome with four

ME-109s attacking us from above. We got one back in return - the 109 was seen going down in a flat spin with smoke coming out of it. The crash could not be confirmed.

July 5 Three enemy fighters made two firing passes just after we completed our bomb run on the Ostiglia fuel dump. They were ME-109s, painted a dark mottled color. The attack started from our four o'clock position. One of our ships was hit, but not seriously damaged. Just after their second pass, a single brave Spitfighter engaged them. The German fighters turned away to engage the Spit and we quickly lost sight of them. Lieuts. Finney and Simpson returned today after being shot down over enemy territory during a bombing mission on April 6. Lieut. Firney gave an interesting and informative talk this evening about their escape from enemy held territory.

July 6 Today's accurate ack-ack greeting holed eight of our ten airplanes. We were under continuous fire from the ground for eight minutes as we approached the Pianora railroad bridge. My plane was one of the ships with fresh damage to the empennage.

July 7 Thunder and lightning accompanied a storm which forced a stand down. Word came back that the R&R ship in Cairo met with a little difficulty when landing. A telegraph message from Lieut. O'Toole said the nose wheel failed, and the date of the plane's return is not known.

The second time I went to Egypt was to pick up our cannon equipped B-25G. The plane made a hard landing at the Cairo airport, and the nose wheel collapsed. When the nose hit the ground, the barrels of the four fifty caliber guns dug a quarter mile long furrow in the hot asphalt runway. The runway was closed for nearly a week. Our outfit became persona non grata at the airport. After they got the nose wheel back up, someone flew the airplane to Port Said Air Depot and they made repairs there.

This was not an R&R trip, nevertheless, I was charged with the usual quartermaster duties. Everyone wanted something from Cairo and I was busy satisfying their requests. My sole companion was a copilot and the empty plane had plenty of room for beer, eggs and other items. We were back in Corsica several days later.

July 8 We played a double header in the German's backyard and they lost both contests. We plan on keeping it that way. Capt. Buchanan departed for the States wreathed in smiles and pursued by all for the equipment that he leaves.

July 9 Church services were again held and enjoyed by all those who attended. During the latter part of the afternoon rain poured down in steady sheets. Major Hackney was joined by other determined fishermen and they returned with some respectable sized trout.

Some of our war weary airplanes were flown to a field that was about fifteen miles south of us. There was no tower; it was just a pasture really. When a pilot had enough missions to be sent home, he would sometimes be assigned to supervise that operation. Part of this easy assignment required the pilot to fly those airplanes in order to keep the batteries charged up.

Lewis, the copilot on our long trip from the U.S., had accumulated sixty-five missions. He was assigned the care of this mothballed wing. There were two or three enlisted men who were assigned to do minor maintenance on these planes. None of men liked to fly on them as honorary copilots. They were engineer/gunners and had seen their share of combat. Consequently, when Lewis took one of these airplanes up he would sometimes go by himself.

At the conclusion of one of these solo flights, the landing gear refused to come down. There was a manual crank to lower the gear that was located in the navigation compartment. He took the airplane up to 10,000 feet and trimmed it out. Running back to the navigation compartment, he inserted the manual crank handle and furiously started turning the twenty or so rotations it took to get the gear down. The disturbance in the airflow by the partially lowered gear caused the plane to slide off into a spiral. He had to climb through the steeply banked ship back to the cockpit and regain control of the plane. As the gear was lowered further down, the control of the plane became more and more difficult.

He was in contact with another airport tower while this was going on and the brass got wind of it. Eventually he got the gear lowered and brought the plane in for a safe landing. A directive came out immediately after this from Air Force Headquarters that no one was to fly a B-25 without someone in the right seat.

July 10 Italy was completely socked in, so relaxing was the key word of the day. Missions or no missions, practice bombing continues and we may be in for a stretch of night bombing. We also did some in-flight target practice today with a towed sock and searchlight. The Officers team again won the ballgame 5 to 4. A USO show at the nearby 306th Group was enjoyed by all.

July 11 The weather over Italy still has us grounded. Beachgoers are now occasionally releasing bug bombs before they sunbathe on the beach. Cpl. Sobansky was nursing a swollen hand after being bitten by one of Corsica's flying bugs. The local cinema presented "Hit the Ice" with Abbott and Costello - mediocre was the opinion of the show.

July 12 Mission results were excellent today. The primary target was the Ferrera Road Bridge and the secondary target was Chivari. Both the primary and alternate targets were hit, and the squadron received one hundred percent on both. Just before reaching the target, the back of the formation was attacked by sixteen enemy fighters. At least one of the fighters was shot down by waist and turret gunners. Two other enemy fighters were claimed as probable.

On the way home a 489th plane developed engine trouble. They ditched the plane in the ocean on the west side of Italy. Witnesses in their formation said they saw two parachutes leave the plane over the Italian coast. The other five crewmen got into a life raft before the plane sank. Several of our planes circled the raft and call for a pickup by the Air Sea Rescue Command. The five were successfully picked up and returned to their squadron. The two who parachuted remain missing.

Around midnight we had another red alert. Not taking any chances, we spent thirty minutes in our now six foot deep slit trench. The recent rains have left calf high water in the trench, and we returned to our tent with soaked pants and boots. Antiaircraft guns at the field fired practice rounds all afternoon, so HQ must suspect that an enemy raid may be in the works. Several planes filled with Cairo Cossacks returned today after their restful sojourn.

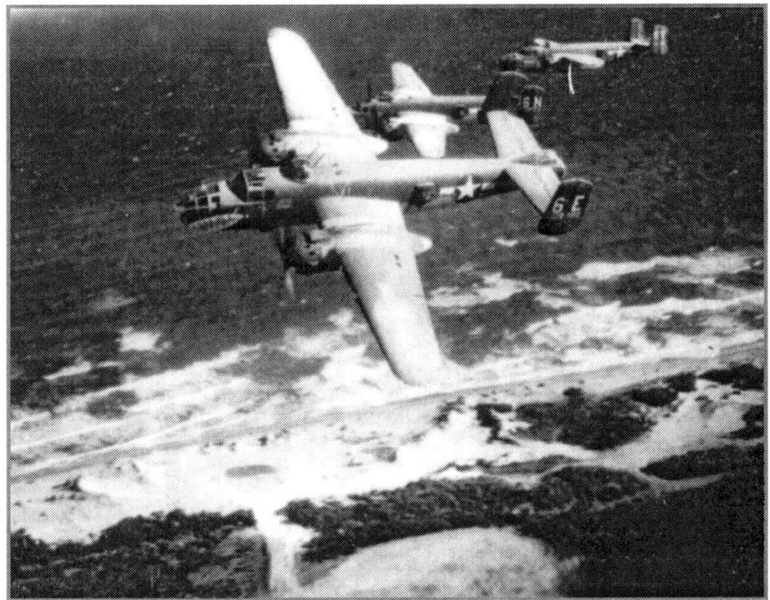

(Courtesy Daniel Setzer)

Yesterday several friends and I visited Ajaccio and enjoyed the amazing scenic vistas. The narrow winding roads carried us through sweet-scented pine forests. Occasionally, we would pass through quiet mountain villages which seemed so estranged from our military life. The highest mountain peaks are 8760 feet and the jeep struggled to clear the pass.

July 13 Ferrera is a railroad center with several intersecting lines. We had good hits on both sides of a bridge that was close to yesterday's target. Four ships were holed and two pilots were wounded. Ship 7H had an engine shot out over the target. In order to get over the Italian mountains, the crew threw out all excess weight including guns, radios, parachutes, flak suits and even their boots. They cleared the pass by less than 200 feet and made a safe return to Alesan airfield.

Everyone has opinions about the way the missions are planned, and some of the guys spoke openly in the squadron Officers Club this evening. They questioned the wisdom of consecutive attacks on a flak heavy target when alternate attractive targets are available. Several bombardiers said that they disagreed with the Intelligence Officers' reports regarding our mission results. It is disheartening when they are not credited for accurate bombing. The bombardiers were sure that the bombs went where they intended them to.

## Distinguished Flying Cross Awarded

Joseph F. Podvojski, 079-5822, First Lieut., 486th Bomb Squadron, 340th Bomb Group for extraordinary achievement while participating in an aerial flight as pilot of a B-25 type aircraft. On 13 July 1944, Lieut. Podvojski flew in an attack upon a railroad bridge at Ferrera, Italy. Upon the approach to the target, shell fragments from intense antiaircraft fire heavily damaged his airplane. Courageously, he maintained his crippled B-25 in perfect formation in the face of this heavy barrage. Lieut. Podvojski enabled his bombardier to release his bombs with devastating effect upon the center span of the bridge. In fifty-five combat missions, his outstanding proficiency and steadfast devotion to duty have reflected great credit upon himself and the Armed Forces of the United States. Homestead, PA.

## Air Metal, Fourth Cluster Awarded

John B. Rome, 081-5392, First Lieut., for meritorious achievement while participating in an aerial flight as pilot of a B-25 type aircraft in an attack upon a railroad bridge near Ferrera, Italy on 13 July 1944. New York, NY.

July 14 Capt. Shealy, Lieut. Cooley and gang returned from Cairo and points east. Of course they were heavily loaded with eggs and booze. Through the efforts of T/Sgt. Sendek, an ingenious contraption enabling target practice for gunners has been completed. A squirt gun stream of water replaces a stream of bullets during moving target practice. Gunners have the added realism of firing from a gun turret with a model sized replica of an FW-190 attacking in a pursuit curve.

Bomb loaders Joe Koloz, Abe Heller, Vin Douglas, Glenn Blair and their friend Buffalo had some excitement today when they were wheeling up a 1000 pound bomb. It jumped the dolly which sheared off its fuse. Despite it being fully armed, Blair defused it amidst the dust caused by scampering personnel.

July 15 Ferrera was hit twice today, making a total of six missions flown there in four days. My squadron led the afternoon flight and came back with one serious casualty. Sgt. Keller, a radio/gunner, was hit in the chest and jaw. Several ships made belly landings and were perforated with flak. Most of the bombs fell in the target area and straddled the bridge. The afternoon mission had its tense moments. Despite our steady bombing, the Germans consistently put up a fierce defense. Reconnaissance photos showed massive damage to the bridge and the intelligence summation was that it was beyond repair.

This target was an important one, and the brass handed out 29 Air Medals (see below). Over a period of time our casualty rate has been lower than other units. Squadron morale is usually high. If our mission losses became similar to those being flown by the "heavies," there would perhaps be a more serious mood.

## Air Medal and/or Oak Leaf Cluster Awarded

The Air Medal and/or Oak Leaf Cluster are awarded to the following named personnel, 340th Bombardment Group, Air Corps, United States Army. For meritorious achievement while participating in an attack upon a railroad bridge at Ferrera, Italy on 15 July 1944. The attack resulted in the destruction of two spans in the bridge thereby blocking this vital link in enemy communication lines. This outstanding achievement reflects the highest credit upon the military service of the United States.

## Air Medal Awarded

Joe L. Boaz, 170-74039, Sgt., Tail Gunner. Petersburg, TN.
Wildore Bousquet, 311-13775, Sgt., Tail Gunner. Woonsocket, RI.

## Air Medal, First Cluster Awarded

Oliver A. Buendel, 182-01172, Sgt., Engineer Gunner. Rungo, TX.
Donald C. Dick, 357-98613, Sgt., Armorer Gunner. Pointer, KY.
Charles A. Maliszewski, 329-13874, Sgt., Armorer Gunner. Jersey City, NJ.
Fleet C. Williams, 140-4353, Sgt., Engineer/Gunner. Prentiss, MI.

## Air Medal, Second Cluster Awarded

Wilbur C. Lantz, 075-3373, First Lieut., Pilot. New Palestine, IN.
Robert H. Martin, 080-9837, First Lieut., Pilot. Roanoke, VA.
Verl J. Miller, 075-3541, First Lieut., Pilot. Atalissa, IA.
Noble H. Byars, 075-6176, Second Lieut., Pilot. Plainview, TX.
Carroll E. Dearborn, 076-0106, Second Lieut., Pilot. Troy, NY.

Robert E. Mac Millan, 075-5383, Second Lieut., Pilot. Troy, NY.
Louis E. Raber, 076-214, Second Lieut., Bombardier. Pittsburgh, PA.
William N. Baskervill, 130-64741, Tech Sgt., Radio Gunner. Worsham, VA.
Gerald H. Powers, 110-69370, Tech Sgt., Radio/Gunner. Boston, MA.
Guy L. Lewis, 37505887, Tech Sgt., Radio/Gunner. Learned, TX.
James J. Allen, 327-71659, Sgt., Engineer/Gunner, Ramsey, NJ.

## Air Medal, Third Cluster Awarded

Fred C. Kirby, 081-5717, Second Lieut., Pilot. Birmingham, AL.
Herbert F. Robinson, 076-5526, Second Lieut., Bombardier. Birmingham, AL.
Theodore R. Olander, 201-01780, Tech Sgt., Radio/Gunner. Jamaica Planes, MA.
George J. Sorbello, 335-53814, Tech Sgt., Radio/Gunner. Canastota, NY.
Charles L. Harding, 332-60406, Staff Sgt., Engineer/Gunner. Elizabeth, PA.
Jack L. Parks, Jr., 381-07409, Staff Sgt., Armorer/Gunner. Amarillo, TX.
Eugene P. Simonson, 372-93815, Sgt., Armorer/Gunner. Buhl, MN.
Lewis S. Young, 202-45731, Sgt., Armorer/Gunner. Newton, NJ.

## Air Medal, Fourth Cluster Awarded

Andrew N. Ryck, 016-83394, Second Lieut., Pilot. Seneca Falls, NY.

Eugene G. Sallen, 075-6821, Second Lieut., Pilot. Fort Madison, IA.
Joseph M. Cline Jr., 081-6051 Second Lieut., Pilot. Gaffney, SC.

General Cannon rightly recognized what a tough series of missions Ferrera was. Group performance had improved markedly since he lowered the boom on us in late April. It was the only 340th mission series I know of where a large number of Air Medals were awarded.

July 16 Stand down today, and we are grateful because it was feared that Ferrera was again to be the target. Swim time and sack time predominated. A USO show was held in the evening with black musicians providing excellent entertainment. We had chicken for dinner and foraged the kitchen for leftovers.

July 17 Today we sent only six ships to the marshaling yards at Alessandria, which these days is light duty. After forming up with twelve other group planes, we bombed it to dust. All squadrons received one hundred percent marks. The rest of the squadron flew a practice mission which as noted is a regular thing. The truth is these days that we fly as many practice missions as actual missions. Later, we played on the beach and in the evening watched “Tampico” at the movie theater.

There is a new odd rule for outdoor movie watching which is that all participants must be covered in mosquito netting which includes their legs! This edict was put in place by the Provost Marshal, who will accept no bribes for an exception. We got a new combat crew in today and welcome them to a happy home.

July 18 France was in sight today, and some of the pilots said they crossed the border while they lined up for our bomb run on the Ceva, Italy railroad bridge. Bombs hit the west end of the approach, but didn't knock the bridge down. My favorite recreational activity, badminton, was installed on the beach. We played several matches and I held my own even with a height disadvantage.

July 19 Foul weather did not prevent Capts. Stith and Meyer, Lieuts. Ottavio and Hartsock from their one plane mission to Rome. I'm sure they will enjoy it as much as I did. The drizzle cleared away, and an evening mission flew with direct hits on the railroad bridge at Sassoulla in northern Italy. Our efforts have been recognized by Gen. Eisenhower no less with echoing sentiments from Generals Cannon and Knapp. The new crews were trained on procedures for escape and evasion should they find themselves behind enemy lines. Our ball games continue nightly and the competition is strong.

July 20-21 Thick fog hung on the coast both days. Capt. Dozier and Lieut. Glade returned from a rest in the States. Their opinion was that thirty days was all too brief concerning the travel time involved, and they are not alone in that opinion. There may be action to improve that situation.

July 22 A weather reconnaissance flight was the only day departure to check the weather over Ronco Scrivia. It turned out to be our late evening target, and six planes bombed the railroad bridge there. Several direct hits were observed on the bridge. On the way back a number of observations were made concerning enemy railroad traffic, shipping, and the condition of bridges, airports and truck movements. Reconnaissance is also one of our expected duties when the mission allows it.

The news of the attempted assassination of Hitler has evoked such remarks as, "Let's leave him for the Russians." It is pretty clear that there is some discord in the Nazi fortress. Today was hot and humid. Summer has definitely arrived.

### Air Medal, Fourth Cluster Awarded

Fred C. Kirby, 081-5717, Second Lieut., for meritorious achievement while participating in an aerial flight as pilot of a B-25 type aircraft in an attack upon at Ronco Scrivia, Italy on 22 July 1944. Birmingham, AL.

### Air Medal, Fifth Cluster Awarded

Constantine D. Stephenson, 120-29061, S/Sgt., for meritorious achievement while participating in an aerial flight as Armorer/Gunner of a B-25 type aircraft in an attack upon a railroad bridge at Ronco Scrivia, Italy on 22 July 1944. Patterson, NJ.

Robert L. Sharen, 322-37571, S/Sgt., for the meritorious achievement while participating in an aerial flight as Armorer/Gunner of a B-25 type aircraft in an attack upon a railroad bridge at Ronco Scrivia, Italy on 22 July 1944. Madison, IN.

July 23 Results on today's mission to the Carbola road bridge were eighty-eight percent. The guys weren't satisfied, they expect one hundred percent. No more passes to Naples are being issued to the squadron for the near future as too many fellows are returning from the city with a S.T.D.

July 24 A huge fuel dump was attacked today based on information provided by the Italian underground. There is a canal that comes in from the Adriatic, and the Germans bring tankers into the canal and unload them into the buried fuel tanks. The tanks are not visible from the air. A road is perpendicular to the canal. The word from our intelligence people was that the tank farm lay two hundred feet from the canal, and right next to the road.

We each carried twelve 100 pound bombs. The bombardier had to estimate where the center of the tank farm was from the canal and the road. When we hit the target there was a massive explosion. Smoke and flames went up to 8000 feet! I had my camera with me and we turned off the target so that I could get pictures of the smoke column. I sent the undeveloped film to Cairo with an R&R crew but never got the pictures back. The combat crews were elated by their early morning success today.

There was the usual swimming, reading and sleeping activities later with baseball in the evening. The brass held an evening meeting and briefed us on Allied progress on the various fronts. A large group listened and applauded loudly. Several new crews have arrived and we have some VIP visitors wandering around; so new faces abound. "Nine Girls" was our evening cinema, a humorous mystery story that was enjoyed by all.

The beach on the edge of our squadron was pretty fair. Sometimes during stand down there would be 200 guys on the beach and no swimming suits were worn. There was a section of the beach further down where the nurses and other WACs had a designated area. They always stayed away from our section of the beach.

Sometimes the area had big wave action on our beach. A few of the guys would bring mattress covers with them on windy days. After soaking the cover, they would run down the beach so that it filled with air. Then they would tie the corners of mattress cover into a kind of air bag. These improvised devices were used to ride the surf. A stream flowed into a pool that was next to the beach. After swimming in the ocean, we could jump into the pool and rinse off the salt. There is some truth in the Catch-22 incident where a soldier on the beach was killed by a low-flying aircraft. One of our planes did buzz the beach killing someone.

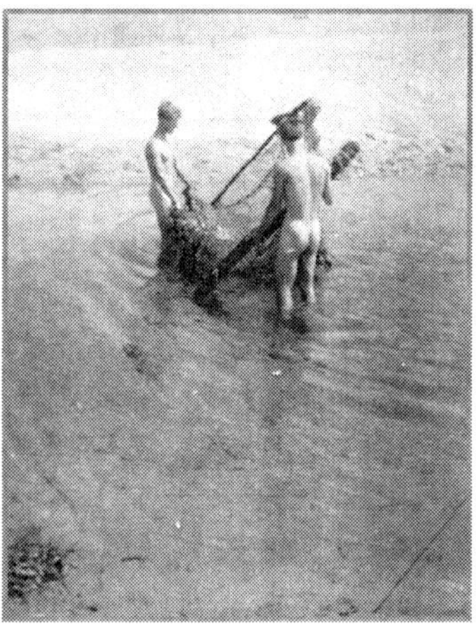

July 25 On the morning mission to Catiglia, our lead ship took a burst of flak which damaged the Norden sight and wounded the bombardier. All of the ships held their bombs and diverted to the alternate target, a nearby railroad bridge. Again they encountered heavy and intense ack-ack, with five more ships being holed. A good bomb pattern covered the west side of the bridge.

Lieut. Merkle just returned from the Capri rest camp to tell us about the following encounter. He swam out to a sailboat where a man in vacation clothing was sunning himself and said "Capico Anglais?" The fellow on the boat replied "Of course." They went together to the beach and were smoking when a Lieutenant Colonel approached and said to this fellow, "General, would you please come over here a minute to meet a few of my friends?" At that point Lieut. Merkle gurgled "Ah-ah-goodbye General," and the general bid goodbye to him.

We enjoyed hamburgers and potatoes with cherry tarts for dessert. The kitchen has benefited from all the fresh foodstuffs. Wow! What a party at the Group Officers club tonight. Seven nurses attended a boogie session and danced till midnight. The party was enlivened by some new records which came from the states packed between cookies.

*July 25, 1944*

*Dear Eleanor,*

*The other morning I was the designated Airfield Officer. I rose at 315AM to be sure that the kitchen was going. At 430AM I and woke my "chickens" for their dawn patrol. Some of them had to be awakened several times, and didn't really get their eyes open till they gulped down a good cup of coffee. I shooed them onto a truck, checked on the weather, made sure that our radio stations were operating and the operator was awake, then went to the tower.*

*They got off without incident and I read a couple of stories in magazines. One of them turned out to be a serial and unfortunately, I found all but the last part of the story. The sun rose across our beach and pretty soon I heard them returning. They buzzed the field to wake everybody up and alighted after an uneventful trip. We had breakfast and I passed out on my sack.*

*It looks as if I will go on a mission tomorrow. I have been asking the operations officer why he doesn't schedule me, but he says, "Aw, you don't want to fly anymore." I guess he finally got tired of my persistent questions.*

*Yesterday a big black raven landed on one of the tents as I was eating. I went outside and talked to him. He allowed me to approach quite close without a sign of fear. I went back to the mess hall and returned with some corned beef. He lit on my arm and ate it from my hand! I gave him some water, and he hopped on one of the beds. He was very hot, and went out and sat on one of the tent poles holding his wings out to cool off in the breeze. I took some pictures of him and hoped he would stay around, but by supper time he was gone.*

*This life affects us all in different ways. Some of the fellows have begun to spend fifteen hours or more sleeping. Some of them turn to building things. A couple of decent houses have resulted. One of them is quite elaborate. One fellow is building a refrigerator. I made a photographic enlarger and numerous useless things. Most of the fellows spend hours at the beach and I go there often myself. I am not exactly hard up for something to do. Nearly every day there is a plane that has received a new engine or wing. I fly it and then sign it off as ready. Sometimes I go on one of the trips to Catania for vegetables.*

*My mother wrote me about her recent visit and said that you are looking good. I've got to see for myself, though. Hope it is soon.*

*Love, Dale*

**July 26** **No doubt about our success today. We collapsed** the Ostiglia railroad and road bridges; an obsession with our crews. Bubbles and I led twelve planes over the road bridge and the other twelve planes hit the rail bridge. Kudos to the line armament crews. Their work is very physical and routine, but we couldn't do our job without them.

We had roast chicken tonight, and the pleasant smell wafting down the line had people queuing up a little early at the mess hall. The evening show presented "Moonlight in Vermont" - a good picture for 14-year-olds.

## Air Medal, Sixth Cluster Awarded

Dale J. Satterthwaite, 080-4516, First Lieut., for meritorious achievement while participating in an aerial flight as pilot of a B-25 type aircraft in an attack upon road and rail bridges at Ostiglia, Italy, 26 July 1944. Oaklawn, Ill.

July 28-29 Showers could be seen falling out of huge cumulus clouds before the rain reached earth today. There were some nickelling missions sent out. The truth about these missions was that they were sometimes more dangerous than armed missions because we flew at lower altitudes and speeds. I got shot up pretty well on several of them. Deanna Durbin played in "To Have and to Hold" at the local cinema and she was "oohed and aahed" by all.

On combat missions we wore standard GI helmets. While on a bomb run my roommate, Coleman Sellers, was struck between the eyes by a piece of shrapnel which killed him. It hit him just below the line of the helmet. His copilot on that mission was Gillette, a man who had flown with me. My opinion of Gillette's abilities was that he was capable, but not confident. Others in my squadron including Coleman felt the same way, and for that reason we did not recommend him as a first pilot. After Coleman was hit, Gillette called the turret gunner to the cockpit while he struggled to push Coleman's hands and feet back from the controls. The gunner was able to pull him out of his seat and lay him on the floor behind the cockpit. After the bomb run was finished, the bombardier got into the left pilot seat. As we approached Corsica at the end of the mission, Gillette called us on the radio and told us about Sellers death.

With a little apprehension, I watched his landing from my cockpit. It was textbook. Later, I invited him over to our tent. Sitting next to Seller's empty bunk, Gillette said he was ready to handle anything after today. He asked me if I would help him get qualified as a first pilot. I looked in his eyes and I could see that something had changed in him. He flew with me on the next two missions. On the second mission I let him do all the flying. The next day I recommended him for first pilot. It was quickly approved.

Coleman's death was one of cruelest blows during my time there. He was along on the June escapade to Rome and knew more Italian than the others. His friendly conversations with locals helped us manage on our limited funds. All of us developed close friendships, and he was particularly close to Steve Cassady. Cassady never got over his loss. Several months later my close circle of friends suffered two more losses. Scott Olson was killed over the Brenner Pass. Ted Somers bailed out with his crew and spent a month in the Italian Alps. He returned through Florence, and was awarded the Silver Star for his heroism. I kept a faded picture of these fellows who could be described as my band of brothers.

July 30 Ferrara Road Bridge was a target that we were not looking forward to because of expected heavy flak. Our mission planning combined with firepower from P-47s reduced the actual danger. We used chaff to defeat their radar aimed guns and it worked. The usual practice missions continue. "The Memphis Belle" was our film tonight. I must say that our crowd appreciated a war picture without flag waving, and it showed some accurate combat scenes.

July 31 Gale force winds created strong surf on the beach. Several ships were sighted off the coast of our island prompting a full out security alert. All troops were ordered to wear side arms, gas masks and helmets. Later, the order was rescinded when it was determined that the ships belong to the Allies and could be preparing to attack France. Summary for the month: We flew successful missions against some strong opposition. The mess hall served better food. Several new crews improved our manpower situation which raised morale.

Allied leaders were afraid that the Axis powers might resort to using chemical weapons. To counter that possible situation, the US merchant ship John Harvey arrived in the southeastern Italian port of Bari on November 28, 1943. On board the ship was 540 tons of mustard gas. There was nothing on the outside of the ship, of course, to indicate what it contained. Only seven US soldiers and their Commanding Officer, Lieut. Howard Beckstrom knew about the deadly cargo. They were all stationed on board after the ship arrived.

On December 2, 1943, Luftwaffe JU-88 bombers attacked the thirty US transport ships docked at Bari. The Germans sank seventeen ships and damaged eight more. This was almost a Pearl Harbor in the Mediterranean. During the bomb attack, the John Harvey caught fire, exploded and sank. The mustard gas containers were ruptured. All those who knew about the secret cargo were killed in the first moments when a bomb hit their living quarters. A lot of sailors from the John Harvey jumped overboard or got into life rafts. Crewmen from other damaged ships joined them in the water. When they came ashore, many of these men were covered in terrible burns and were having respiratory problems. The doctors who treated the victims could not figure out why they were so badly burned. Finally, one of the physicians onshore realized that the burns and internal injuries were caused by mustard gas.

The USA clamped an information blackout concerning the mustard gas release. The number of civilians that died from gas exposure was also kept quiet. Winston Churchill ordered British medical personnel not to tell what they knew about the incident. The cover story said that the dead either died from burning oil or bronchitis or lung problems. Insiders in the military later confirmed that poison gas was a major contributor in the burning and poisoning of 328 soldiers and sailors of which a full 96 died. The winds must have been blowing away from the town which prevented a real disaster.

Since I participated in a mock exercise to drop mustard gas, I had to assume that B-25s might be the airplane of choice if it were used. Learning about this terrible incident put a cold chill down my back. I'm very grateful that the Germans decided that chemical warfare was equally risky for both sides and did not use it. My friends and I now knew what it felt like in a high explosive and frag bomb attack. Here was a stark reminder of the destructive power of chemical weapons and how dangerous they were. Dropping conventional bombs was a necessary evil. Delivering mustard gas to the enemy was an altogether different thing.

For a moment indulge me in a scenario situation where the Germans had not succeeded in destroying this ship. Alternately, after the Bari attack the Allies could have positioned another ship load of the gas in the Mediterranean. The John Harvey was anchored just fifty flying minutes from the Foggia airfield. Hitler in his madness might have decided to arm some V1 flying bombs with chemical warheads directed towards London. After the devastating loss at Kursk, the German High Command could have decided that chemical weapons were their only option to curb the Russian onslaught. Churchill was on record stating that if the Germans used poison gas on the Eastern front, the Allies would reciprocate with chemical weapons delivered on Allied planes.

If Col. Chapman had assembled the Group and asked who had participated in the mock exercise with mustard gas, would I have put my hand up? The true answer is probably. I would possibly have found myself writing a goodbye letter before leading a near suicidal mission. We would be equipped with a delivery system far more lethal than was available in World War I. Fortunately, even in their desperation Hitler and the high command were not willing to unleash these weapons.

The squadron had some business to conduct in Bari at the end of July and I volunteered to take care of it. Mission and training flights occupied the squadron pilots on the day I intended to make the trip. The maintenance shop was not busy and a crew chief agreed to go along in the copilot seat. Early the next morning we departed Corsica with the intention of returning the same day. Our flight path took us over the Italian mountains. After climbing to 14,000 feet, we passed over the peaks and continued down the east coast to Bari.

Summer cumulus clouds began to fill the afternoon sky as we departed Bari on the return flight. They blocked our view of the mountains while we proceeded up the coast. It was clear that we would not be able to fly under the overcast while traversing across Italy. I made the decision to get up on top of the clouds. Despite some minor icing, we climbed through the clouds on instruments with the engines at full power. As mentioned earlier, the oxygen equipment had been removed from the planes. We were wearing summer flight clothes and it was very cold up there. Our plane crested the clouds at 18,000 feet, and the lack of oxygen made breathing difficult. My stateside training in the altitude chamber prepared me for this situation and we checked each other for signs of hypoxia. Our fingernails were blue and it was miserable. We flew at that altitude for about twenty minutes and were able to let down on the other side.

That was the highest I ever flew in a B-25. We did fly some longer missions where we stayed at 15,000 feet for as long as four hours. We would come back really exhausted and usually sleep for a while afterward. A B-25 was capable of flying as high as 25,000 feet with the high-speed supercharger engaged, but it was almost never used at high altitude. Even at 15,000 feet the airplane was kind of mushy on the controls. While flying in formation the pilots behind the lead ship had to anticipate turning maneuvers.

When we came down from combat missions, crewmen were issued two ounces of Old Overholt rye whiskey in a tin cup. Our strict orders were to consume the alcohol immediately. Some of the fellows kept an empty coke bottle in their flying suits and they would save their shots for a party at a later time. It was strictly against the rules. If we had been on a long mission at high altitude, that liquor would really hit us. Most of the guys would collapse in their bunks afterward.

As newer B-25Js arrived from the States, some of the older C and D ships were sent down to the depot in Alexandria, Egypt to have armor installed in them and also to get new waist guns and tail guns. The tail gun was mostly a scare weapon and could only swivel about fifteen degrees.

Air would come in through the waist gun ports and go out the tail like a wind tunnel. The tail gunner had to put straps around his ankles or his pant legs would blow up by his knees. All the gunners were assigned heated flying suits because it was so cold in the back of the plane. These were British suits which plugged into a 24 volt outlet. The suits were a little bit on the shabby side, being hand-me-downs. On almost every mission one of the gunner's suits would catch on fire and have to be extinguished! This was especially tough on the turret gunner because he would have to climb down for help. The brass had had issued orders that heaters were to be removed because they could explode if hit. Pilots and bombardiers wore woolly bomber jackets and stayed reasonably warm.

There was a set of "civvies" that the squadron had us all put on and be photographed in. We put that photograph in our bailout package that all crewmen carried when they were flying missions. Guys who bailed out would pass the picture to the underground resistance fighters that they met to get an ID made. We carried maps and Italian money in that pack also.

While I was in Corsica, I acquired a very nice gold-plated watch. It had a stopwatch function built into it and was beautifully made. I was in the bar talking to "Trigger" one day and he really wanted that watch. He had a Lugar pistol in his collection and he was willing to trade. Besides the Lugar, I had a twenty-five caliber Colt automatic which was purchased from an Italian who befriended me. As I recall it did not have any clip or ammunition, but it was kind of a nice thing to have in the streets of Cairo were I was a little uncertain about the native population. I never had any occasion to pull it out. The Lugar was a really nice pistol and was very accurate. It had great balance and I had a lot of ammunition for it.

Narrow trails ran along the ridges on the rugged mountains which were near Alesan airfield. They reminded me of the impressive scenery which surrounded the Greenville, North Carolina base. My friends Mark Somers and Sam Streckert went with me on a three day camping trip. We knew that wild boar roamed the hills, and we were determined to augment our fresh meat diet. I brought my Lugar and Sam had a rifle. We found the high country air to be refreshingly cool after the heat of the summer. Leaving our small camp at first light, we saw boar tracks and droppings. Since we were unfamiliar with the geography, we opted to hide in a glade and wait. It was not long before a boar wandered down the trail and Sam made an excellent kill with one shot. We carried the boar back to camp and quickly had the back loins on a spit over a fire.

Sam remained at the camp while Mark and I walked up a lovely stream nearby. Several large trout were visible in the shadows of a deep pool. We didn't have fishing gear with us, so I waited until one of the fish approached the surface and made a headshot with my Lugar. After a glorious lunch, we continued our exploration of those beautiful unsettled hills. Our remaining days passed in a similar fashion, and we returned to camp each night tired and ready to sleep. Memories of that peaceful time remained with me forever.

August 1 Thick fog again blanketed Alesan field. This evening Major Hackney, the X/O, and the Flight Surgeon threw a party for some of their friends and I participated. The Major had just returned with a bushel basket of lobsters which he obtained while on a trip to the south side of the island. One of the fellows had a bottle of 150 proof rum which was passed around. After several shots, the party quickly turned boisterous. As the merriment continued, some of the fellows broke out the Old Overholt whiskey that they had ferreted away after missions. Speaking for myself, it was one of the few occasions where my consumption exceeded my capacity.

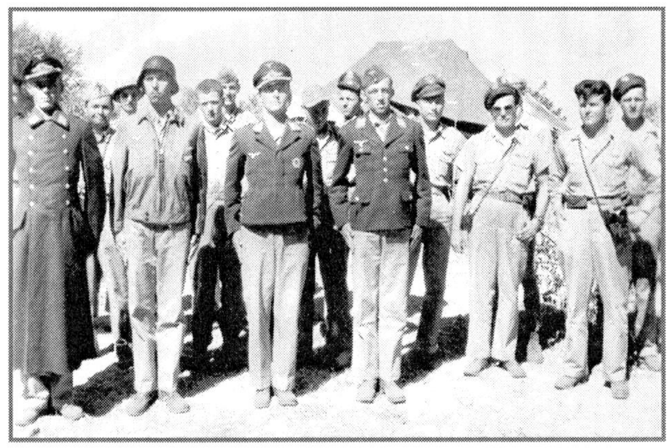

**Our alternate German dress day**
(Courtesy Daniel Setzer)

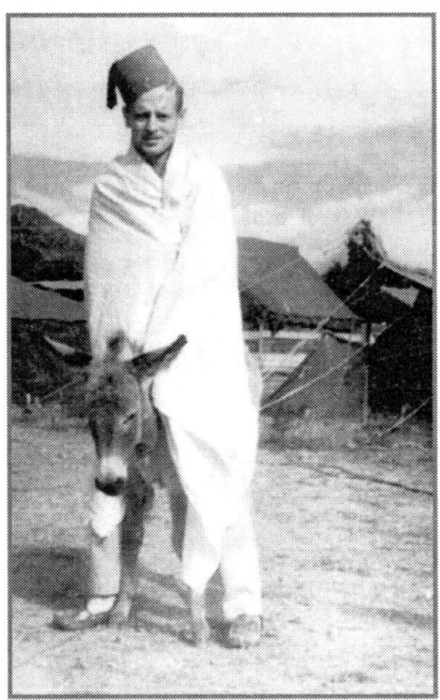

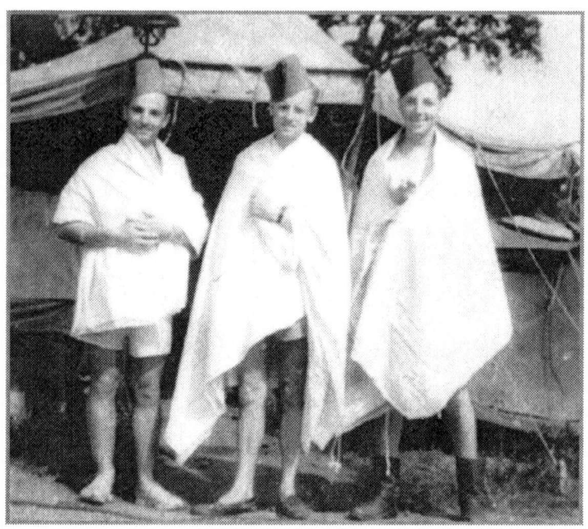

August 2 We went to Nice, France today with seventy-two airplanes. The flak was very heavy, and most of the airplanes came back holed. As we rolled out on the bomb run, A/A fire came up from two batteries straight ahead of us. Shells were coming towards us at our altitude. Over the intercom Bubbles said, "I can't change course, we've got ten seconds to go!" About that time the flak started to hit us, and it sounded like someone was pounding the aircraft with a sledge hammer.

We were flying in close formation and 6E, the plane piloted by Lieut. Hill on my left, took a cannon shell blast on the trailing edge of the right wing. The explosion blew most of the back edge of the wing off. I felt the concussion, and some of the debris struck my plane. Without much lift on the right side, the plane did a snap roll in my direction. I thought we were going to collide as he rolled, but somehow the left wing just missed hitting our wing. They fell upside down toward the sea. I couldn't see their path down, but thought they had no chance of surviving that inverted dive.

We were about 100 miles away from our base in Corsica when Lieut. Hill called in on the radio. In spite of the tremendous damage to the wing, the engine was not affected. They managed to get straightened out by throttling the left engine way back and bringing the right engine on the damaged wing to full military power. As they limped into the airport, the crew fired a red flare to indicate wounded on board. I pulled my camera from the case and took a picture of the airplane as he taxied in with all that damage. The hole in the wing was bigger than the span of a man's arms. During the violent snap roll maneuver, the bombardier was pitched backwards and his body smashed into a bulkhead. He had a broken arm which was the only injury on board. I thought Hill deserved a Distinguished Flying Cross for getting that plane back. Intelligence confirmed that the bridge was destroyed.

After the mission there was much speculation about an invasion from the Mediterranean side. Naturally, there were many bets placed on that.

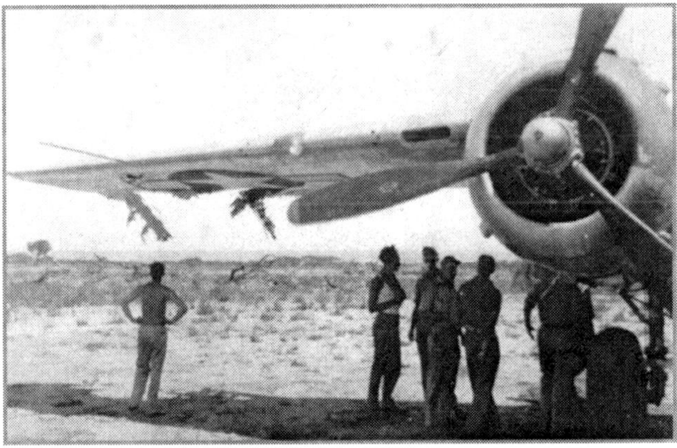

August 3 Our mission was again to Nice, France. For some reason there was no flak today which, after yesterday's greeting was a total surprise. The bridge, which was two miles from yes-

terday's target, was destroyed. "Rosie the Riveter" was at our evening cinema and was enjoyed by the majority of spectators.

August 4 We got our PX rations today - five candy bars, cigarettes and two bottles of beer. The morning mission to the marshaling yards close to Nice had good results. Sgt. Foster took a bet at the club tonight and ate a live grasshopper for a two dollar drink book. The only difficulty he complained of was that the insect was quite active, and insisted on kicking his lips during the mastication procedure. He may be war weary or just plain crazy.

August 5 The ancient "red sky in morning" warning proved true with strong afternoon storms. A jovial and often noisy party was held at the Group Officers Club. Lieut. Dombrowski, who was believed lost since June 22, returned to the squadron today. He was quite severely burned about the face and head. His hair is starting to grow back after being completely burned off. He spent over a month in the mountains of occupied Italy. Several good meals have lessened his gaunt appearance; apparently food was pretty scarce.

With the help of some partisans, he approached the front line. They directed him to a house where he could rest before going across the line to the Allies. An older man and a young boy were occupants of the home and they shared their meager meal with Dombrowski. Just then, a German motorcycle with a sidecar and a truck pulled up to the door of the house. Quickly, the youngster motioned the airman to follow him to the attic which was accessed through a trap door in the ceiling.

The Germans entered the house and immediately evicted the older man. They set up a machine gun in the window and set the young boy to work cooking and cleaning their gear. In the middle of the night the young boy bravely slipped some water through the attic trap door for Dombrowski. The Germans remained in the home for two full days, with the American praying that the Germans would not explore the attic for supplies. Suddenly, they packed up and left as suddenly as they had come.

The older man had been observing from down the street and returned to the house. He motioned the airman to follow him to a nearby home where an English speaking partisan told him they would get him across the line in the morning. At the crack of dawn, the man led him down a narrow street. He pointed to an entry two doors down across the street and said, "Go there." Opening the door with some trepidation, Dombrowski was amazed to see American soldiers.

August 6 Three ships flew an afternoon frag mission. The rest of the fellows flew practice missions, which included ditching practice and dingy drills. We had chicken for dinner and there were no leftovers.

August 7 We were off very early to strike the French Le Voultre Bridge. The first bombs scored direct hits which destroyed the northern part of the bridge. The second box of planes was equally accurate and took out the southern section. The trailing flights were struck by A/A, and one plane belly landed at Alesan field. The bridge is definitely destroyed. Cancellation of all leaves for the next month rekindled rumors of a French coast invasion.

Our daytime entertainment consisted of squirt gun target practice in the turret trainer. This device sounds silly, but our gunner crews have become much more proficient using it. It helps them visualize accurate deflection shooting. Col. Chapman, Lieut. Col. Bailey and some majors and various correspondents tried the device out today. Some of their nervous trigger fingers made a poor showing. After a while however, some of them registered some pretty good squirts.

August 8 Headquarters drafted twenty of our bomb loading crewmen into B-29 heavy bombers today. It's the first time they've done this and the "victims" are not happy about it. Some of those fellows are suggesting that their backs may suddenly go out.

The early morning mission to a French railroad bridge near Avignon was credited with one hundred percent accuracy. Over the target, a 488th plane was hit by flak and went down flaming. Five chutes were seen to open. Our crewmen used to think that they would soon be homeward bound after completing thirty-five missions. Now, guys who have flown that many missions are seeing their chances of rotation look slimmer.

My friend Ted Wheeler had a 16 mm movie camera. He had some color film for the camera which was rare and hard to come by. Ted was a skillful pilot, and the two of us decided that we were going to do some joyriding over Italy in a B-25. Our plan was to make a low level movie with this camera. There were just the two of us in the plane which we flew from Corsica over to Pisa.

Ted put us in a steep turn around the Leaning Tower. The echoes of our raucous engines bounced off roof tops which were only a few feet below us. I operated the camera out the top hatch of the airplane with the top of the Leaning Tower angling above us. After several orbits, we arced away from the tower and hedgehopped across the city. I was in the nose operating the camera while Ted flew past rural landscapes. Continuing to play daredevil, Ted positioned the plane at low level over the highway to Empoli. I have to admit that we caused the sudden redirection of traffic on the highway. The movie went back to Los Angeles in Ted's baggage and I never got to see it.

As I mentioned, poker games started up at payday in the Officers Club and ran for days. The game would only end when some of the fellows had bet their pay away. Ted was a particularly good poker player, and he told me that he was sending home an amount equal to his pay just from his poker winnings. Sometimes the fellows would play a game called "Red Dog" and I was more likely to join in. Four cards were dealt to each player who bet that their hand would beat the dealer's hand when a fifth card was dealt to them. I won seventy dollars on one occasion and lost the same amount the next time I played.

August 9 Command has asked us to drop bombs when we fly to France even if the target is partially obscured. Today the weather over the Ventimiglia railroad bridge was definitely unfavorable, but we were credited with eighty-three percent accuracy. The bomb pattern hit the west approach and left large holes in the bridge deck.

Tonight's menu was fresh ham and potatoes. A steady shower canceled the cinema and so the Officers Club was crammed with customers. Lieut. Cochran gave the squadron a thorough buzz job this afternoon with a P-47. We are so used to his buzz jobs that unless the plane takes off the top of a tree, it is not exciting.

August 10 Rain showers increased in intensity in the early morning, which flooded many tents. Shoes and gear floated onto the nearby roads. Unfortunately, the Special Service tent containing unsorted mail was also flooded. Slit trenches filled up with five feet of water. This onslaught was lightened by much laughing while the occupants salvaged their belongings by flashlight. Judging from the blankets and clothing hung out to dry this morning, there weren't many who missed the discomfort. Nature capped off the show with a huge waterspout just off our shores. The evening weather cleared enough for "Gaslight" to be shown at the cinema, and it received high acclaim.

August 11 Our mission today required precision targeting to have any success. The hardened coastal gun positions on the French coast were not affected by a near miss. Most of the bombs did score a bull's-eye. Nearby, fighter-bombers strafed a nearby radar station. The afternoon mission put up sixty-eight aircraft. Fifteen of our friends are heading back to the States tomorrow and of course we held a big party to send them off.

August 12 Today's mission was unique in that we bombed a seaplane base at Lake Cuomo which was being used by the Germans for reconnaissance flights. I had a pretty good view of the area and saw several seaplanes taxiing away from the base at high speed.

Florence is still on the front lines and fierce fighting is reported in the area. Allies are pushing further in France following the cleanup of Brittany and the fall of Nantes. Some clever soul has already located a 486th Rest Camp in Paris with a pin on the targeting map. Fresh hotdogs garnished with hot mustard were served for dinner today and each man got three!

August 13 Intelligence gave us a ninety-six percent on yesterday's mission. Bravo! Our combat crews are doing an excellent job this month. Our squadron had a scheduled stand down day. The afternoon sun was very hot, and a good portion of the squadron cooled off at the beach. We were again graced by the presence of seven nurses this evening at the Officers Club. The nude murals on the wall caused them no consternation.

August 14 Combat crews at this evening's mandatory gathering were told that the invasion of southern France would be initiated at 0800 hrs. tomorrow. The location of the invasion was revealed, and also plans for air, land, and sea forces. We were told that tomorrow's briefing would be at 0400 hrs. so most of the crew retired early.

For several nights we have practiced making airborne formations, which is very difficult and dangerous in the dark. Our goal was to be over the southern French shore at daybreak for the start of the invasion. That was a bit of a challenge because it was the only night flying that we did. Our stated purpose was to take out shore batteries near the French Riviera. The Allies again tried to disguise the actual location of the invasion and so we hit many targets away from the actual landing zone. We found out later that many of the German cannon emplacements were made of wood. They were also not adverse to employing deception.

August 15-16 The 340th Group sent fifty-two bombers into the air over the southern French coast line near Antheor this morning. On the way to the target, I looked down on the water and saw an American landing ship that had been converted to be a small aircraft carrier. On the deck were three observation planes. I had never heard of these mini carriers and that was the only one I ever saw. There were dozens of other ships heading towards the beach. The damned weather which blanketed the coast meant only a few ships dropped their bombs. There was very little flak and everyone returned safely.

The day was still young, and another large mission was dispatched to bridge targets at Avignon. A French Major General and his aide-de-camp accompanied the afternoon mission after they had been introduced to the squadron by Col. Chapman. The mission was rough; three ships did not return and most planes were holed. Two ships went down over the target and one over the sea. The plane piloted by Lieut. Hoschar was struck in the right wing which flew apart, setting the ship into a flat spin. No one was seen chuting out, but chutes may have been overlooked because of the excited state of the crews due to heavy and intense flak.

On the return trip, pilots Smith and Morrison spotted a 488th ship going down. When the crew landed in the water, they each dropped spare dinghies and radioed fixes for air-sea rescue. Squadron members were understandably not happy and groups of men could be seen about the area in discussion, quietly and soberly talking about the mission. Quite a few boys drained their sorrow with some beer and whiskey. In fact, singing could be heard during the small hours. The squadron's turn for stand down tomorrow will be welcomed. Despite the grim news, some of the fellows went to the USO show at the adjoining army brigade because our USO shows have been discontinued until further notice.

August 17 Steady drizzle fell from low clouds, and a cancelation decision was rendered in the early hours. There were two large sacks for mail call which cheered everyone up. Eight new pilots arrived and were assigned to fly with experienced guys. In the evening, Col. Chapman came into the Officers Club and informally praised the job that the engineering section was doing keeping the planes in good flying condition. That was good news to Capt. Stoler and me.

August 18 Steaks sizzling on a grill created a mouthwatering aroma that wafted down the flight line. Everyone lined up outside the mess tent early, which was unusual because the food has been none too good lately. We fault the quartermasters, not the efforts of the cooks. More than likely it has to do with the big drive in southern France. Nine candy bars, two cokes and one beer issued to each man quelled the grumbling a little.

Last night the armament section was handed a nightmare load. Nineteen ships were armed with double clusters of frag bombs, twenty-eight clusters per plane. The crews started loading the bombs, but suspected that they would be told to unload it. Operations officers gave them smiling assurances that the bomb loads would not be changed. For three hours grunting and groaning they wired all those clusters in the airplanes. At the first light of day the announcement was "Frag mission canceled for the 486th!"

The order sent the ground crews sky high - unloading six ships for a pamphlet mission. Pamphlets! Ugh! They won't kill any Germans. And besides, Axis Sally said the paper wasn't good enough to use in Nazi latrines. There was a near mutiny. Capt. Bridges had helped to load the bombs and he said he was damned if he was going to pass that order on. While the armament section silently applauded, he phoned Operations and told Capt. Dozier that if they wanted the ships unloaded, he would take them up and jettison everything into the ocean. He was unfortunately overruled by Maj. Hackney and Col. Chapman. Stripes and bars will never win against eagles and leafs. To make it a perfect day, they also decided to unload the other thirteen airplanes.

August 19 At 0530 hrs. the first planes lifted off from Alesan field for a mission to the Rhône Valley in southern France. This was a bridge attack at Orange, France. There were indications that the ground troops in that area are doing well and don't need our help. Our crews returned disgusted, because as one crewman put it, "cloud coverage was about 11/10ths over the target." Consequently, another mission went out at 1600 hrs. to the same target and they were successful. The north span of the bridge is down. The evening found the weekly dance at the Group Officers Club a lively affair and four females were present.

August 20 Four enemy planes on an airfield were destroyed today. There were fifteen planes spotted at the field so results were a little disappointing. The Armament baseball squad won the play-off for the 340th tonight and will play in the finals at Ajaccio.

August 21 French targets have occupied us for the last two weeks. Today our planes returned to Italy and knocked down the railroad bridge at Parma in the Po Valley. Both six plane boxes crossed the bridge approximately at the center, with direct hits observed. This mission was a milk run with little opposition. Mail was again quite plentiful with lots of smiles all around.

August 22 Stand down. The happy reason is that there seems to be a shortage of targets. Lieut. Sellers returned from German held Italy last night. This morning he related some of his escape experiences to a large audience. Two new crews arrived, and turnover may quickly increase because many crews are reaching the seventy mission mark.

S/Sgt. Iwan returned to the organization today after a thirty day leave in the States. He enjoyed the furlough immensely, but was quite burned up at the excellent treatment being rendered the P.O.W. at American camps. He claims that it is difficult to get noticed in the PX at Fort Patrick Henry due to the sizable number of prisoners purchasing whatever they desire. We are sure that arrangement is quite different from anything our men have run into as P.O.W. guests.

August 23 It looked as if we would stand down when suddenly a mission was called for Avignon, the dreaded target. The mission was so unexpected that the bomb loaders were overwhelmed, and volunteers from the gunner crews helped load the bombs. We took off with great apprehension, and were amazed to find no flak as we arrived there. After dropping our bombs, we accidentally strayed over Marseille on the return flight where flak struck three planes. The bullets may have come from our own troops. Everyone returned safely to Alesan field.

August 24 German troop strength has increased around Avignon and we flew a mission to suppress their gun positions. After the bomb run, the accompanying P-47s went hunting for trains. Several minutes later three ME-109s made an appearance, but did not attack. Today's great news is that Paris has been liberated. Further, Marseille is also in Allied hands. The day was again quite warm and the evenings are very pleasant except that the mosquitoes are now becoming too numerous.

*August 24, 1944*

*Dear Eleanor*

*We are very busy now as you may be hearing from the papers or radio. I hope it hastens the end of this thing. I could probably come home sometime in September or October, but I've been promised the rank of captain if I stay through November and I intend to do that. I won't have to fly many more missions, however. I expect to stop around seventy and I have sixty-one now.*

*The weather stays the same. It has been so beautiful for such a long time that the cloudburst the night before was almost welcome. It did result in our shoes and various other articles to go floating through the tent and down the hill. I spend as much time as I can at the beach soaking up sun. Usually there is a crowd of us. We take some freshwater, a rubber boat and a blanket to lay on. Bathing suits are quite superfluous. The few nurses or Red Cross girls have their own stretch of beach a few hundred yards away and they stick to it. It's a sort of unwritten and unspoken agreement.*

*Next day. Your letter dated July 16 came the other day and I hope to receive another one soon. I talked to some of the "wheels" and learned that they will put my promotion in next month. I won't depend upon it too much though. Look what happened to my thirty day leave! I am an instructor pilot now. I have two junior birdmen from Dallas, Texas who are progressing quite rapidly. I didn't teach them today because I was recuperating from yesterday's mission. Tomorrow is the second anniversary of our squadron and they are presenting me with a Distinguished Flying Cross and several other medals. Of course, there are many other fellows getting medals as well.*

*The generals have decided not to send fellows home for thirty day leaves anymore. I guess it is both good and bad news. I probably won't have to return when I get done. Please look for a column by Ken Dixon. He writes for the Associated Press and just spent a week with us writing about various characters in the squadron.*

*I have been giving some thought to postwar plans. I believe I would like to go to school again if I can't find a flying job. Would you like to live in a college town? I think of you always. It makes the day shorter and the nights sweeter and all of this worthwhile.*

*Love, Dale*

In truth, I received more letters from home than I sent. Packages were sure welcome. One of them contained hard salami. In order to buy that, the family had to give up some of their meat rations. This sure went over big with me and a few close friends. We also got cookies which survived the trip pretty well. There wasn't much sweet stuff to be had in Corsica outside of the packages from home.

Richard Sutton, a bombardier with the group, had been a refrigeration specialist before he went in the service and he learned that you could get a dry ice cream mix from the quartermaster. There was no ice to be had and he decided rig up a means of freezing some ice cream. He took an oxygen regulator and converted it for Freon. One of the hospital staffers agreed to give him a flask of Freon. Finally, he scavenged an airbrake compressor from a truck. It was a pretty involved assembly which worked well, but soon the Freon dissipated away.

I was going to Naples and word got around the squadron. Richard asked if he could go with me. He went down to the harbor in Naples and talked some people who had refrigeration aboard their ship out of a big tank of Freon. I came out to the airplane to go home that evening and he was standing there with this shoulder high cylinder. We went back to Corsica and he connected the tank to his ice cream freezing system. Much to the delight of the squadron, he was able to make ten gallons of ice cream. The Freon escaped so easily that it was our only batch.

We didn't have many sources of news from home. The occasional Stars and Stripes newspapers that came our way were passed around the squadron. There wasn't much news from the US in the military paper. Our squadron issued everyone thin onionskin style stationary to write home on. Officers were allowed to censor their own correspondence. Occasionally I drew the duty of censoring enlisted men's mail.

We became friends with an officer who ran a large G.I. laundry about twenty miles away from us. He had to censor the letters sent by the enlisted soldiers there. He told us about this one letter written by a black soldier. It had a drawing of a dove on top of the letter. Inside the envelope was written the following:

*This dove brings you my love,*
*and also this letter. May he not lose a feather*
*till I hold you in my arms*
*and our shoes lie beneath the bed together.*

**August 25** **Today is the second anniversary of the formation** of 340th Bomb Group. At 1400 hrs. the men were assembled for a formation which was led by Gen. Knapp and Col. Chapman. Unfortunately, Gen. Cannon was unable to get here as was the original plan. The 340th Group was presented a Presidential Unit Citation. Many fellows received medals at the ceremony as well. The general said that this group had done the best pinpoint bombing in the European theater.

At the conclusion of the ceremonies, some of the guys went to the beach and some to the bars to whet their appetite for a nice chicken dinner. At 1900 hrs. the outside amphitheater was packed for the USO show. After the show the entertainers mixed it up at both the Enlisted Men's Club and the Officers Club, where participants partied with enthusiasm aided by our bar which set up free drinks all night.

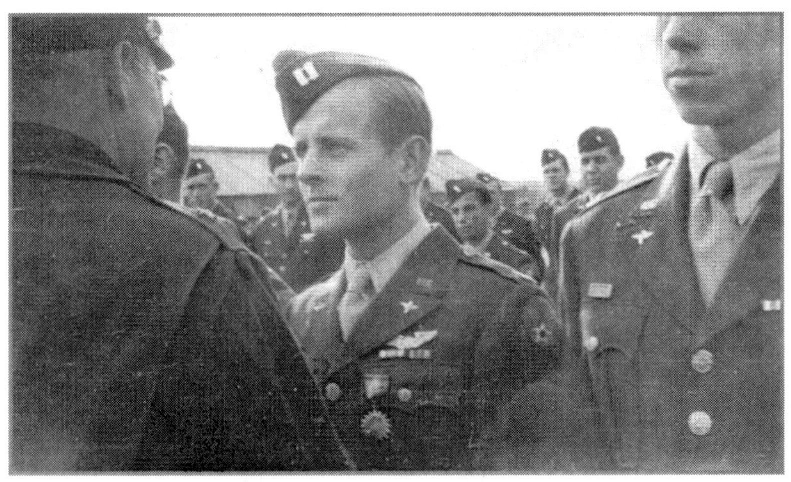

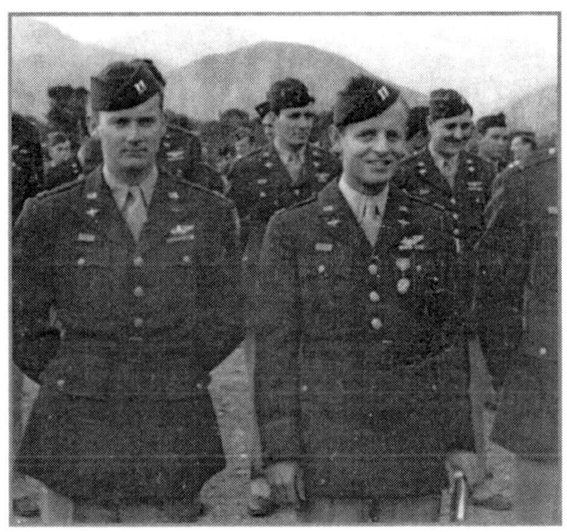

# 340th Bomber Group Marks Second Birthday

MAAF HEADQUARTERS, Aug. 27—The 340th Medium Bombardment Group, which thinks its July average of 97 bombs on target out of every 100 dropped is just about tops in accuracy, celebrated the second anniversary of its activation by receiving 180 awards and decorations from Brig. Gen. Robert D. Knapp, Auburn, Ala., wing commander, it was announced today.

The Group, accompanied by Col. Willis F. Chapman, Jackson, Mich., flew its 500th mission in southern France on Aug. 15, and recently was cited by President Franklin D. Roosevelt for its services in the Tunisian and Sicilian campaigns.

Graphic evidence of the Group's bombing precision was presented to General Knapp by Col. Chapman in the form of a 31-day diary of target area photos, which showed that no target had been missed during July.

Among the awards handed out were a Distinguished Flying Cross and a Silver Star to Lt. Warren E. Barnard, Somerville, Mass., bombardier, who participated in the effective attack on the Itri tunnel during the final push on Rome. Col. Chapman also received one of the 32 DFCs presented by General Knapp.

A Bronze Star went to Pfc. Celse Castenda, San Antonio, Texas, for heroism during a German bombing and strafing attack on the Group's base during which several were killed and wounded. Fourteen others also got Bronze Stars, 11 received Soldier Medals, 34 Purple Hearts and 87 Air Medals and Clusters.

The 340th was activated at Columbia, S. C., in August, 1942, and came overseas in time to bomb the Mareth Line in Tunisia. Two of its three commanding officers have been shot down in action, one being a prisoner of war. The Group tops all other Mitchell units in this theater in bomb tonnage, with more than 14,600 to its credit.

(Courtesy Stars and Stripes)

August 26 Group stand down was no doubt appreciated by numerous owners of hangovers. The day was warm and aside from a few practice missions, the usual activity prevailed. In the evening our outdoor cinema presented "Crazy House" which began late causing little concern and then broke down several times which did cause some grumbles. However, the picture was humorous and enjoyed by all. Romania surrendered to the Allies and declared war against the Nazis. Some of the other Balkan states may soon follow.

Occasionally we would venture twenty miles up the coast to Bastia for a drink and dinner. There was little night life in the town, and our brass strongly recommended that we not remain there after dark. They suggested that it would be a good idea to carry our side arms while visiting. Generally, the Corsicans were not very cordial. They hated the Germans; they didn't like us much, and didn't even seem very agreeable to their own citizens! Given that, I was not aware of any outright aggression to Americans.

In the mountains about four miles from our base was a little village where we had our laundry done. There were several young ladies who lived in the village. Some of the fellows and I befriended them and spent several chaperoned evenings with them. I have pictures of them, and enjoyed their company. We did our own dry cleaning. We would stretch the garments out on planks and scrub them with 100 octane aviation gas. 80 octane gas would not do because it had a reddish tint and would stain the clothes. The 100 octane gas had a bluish tint and seemed to do a good job.

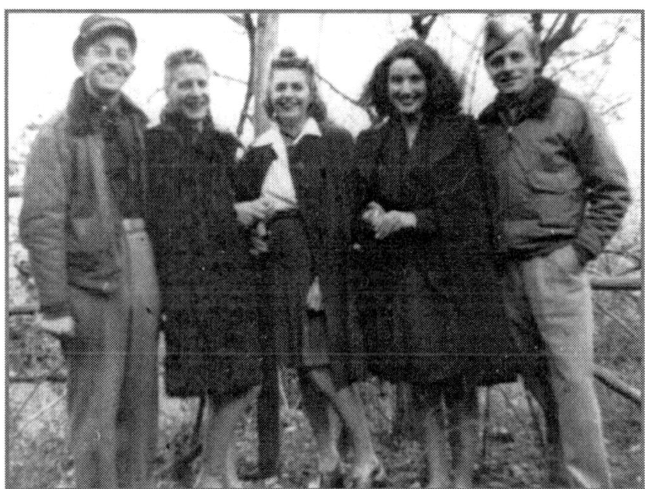

August 27 Usual church services were well attended and presented by Chaplain Cooper. Chappy is a regular fellow who was liked by all. Practice missions on the usual schedule - "Sunday, Monday & Always." Three truckloads of men attended the movie at a nearby army unit and enjoyed the picture "Double Indemnity."

August 28 Lyons, France was our target today, and it was a long, long way. Only six of the twelve airplanes dropped their bombs through the clouds with debatable results. Afternoon beach lounging was the preferred recreational activity. Many attended the evening cinema, and on the return walk home a sergeant was struck by a Jeep and injured severely. Capt. Wathen had him taken to the hospital. Unfortunately, it takes lessons like this to convince some men not to drive too fast and too foolishly.

August 29 Twelve planes laid a good pattern across the railroad bridge near San Marino, Italy. Three cases of beer are to be raffled off Saturday night in order to procure the funds for instruments and equipment for a squadron band. It costs ten francs to get in the pool.

August 30 Crews were awakened in the misty morning and planes were readied only to hear that the mission had been canceled at 1330 hrs. There was much moaning and groaning about the wasted time. Everyone got into recreation mode very quickly. The Ploesti oil fields were Germany's main source of oil, and one of the greatest prizes of the war. They were occupied by the Russian army today.

August 31 Today's early briefing had crews making up for yesterday's easy living. We flew north of Venice which was a five hour mission, our longest yet. The results were good and we knocked the bridge down. Heavy and accurate ack-ack harassed the formation, and one of our ships was hit but returned to base.

A French crew flying a B-26 stopped at our field today to refuel. A few pictures were taken, and Lenny Tetreault found out that one of the airmen was from Marseilles and one from Brest. Several men departed for Foggia to meet the medical disposition board. It is rumored that we will lose them all, but their families will be jubilant.

September 1 Our morning mission was to a road bridge in Italy with twelve planes. The squadron got only fifty percent because one six plane box missed the target, and the other made a bull's-eye. They sent a camera plane out to take pictures after the mission. Lately they are using P-38s for that job, and they are based at a northern Corsica airfield. The weather remained warm and there was lots of beach action in the afternoon.

September 2 Today Col. Chapman told me to fly to Rome. He instructed me to check in with Radio Roma and said that they were interviewing several pilots. I'm not exactly sure why I was selected to do this. At the radio station I met two pilots who were there for the same reason. We were there to make a recording which would be sent to stateside radio stations.

The other two pilots had interesting stories. One of them was an L-4 courier pilot. He was attacked by an ME-109 and survived by putting the maneuverability of his plane to full advantage. He suckered the fighter into pursuing the little L-4 into a canyon that the ME-109 could not fly out of. The German attempted to turn around inside the canyon and cracked up. The other fellow was a P-47 pilot with three victories in a single day. I contributed some information about our missions to knock down the bridges at Avignon.

The Borghese families were rulers in Rome for some time. This Radio Roma assignment gave me an opportunity to tour the Borghese Palace. Inside the palace I came across a portrait studio manned by a photographer who had a Leica camera with a 180 mm lens. He offered to do my portrait and I accepted. The thing that I recall about that tour of the palace was that there was a billiard table, and it had real ivory balls on the table. When two of the balls clicked together, they made a different sound than the plastic balls do. It was a very elegant table.

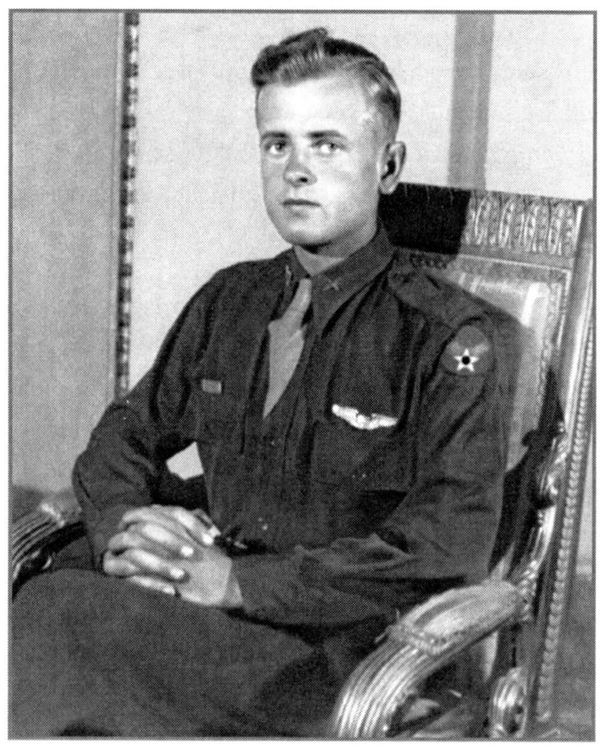

*September 2, 1944*

*Light of my Life,*
*A note from the Eternal City.*

*I am in Rome making a recording that will be broadcast over Detroit radio stations sometime in the morning when no one is listening. After telling them about one of our missions, I read a three-minute speech urging civilians to buy bonds. Rome is warm, pleasant and busy. The population is busy ignoring the war and attempting to extract all the money possible from the pockets of the rich Americans. Anyway, I wish you were here and I love you.*

*Dale*

We used our precision bombing techniques to great effect in the sinking of a German light cruiser the "Taranto." The cruiser was not being used by the Germans as a fighting vessel, rather they were attempting to tow the ship to the mouth of La Spezia harbor and scuttle it. They wanted to prevent the Allied forces from using the harbor to offload heavy equipment and munitions.

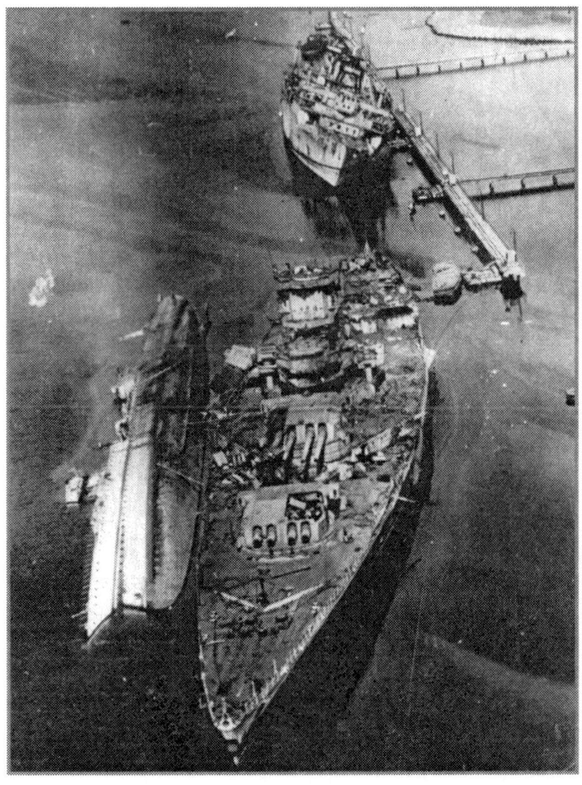

(Courtesy Daniel Setzer)

In our mission briefing, they told the first flight of six airplanes to hit the bow of the ship. The second flight was to hit amidships, and the third flight the stern section. That is exactly the way we hit it. It turned over and sank about twenty minutes after we bombed it. The 340th was recognized with a second Presidential Unit Citation for this mission.

> RESTRICTED
> HEADQUARTERS TWELFTH AIR FORCE
> DISTINGUISHED CITATION OF UNIT
>
> Under the provisions Of Circular 333, War Department, and Circular 89, North African Theater of Operations, on 10 July 1944, the 340th Bombardment Group is cited for outstanding performance of duty in action against the enemy In the Mediterranean Theater of Operations on 23 September 1944.
>
> Culminating a long and unbroken series of flawlessly executed bomb attacks on pinpoint and area targets, the 340th Bombardment Group sank the enemy light cruiser Taranto on 23 September 1944. The 340th distinguished itself by extraordinary heroism and professional competence in the face of vigorous enemy opposition. Their achievement places them above and apart other units which participate in similar operations. When aerial reconnaissance disclosed an enemy plan to scuttle the Taranto at the entrance of La Spezia harbor in Italy, the 340th Bombardment Group was ordered to destroy this warship with all speed before it could be moved into position. Acting swiftly and with utmost thoroughness, the Group's operations, intelligence and maintenance personnel skillfully planned the attack, briefed the crews, and readied their planes for the assault.

At 0800 hrs. on 23 September, twenty-four B-25s of the 340th Bombardment Group took off without escort from the bases in Corsica for the heavily defended La Spezia area. A heavy antiaircraft barrage from the ring of powerful enemy batteries which encircled the harbor targeted their planes. Nevertheless, gallant pilots displaying outstanding courage and flying ability resolutely held their aircraft in tight formation throughout the attack. Highly trained bombardiers, who were undeterred by hostile fire, expertly synchronized their instruments. They released the thousand pound bombs with unerring precision, scoring numerous direct hits on the target. Compact bombing patterns from the first three flights covered the bow, beam and stern of the cruiser with devastating effect, capsizing it before the last flight could release its bombs.

This outstanding achievement was made possible by unsurpassed teamwork. The successful attack combined exceptional planning with indomitable courage, superior flying skill and precision bombing. The enemy's attempt to block the entrance of this strategic harbor and naval base was completely frustrated. Personnel of the 340th Bombardment Group displayed heroism and extraordinary professional skill which reflects the highest credit upon themselves and the military service of the United States.

By command of Major General Cannon,
Charles T. Meyers, Brigadier General, USA
William S. Dick, Colonel, AGD, Chief of Staff.

This was one of the few successful attacks on ships from American bombers in formation. We flew three practice missions before the actual attack.

One of our planes went over to Cyprus to pick up a load of liquor for the officers club. On the return flight they were flying on top of an overcast, and the tower heard them call for a fix. The tower responded, but the pilots did not confirm the bearing sent to them. The calls from the airplane got weaker and weaker and finally disappeared. Everyone assumed that they went down.

A month later the crew of that airplane came strolling in to camp. Their story was that their radio compass failed, and they were unable to hear the bearing the Alesan tower had broadcasted. Running critically low on fuel, they let down through the overcast hoping to ascertain their position visually. They saw an island, and it had an airport with an Allied airplane on it. After landing, they climbed out of the airplane were greeted by some men with submachine guns. The island was Mallorca which belonged to the Spanish government. The soldiers put in enough fuel to make it to the Spanish mainland and they put an armed soldier on the plane.

They flew over to Valencia, Spain and landed. The Spanish government took control of the aircraft and they turned the crew over to the American Embassy. Even though Spain was technically neutral, they allowed the crew to go down to Gibraltar and from there they crossed over to Morocco. Officially, the crew was sworn to secrecy about the return trip. The Spanish of course confiscated the liquor which was valued at $3000. The word was that the Spanish told the Americans that they could use the airplane as a staff ship inside Spain. However, the plane had to remain in the country. It remained with the Spanish after the war was over.

September 3 Heavy clouds covered our airfield until midafternoon. A mission departed to bomb a rail bridge north of Bologna, Italy. Returning crews said that the approach to the bridge had been damaged, but remained standing. A more detailed assessment required reconnaissance photos. The latest Cairo Cossacks returned today bedecked with souvenirs of all kind. An orchestra at the Group Officers Club was well received and did a similar show at the enlisted men's Red Cross Club.

September 4 Our Missions to bomb rail bridges in the mountainous north of Italy continued today with one hundred percent hits on a bridge near Modena. These targets require greater accuracy because steep hills deflect any bombs that are slightly off target. Sgt. Krause, alias "Bombline," who updates our war situation maps, has been very busy lately because of many Allied gains. The evenings are becoming cool, which makes it more comfortable for sleeping.

September 5 The weather is again clear and comfortable. Good weather was also over the target which was a bridge near Parma Reggio. Support columns on the bridge collapsed, and the mission was judged a complete success. Climbing out from the target, we heard a distress call from a B-26 over the Po Valley. One engine had stopped running and they were struggling to gain altitude. These planes did not have good performance with one engine. We heard the pilot tell the crew to bail out. The victorious Armament baseball team is now playing in the Island finals in Ajaccio. They lost the first game, but won the second one. We are eagerly awaiting the results of the next game.

September 6-7 Weather prevented missions, and several groups of lucky crewmen began their return trip to the states. One of them was Cyril Staub, my friend and partner. A noisy, rather drunken gathering at the Group Officers Club roasted a goat in their honor. I was overjoyed to see Cyril depart safely. We had shared so many perilous moments and good adventures. It was as if I were splitting a part of myself knowing I would probably not see him again. I said to him, "This is the last time anyone will call you Bubbles." He smiled and said, "My girlfriend latched on to the name, and I will hear it all the time!"

Fourteen officers and sixteen enlisted men departed on planes which buzzed the area, shaking the headquarters tents with prop wash. The newly organized squadron band has been rehearsing the last few days, and it will be some time before they sound like much of anything. They haven't got enough instruments and the players are pretty rusty.

September 8   Low fog brought about another stand down. At 1430 hrs. everyone who was off duty went to see the championship game between the 340th team and the Ajaccio baseball champs. Unfortunately, the Armament team came out on the losing end of a 5 to 3 score. The evening show was "Captive Women" - A real stinkeroo.

September 9   Clearing weather finally allowed a frag mission this afternoon, which was flown in support of troops on the east side of the Gothic line (north of Florence). Results were good. Lieut. McMillan landed late due to flak related nose wheel trouble and consequently, made a tail down landing. "The Great Moment" with Joel McCrea played at the Group movie tonight along with a twenty minute film about the Vesuvius eruption. Everyone was thrilled to see the 340th on film, even if it did take the eruption of Vesuvius to bring it about. It appears that soon the snap of fall will be in the air.

German radar directed fire was becoming an increasing problem over Italy. We are using decoy ships, which break away from the squadron and come over the target from a direction well off the bomb run course. Those planes throw out chaff. The timing of their approach is carefully synchronized to happen just ahead of our arrival. Employing these methods reduces the damage to the main formation. The guys assigned to that risky task are not often recognized for their bravery.

September 10 Early chapel services preceded the morning mission. Unfortunately, the crews could not locate their target which was an ammunition factory. It was rare for us to not locate our targets. On an earlier mission, two similar canyons diverged and I mistakenly lead the flight up the wrong canyon. We diverted to our alternate target. I received some rebukes for that error. I am training a number of new copilots and several of them will be ready for first pilot duties soon.

September 11 A frag attack on enemy positions in the mountains north of Brescia had excellent results. The flow of fresh vegetables from the south has ended. Our food supply mostly comes from canned goods, with the usual objections about meals. In the evening we were entertained with a musical comedy, "Trip around the World". Some of us are quite amazed at the variety of cinema that makes its way to this small corner of the war.

September 12 We have been departing on missions at dawn because the weather is usually better during morning hours. Today we brought down a bridge near Piacenza. Later, we flew a training mission with several new replacement crews.

September 13 Our string of successful missions continued today when we bombed the marshaling yards at Monza. The formation was over the target at 1215 hrs. and bombs cratered the tracks for 600 feet. Three ships returned with moderate flak damage.

Today's evening meal was an example of the deteriorating quality of our food. The steak was practically indestructible. One soldier acidly commented that, "It was so tough that teeth and fillings lost while attempting to eat it should be replaced at government expense." In addition, many in the meal line complained about the microscopic portions before sampling it.

September 14 Heavy and intense flak greeted us at Rimini, where our frag bombs covered the entire target with a well-placed pattern. One crew member was slightly wounded and eight of the bombers were holed, but all planes returned safely to Alesan field. The cooks have procured a lamb for tonight's meal, so all may be forgiven. The chow line started at 1600 hrs. Mosquitoes are using us for fresh meat as of late despite the slightly cooler weather.

September 15 We were up at 0400 hrs., and ready to start engines when the stand down order came. The groans and cursing from the flight line could be heard some distance. There is some apprehension about our target which is the Bologna marshaling yards. Two mission cancellations have heightened this concern. Our film tonight was "Sing The Blues," a musical comedy that a few people walked out on. It had humorous parts and good music, but we wish they would leave the corn out.

September 16 Again we were ready for wheels up at daybreak, and the mission proceeded to Bologna where we plastered the marshaling yards and gun positions. Several ships were holed, but everyone returned without serious damage. Weeks later an intelligence report for today's mission stated that, "The marshaling yard center and nearly all the vehicles including thirty motor tank trucks were destroyed. There were 130 enemy casualties." We had steak again (better tonight) and some of the fellows took a cool swim on the beach.

September 17 Today's mission to troop concentrations near Rimini was a tough one. I led the combined formation against gun emplacements there. Forty-eight planes participated in the attack, and the bombs hit dead center and immediately west of center. Ship 7N took an A/A burst along the length of the ship, causing an engine fire and fuel leak. They feathered the engine and made an emergency landing at Fano. Two days ago the same crew made a crash landing.

## Distinguished Flying Cross, First Cluster Awarded

Dale J. Satterthwaite, 080-4516, Capt., 486th Bomb Squadron, 340th Bomb Group.

For extraordinary achievement while participating in an aerial flight as pilot of a B-25 type aircraft. On 17 September 1944, Capt. Satterthwaite flew in an attack upon an enemy troop and supply concentration near Rimini, Italy. Upon the approach to the target, intense antiaircraft fire enveloped the formation, damaging seven B-25s. Displaying great courage and superior flying ability in the face of this accurate barrage, Capt. Satterthwaite maintained his plane on perfect course, thereby enabling his bombardier to release his bombs with devastating effect upon this vital military objective. On more than seventy combat missions his outstanding proficiency and steadfast devotion to duty have reflected great credit upon himself and the Armed Forces of the United States. Oaklawn, Ill.

With the exception of 7N, all planes returned on that mission. I had some fresh holes in Sahara Sue II. One of the planes took a hit to the right propeller and the prop governor ran wild. They ran the left engine at full power to keep the airplane thrust balanced and returned to Alesan field. Over the airport they feathered the right engine and made a good single engine landing. Another plane belly landed with two injured crewmen aboard.

The Gothic line was the Germans last line of defense in Italy. Hitler had concerns about the state of preparation of those defenses. To downgrade its importance in the eyes of both friend and foe, he ordered the name, with its historic connotations, changed. He reasoned that if the Allies managed to break through, they would not be able to use the more impressive name to magnify their victory claims. In response to this order, General Albert Kesselring renamed it The Green Line. The Allies named their assault on these fronts Operation Olive, but it's more commonly known as The Battle of Rimini. That city was indeed heavily fortified and a dangerous destination for our bombers. According to Lieut. Gen. Sir Oliver Leese, Commander of the Eighth Army, "The battle of Rimini was one of the hardest battles of the Eighth Army. The fighting was comparable to El Alamein and the Gustav Line (Monte-Cassino)."

September 18 Col. Chapman sent a ship to Sicily today with orders to bring back fresh produce. Twelve planes from 486th participated in a morning attack on the Gothic line with good results (ninety-five percent). The flak was accurate, and damaged Lieut. Cooley's ship to the extent that he considered telling the crew to bail out. Fortunately, the fire in his left engine went out and he was able to return to Alesan field. He told us that his crew remained cool and bravely faced the danger. When I see the new replacement crews with their young faces, I feel old and a little tired.

September 19-21 Clouds formed a solid mass in the Mediterranean. Training missions occupied most of this time. I busy myself in the maintenance tent helping the mechanics and flight testing repaired airplanes. Those duties blessedly shield me from the worst enemy of all - boredom. Many crewmen are not as lucky.

The rumors of our relocation to southern France are apparently not true. There is some disappointment about this as a change of scenery would be welcome, and would shorten our missions. A Twelfth Air Force order requires the 340th Group to return all Italian workers to the mainland. They will be sadly missed, as the dreaded KP Duty will again fall on the enlisted men. No doubt much complaining will result.

September 22 We are back in the air today, and blast a bridge near Piave Susgana into the river. The evening cinema presented "Shine on Harvest Moon" which was a nice two-hour diversion.

September 23 Perhaps to inspire us, we were assigned an ammunition dump for our target today. We struck it with such accuracy that the explosion rocked the ships at 9000 feet which gave us all a great sense of satisfaction. A black band played excellent boogie woogie in the enlisted men's dayroom this evening.

My gasoline burner design placed inside GI stoves has become a fixture in most of the tents. It became a topic of discussion one evening because a tent was nearly destroyed when too much gas was thrown on the burner before it was lit. A fearsome blast forced Hammond and Jennings out of their burning entrance. Harry Strait rushed an extinguisher over from a nearby plane. All were cautioned not to exceed a half cup of gas when lighting the burner.

September 24 Rimini remained a hot target, and we encountered heavy A/A and a German smoke screen which limited our damage assessment. Several crewmen sustained minor flak injuries. To lessen the pain of KP, soldiers assigned the duty are receiving

$15 a month extra. After all these months they find it a little difficult to go back to pot washing, but the extra income equals a twenty percent raise for some of them.

September 25 An early mission again to Rimini was canceled over the target due to a heavy overcast. Two dachshund puppies which were purchased in Rome are up to mischief in every corner of the squadron. It is really a treat to see pure bred dogs after the many mongrels that we have adopted. The breeding papers for the dogs are in Milan, which is still an occupied city.

## Soldiers Medal Awarded

Vallie W. Malone, 384-31911,Tech Sgt., 489th Bomb Squadron, 340th Bomb Group, for heroism. On 25 September 1944, when a solid overcast over the target area prevented Tech Sgt. Malone's formation from carrying out its assigned mission, his leader turned toward home. Approaching his base violent air turbulence severely rocked his aircraft, which loosened the bombs from their shackles. When the bombardier attempted to jettison the bombs, one failed to release and hung up in the bomb bay. Realizing the danger of explosion, Tech Sgt. Malone immediately removed his parachute and lowered himself into the open bomb bay. With a comrade holding him suspended by his foot, he succeeded in effecting the release of the bomb. His selfless devotion to duty in the face of grave hazard reflects the highest credit upon himself and the Armed Forces of the United States. Dallas, TX.

When Florence was liberated, many of us on Corsica wanted to go there, but nobody could get clearance to go unless they had business there. At that point most of the fellows had gone to Naples and Rome for R&R. Twelfth Air Force established their headquarters in Florence. I had been expecting my promotion orders for captain for some weeks, but they had not come. Finally, the X/O said "Why don't you go over there and get those orders yourself?"

I made arrangements to fly over there, and I let it be known that I need a copilot for the flight. One of the squadron pilots volunteered and we flipped a coin to see who would fly over. He won the toss, and I told him that I would fly back. We went to the operations office and got information about the field at Florence. They told us that the field was near the town and the runway was 4500 feet long.

As our plane neared Florence I requested landing instructions, but there was no answer. Finally, an airfield about fifteen miles away called us and said that the radio at Florence field wasn't working. We made a downwind leg and turned to final. Just as we made our turn, an airplane started taking off from the opposite direction. I reached down and retracted the landing gear so that we could go around. The guy who was flying continued on the approach. I asked him, "Are you still going to go in and land?" He said, "Yeah, I can make it."

We narrowly passed above the airplane that took off. Meanwhile, I lowered the landing gear at the same time the flaps were coming down. The gear indicator indicated that it was down and locked just as the plane started to flare. We came over the end of the runway threshold at about 170 mph. Normal speed was in the range of 130 mph. I thought he still had time to abort the landing, but we continued to settle. Touchdown occurred at about midpoint down the runway. He jumped on the brakes and the plane began to slide. Leaving the runway, we blew out a tire and slewed into a muddy field about 400 feet. The wild and bumpy slide fortunately left us right side up. Crewmen took a tractor with a large rope to the plane and tried to tow it, but the blown tire made it impossible.

Operations told us they would have a wheel and tire flown over from Corsica. While talking to them we found out that the runway was actually only 3800 feet! After cleaning the mud off our boots, we went to Twelfth Air Force headquarters and I got my promotion orders. We were supposed to return to Corsica the next day, but remained there for five days. The Florence Art Museum was open and Michelangelo's statue of David was on display. Most of the other art was sequestered in hiding places.

Florence was the closest city to the front lines, so any airplane in the area that had an emergency came there to land. Consequently, there was always some kind of excitement going on at this field. The next morning a P-47 trailing smoke attempted to land and wound up off the end of the runway near our plane. Later, a British Beaufighter started to take off and was nearly airborne when it veered off the runway, striking a large tent which knocked it down. The plane then bounced off the top of an ambulance and wound up stuck nose down in the mud with an engine on fire. We were about a half mile away and started running toward the burning plane.

Firefighters stationed at the field were using a weapons carrier with a large CO2 bottle on it as a fire engine. That unit arrived, and the men sprayed retardant on the burning engine after pulling the pilot to safety. They had nearly extinguished the fire when the crew got a call from the tower asking if they needed back up equipment. They told the tower they thought they had the blaze under control. Just then, the CO2 bottle ran out and the fire quickly started to grow. Ammunition from the plane's four 20 mm cannon started to cook off, making the scene look like a fireworks display. Everyone quickly backed away and the Beaufighter was completely destroyed by fire.

On another day we watched as a Spitfire taxied out for takeoff. The fighter was waiting on a nearby taxiway as a C-47 landed. There were steep hills on one end of the runway. For that reason, takeoffs usually departed in the opposite direction of landings. That is why we encountered an oncoming airplane on our approach. When the C-47 landed, its wing hit the Spitfire, spinning it around. The guns on the Spitfire went off, raking the C-47 from one end to the other. Fortunately, no one was on the C- 47 except the pilots who escaped injury.

September 26-29 No bombing activity on account of weather. If this weather is any indication of what is in store for us during the winter months, we shall all be spending our time putting up tents as the wind blows them down. Some felt it was the worst three days of weather since our arrival on Corsica. Thanks to the Colonel, we again have fresh vegetables. One of the fellows shot a small bear near the high country area where my friends and I camped. Those who sampled some of the meat found it very greasy. Some enterprising fellows smoked it for jerky, which was pretty tasty.

September 30 Voting for the US election is in process, and is a nice reminder that we still have lives in another part of the world. It does seem odd to be registering our political opinions from Corsica. It is a certainty that the soldiers who fight for Germany have no choice in their leaders.

This afternoon the weather lifted long enough to relieve our stand down siege. A frag mission to the hills north of Rimini had good results with moderate flak. Orchestra practice occupied part of the day, and the band is beginning to sound pretty good. It shouldn't be long before they put on a show.

October 1 Shaggy and unkempt is a description befitting most of the Group. When the Italians departed, we lost our barbers along with the kitchen staff. A corporal has been assigned the job of barber, but one man certainly won't be enough for the job.

The first of the month brought clearing weather and two missions were flown today. In the morning forty-six planes bombed the Piacensa, Italy encampment and most of the buildings were damaged or destroyed. A second raid of eighteen ships made afternoon visit to the Magenta Railroad Bridge. Damage assessments were difficult due to intense flak, but returning crew told us that hits were scored on the east approach. Lieut. Donovan was seriously wounded and his ship was forced to make an emergency landing near Pisa. One of the other ships stopped there and picked up the rest of the crew.

October 2 Strong winds and threatening skies make combat flying impossible. A new Twelfth Air Force rule declares that all crew members who are up for awards must remain with their overseas units until the medals are awarded! Part of the problem is that Twelfth Air Force headquarters is in the midst of moving which puts a real snafu on all paperwork. The implications are that stateside rotation will be put off for troops that have completed their tours. Many are asking that they be put in for no more awards because going home is much more important.

October 3 Every ship in our formation was hit today as we returned to the Magenta Bridge, and there were some close brushes with death. Miraculously, Lieut. Henry Smith was the only man wounded by flak. One other gunner did experience something close to a miracle. A large piece of flak went completely through his flack suit, and halfway through a Bible which he carried in his left shirt pocket. I am sure that he and others are considering the significance of his good fortune. This target has been stubborn and still stands, although we had hits on both ends of the bridge. Successive hamburger and meatloaf dinners for six days have us all hoping for some variation for our evening meals.

October 4 In spite of the miserable weather, hardly a man missed the fresh eggs for breakfast. The quartermaster amazed the entire Group by issuing 2700 fresh eggs. To top it off we had steak for dinner.

The second accident in less than a weeks' time destroyed a jeep driven by Lieuts. Graber and Love. Both have broken legs with possible internal injuries. They were observing the standard speed limit for most Corsica drivers which is twenty miles an hour too fast.

The Magenta Bridge has become a dreaded destination with 88 mm cannon fire coming from several hills. Today seven planes were holed while on the bomb run, and ship 8F was ditched about a mile north of the tip of Corsica. Lieut. King, the pilot was drowned and Sgt. Berger, the tail gunner, never came up. He must have gone down with the plane. The rest of the crew is in the hospital suffering from exposure.

October 5 Lieuts. Rushton and Sperling are getting a little practice in as airline pilots. They have been tapped to fly a Service Command General around the country for a while. It will be a break, and they will see a lot of Europe throughout their tour with the general. Stand down orders surprised us today. Italy must not have shared our clear skies. Downtime was used to lay a concrete floor in the armament shop yesterday, and paw prints were found on it this morning. One of our "pets" passed through the area at high speed.

October 6 We struck a power station in downtown Trento, Italy. Targeting was one hundred percent. This was important because there are three hospitals located in the area. Not one of them was hit.

To date the 340th Group has flown 578 missions; 11,400 sorties of which 9,923 are classified as effective sorties. Our planes have dropped 16,252 tons of bombs. Seventy-five airplanes have been lost to enemy flak. Four hundred and fifty airmen were aboard these lost ships. (Per Group notes) The figures do tell a tale, but it does not really show our man hours and our blood, sweat and tears.

I made several more flights into Cavatina airfield near Rome, and also made several more flights to Florence. The steep hill at the end of the runway had apartments terraced into it. On takeoff, we would be zooming 100 feet above those apartments. They must have been a tough place to live. Combat action remained close to the field. We stayed at a nice hotel where the food was good and a strolling violinist worked the evening crowd. We did the usual tourist things including the Ponte Vecchio Bridge with its shops.

*October 8, 1944*

*Sweetheart,*

*This note is from Florence. I wrote a long one, but didn't quite finish it when I was still on Corsica. My return has been delayed, and I am rather enjoying the scenery and shops of the old city. I don't expect to be on this side of the pond much longer. I am ready now to return at the first opportunity. Meanwhile, I send all my love.*

*Someday perhaps we can return here and stay at the Grand Hotel overlooking the Arno River. It is famous for an old bridge which has houses on it. We might walk by the old palace, which is where I am writing this letter. We have many good things and many great days ahead of us.*

*I love you, Dale*

**October 7-10** Everyone in Corsica is bored and frustrated with a succession of stand down days. Fall weather in Corsica is not for the birds. During the summer most of the fellows made a beeline for the beach when a stand down was declared. Without those activities, time hangs heavy and many members spend the greater part of the day in their sacks. Even the flights to Rome for R&R have been grounded. A wire from the Rome airport stated that due to weather, our stranded personnel on leave in the city have depleted their funds. Some of them are desperate to return to Corsica. Many of us would rather be broke in Rome than deal with the inactivity on Corsica. The war rages on somewhere while we twiddle our thumbs. We have not received any mail this month which is adding to the general discontent.

October 11 Major Hackney bowed to pressure from squadron pilots and assigned a mission today, even though the clouds remain dominant in the skies. The other squadrons looked on somewhat jealously as we departed Alesan field. Our target was a bridge near Chivasso in the Italian Alps. Determined not to bring our bombs back, we circled twice before dropping our bombs through a small break in the cumulus. Some hits were observed on the approach to the bridge which remained standing.

October 12 All Group squadrons were in the air today to bomb supply depots on the outskirts of Bologna. Although clouds covered the target area, the forty-eight ship formation scored many direct hits. Two of the participating aircraft were holed.

We returned to Alesan field in the middle of the afternoon to find a typical fall day. Across the road, farmers were gathering their harvest grain. In the distance, the sea is placid in its azure hue. The air has just a touch of chilliness to it, and the sun is reluctant to make an appearance. Outside the headquarters tent some boys are playing touch football after a strenuous morning of flying. Two planes finally got over to Rome today and picked up our weary vacationers.

October 13 Friday the 13th dawned soggy, but our spirits were buoyed when a huge shipment of packages and newspapers arrived from the states. Letter mail was still missing and everyone wonders where it is. The poor corporal assigned to sort the mail was harassed endlessly by those who were eager to get their hands on the waylaid parcels. The intermittent mail has many of us thinking that there may not be another delivery until Christmas. Mail from the folks at home is still the Army's number one morale booster.

October 14 There are many new inhabitants in the squadron, and they are of the rodent variety. Mice have made an invasion. There are hundreds of them, and our maintenance shop has gone into mouse trap production. Trap designs vary, but most of them are constructed from arming wire and C ration boxes. One man has a classy job made of Plexiglas. In the evening clearing skies allowed an evening movie. "Uninvited" with Ray Miland and Gale Russell was enjoyed by all.

October 15 Morning fog and some light rain did not prevent a raid to a railroad bridge at Largenta, Italy. Cloud cover prevented us from bombing the primary target, so the squadron attacked the marshaling yards at Ronco Scrivia. Visibility was limited, and some of the ships opted not to drop bombs. Thirty 1000 pound bombs were dropped which destroyed the southern end of the yard. All planes returned safely. Those who rely on a steady supply of tobacco have a problem because our supplies have dried up. A number of fellows wrote home asking for cigarettes as a Christmas present.

October 16-18 We wonder if the nearly constant rain has set new weather records. Football is still a big sport. Maj. Cassada was the referee for the Gunners and Headquarters teams, and two of the gunners got a bit heated. The Major stopped one scrap on the field. After the game was finished, the two went off into the woods and had it out. One of them ended up with four stitches taken over his right eye. On the whole though, good sportsmanship has been displayed on the football field. Most of the fellows have enjoyed the season.

October 19 Strong cross winds challenged our crews on take-off, but all succeeded in getting into the air. Magenta Railroad Bridge was again the target, and the enemy was ready and waiting for us. Heavy A/A barrages did cause significant damage. The 486th had ten ships holed, but no injuries. The 487th wasn't so fortunate. Five ships were holed, three men wounded and Lieut. Meek, copilot on 7Z was killed. Lieut. Bloomberg was wounded for the second time on this mission and is ready to quit flying. Intense flak, as well as smoke from the other bomb patterns made the success of the raid difficult to determine.

Two trucks and one plane went over to the other side of Corsica to procure wood for our mess hall. The plan was to tear down a building that was out of use. They were met by a detachment of French soldiers who told them the building could not be torn down. Thus, they returned empty-handed.

October 20 Today's mission was certainly no milk run. Forty-eight planes attacked the supply depot at Imola, Italy. Intense antiaircraft fire holed nine of the ships. Minutes later, four FW-190s approached the rear of the first formation, but turned off when fired upon. Returning crews said the bombs hit the target. Some of the fellows who volunteered for combat crew status in order to expedite their return to the states have had their eyes opened on the last two missions. Staff Sgt. Paul McMillan, a former Mess Sergeant, flew his first mission yesterday and was in one of the flak damaged planes. A number of crewmen donated their Old Overholt whiskey to Paul after the raid. He received some well-deserved jibes that mess food was more dangerous than incoming shells.

October 21-22 Blustery and wet fall days with no missions.

October 23 Reasonable weather returned today, and we carried paper rather than bombs to the enemy. Twelve ships were loaded with "nickels" for Bologna, Ferrara, Ravenna, Forli and Imola. Antiaircraft fire holed five ships and wounded Lieuts. Cuthbertson and Lyle. Despite this, the "nickels" were successfully dropped in their respective areas.

The 340th Group orchestra made its debut last night at the Red Cross Enlisted Men's Club. It was pretty good performance, considering that it was the first time many of them have played together. At each new rehearsal new members were added. Col.

Chapman was present at the debut and showed his approval by requesting that they play at the Officers Club on Monday night.

October 24-27Several inches of water cover the floors on most tents from steady and relentless downpours on the 25th. Many of the guys spent the entire evening of the 26th battling the water and some of the tents were completely washed away. The Red Cross Club was submerged under three feet of water. Fortunately, the skies cleared on the 27th and the unfortunates who were washed out hurriedly transferred their tents to higher ground. Progress in Italy remains rather stagnant and the allies are still eight miles from the key city of Bologna.

October 28-29On the 28th a clear sky broke for the first time in five days. Alesan field was so water logged that planes could not take off with a bomb load so another stand down was declared. The field remained an unusable mess on the 29th, and the engineers are frantically working to install steel mats. Many roads in our area were washed out and need to be re-graded. S/Sgt. Lippert of our photo section received a direct commendation from General Knapp for perfecting the installation of a twelve inch camera in the nose of a B-25. The purpose of the camera is to take pictures from the IP to the target. The pictures will be used to determine if we have to go over that target again.

*October 29, 1944*

*Light of My Life,*

*The latest letter from my mother's tells me that we have a house! She found this modest bungalow in the course of her real estate activities. In case you don't already know, let me read you her description of the place: Roses surround the outside with several large oaks in the yard.*

*The kitchen has large white cupboards and small cute windows. It has a large living room, small screened porch and a bath. I don't know if we will ever live in it or not, but it sounds to me like it will be a good investment. Anyway, it will be paid for in a year. Tell me what you think.*

*I am eager to get home and see this house, but mostly it's you I want to see. Boy, my remaining time here still feels like a year even if it's hopefully just a few weeks. I think you understand my point. Weather is bad. I am a transport pilot whenever I feel like it, which is whenever there's a trip to a place I haven't seen.*

*I have a gift that I'm going to bring home with me. It isn't a ring. I thought I had sent it to you in my last letter, but I found it while rummaging in a footlocker. I know you don't like secrets, but I feel ornery tonight. I wish I were there.*

*I am being held up here for a cluster on my DFC Medal, and several clusters on my Air Medal. I wish they'd take those medals and ______!*

*Love, Dale*

**October 30 Stand down was again the order of the day,** although local training flights put many planes and men in the air. We had a heavy shower this afternoon, but it didn't last long. The remainder of the day was cold but rather pleasant. Mail came in this week. Dates on the letters vary from three months old to recent and everyone is pretty well caught up on back mail.

October 31 Training and practice missions were flown with no bombs delivered.

November 1-3 Corsican weather has steadily improved, but we are still grounded by bad weather hanging over most of Italy. There is reportedly a foot and a half of water on the Rome runway. A weather reconnaissance flight over Italy came back to report that the weather was "worse than flak," so it really must be really bad.

We envy the lucky six who just returned from Cairo and Alexandria. Everyone on the trip claimed to have had the time of their lives. Both ground and combat personnel are getting restless and tired of nothing to do. I busied myself with what maintenance and engineering duties that I could find. There are new crews arriving, and I took several new pilots on training rides. Many of us are hopefully nearing the end of our deployments and it is important to get the new pilots prepared.

November 4 Bombs were at last loaded in our B-25s, and the target was the marshaling yards at Asti, Italy. We plastered the center of the target and many buildings were left burning. Antiaircraft fire was heavy, and ship 9E was hit by flak a few minutes off the target. It crashed into the city of Alessandria. Parachutes were seen before our crews saw the ship hit a building.

November 5 Crewmen doubled checked our fuel tanks to make sure they were full for today's mission. Padua East Railroad Bridge was the target, and the round-trip distance exceeded any prior mission we have flown. A plane piloted by Lieut. Brandle inexplicably veered into a cloud bank while we were enroute and was not seen again. Both formations put bombs directly on the target, but smoke and dust made it impossible to see if the bridge was down. "Beautiful But Broke" with Joan Davis played at the movies tonight.

November 6  We flew two raids today. In the morning over two hundred 100 pound phosphorus bombs were dropped on the gun positions at Trento, Italy. Ack-ack was heavy, intense and accurate, damaging three ships. We observed six ME-109s several miles away from the formation. One of the enemy planes climbed higher and then dove toward us. Our gunners fired on it when it came in range. The fighter pulled out of the dive under the formation, rolled upside down, and went down with smoke trailing from its fuselage. Both S/Sgt. Woods and Sgt. Whipple claimed the kill, but the actual gunner will probably never be determined.

Ten minutes later the remaining enemy fighters approached our planes from the six o'clock position, but broke off when all of our available guns fired on them. In spite of the opposition, it did not prevent a successful raid. Photographs proved that the gun positions were well covered by our bombing pattern. The second raid was not quite so successful in their attack upon the Borgo eastern railroad bridge. Their pattern hit approximately 100 yards east of the approach to the bridge. All ships returned safely.

Gen. Cannon was at the 340th Group yesterday for the celebration of our 600th mission. He commended the terrific bombing being done by the 340th (his words). "Pistol Packing Mama" was shown at the Group movie tonight. The unanimous opinion was that it was the worst picture we have seen.

November 7  Twenty-four ships took off this morning to bomb Latisana Railroad Bridge in northern Italy. Flak was nil, and the formation placed an excellent pattern scoring direct hits. When we returned to Alesan field, we were debriefed by a new officer,

Lieut. Bahm. He is better known as "Frag," a nickname he got when bombs blew up on his P-47 as he bellied in.

The seventy mission requirement continues to be a topic of discussion in the squadron. Ground crew who switched to combat status in order to lessen their deployments are understandably disappointed. While Col. Chapman received the brunt of criticism for that decision, I know that it came from much higher up.

November 8 President Roosevelt's reelection naturally sparked a discussion amongst his supporters and detractors. Whatever political differences we have, our hope is that he brings us through this war as quickly as possible with a lasting peace. No flak or airborne opposition impeded our mission to the Pinzano Railroad Bridge in northern Italy. Bombs cut the railroad track and cratered the approach to the bridge. An evening dance at the Officers Club was well attended.

November 9 For the first time in a year our planes were over Yugoslavia on a raid to the Zidanimost Railroad Bridge. There was no enemy opposition, and both formations covered the south central portion of the bridge with four or five direct hits observed. Everyone returned safely from this nearly five-hour mission.

Basketball games are again being played in the better weather. Our court is very good despite the crude materials used to construct it. "Bride By Mistake" starring Lorraine Day was the entertaining picture shown at the movie tonight.

November 10 Cittadella Bypass was the target for a midday mission. Our pattern cut the eastern end of the bypass and made direct hits on the target. No A/A was encountered over the target although a slight barrage was met enroute.

A gale with a seventy mile an hour velocity swept through last night leaving the mess hall tossed and torn. The mess tents were in the midst of a changeover to make more headspace. Three of them were blown down, and the Enlisted Men's Club also collapsed. Four other tents also took to the air. Fellows not occupied on the line spent the day working on details to put things back in shape. Lieut. Brandle's ship is now considered lost.

November 11 Careless driving again claimed some victims as we prepared for a morning mission. The carry-all driven by Lieut. Carlson was smashed by a two and a half ton truck. He was seriously injured, and will remain in the hospital for many weeks. His passenger, Lieut. Clark, suffered a fractured nose. The big truck ran them off the road and then crashed into them.

Thirty-six bombers departed today to attack Pontetivone Railroad Bridge. The target was completely plastered, with hits on the center portion which felled the bridge. I flew as copilot on this mission, and was happy to be along for a young lieutenant's debut as first pilot. All planes returned safely.

November 12-15 Italy was socked in from Naples to the Alps, and even the regular R&R flights did not depart. The former baseball teams are now playing football. "Louisiana Hay Ride" was shown at the Group movie on the 15th. It's getting a little chilly for open air movies, but as long as the movies are shown we will be there.

November 16 Direct hits were observed on the Faenza Road Bridge, which was our target today. The afternoon mission with twenty-four planes was judged very successful. Inaccurate antiaircraft fire caused no damage and all planes returned safely. Earlier in the day a nickelling mission was flown over northern Italy with no problems. Twenty men awaited departure from

Alesan field today to Rome for R&R, but the airport there remains closed. Weather has again extended the stay of our crews who are on leave in the eternal city.

November 17 Mission plans again take second fiddle to high winds which whip the leaves into a fury.

*November 17, 1944*

*Dearest One,*

*Tonight I am blue. It is because you are just a little further away than I had thought. I'm afraid that it is unlikely that I will be home for Christmas. I looked forward to it so very much. I am desolate. "Red tape" is preventing my departure. I must wait until all pending awards have been presented to me before stateside orders can be cut. Just the other day we learned that a careless clerk waylaid the award paperwork which will result in a four week delay.*

*Today I received my eighth Air Medal cluster from General Knapp, but I must wait for the pending DFC. It balls up all my plans of course. I have Christmas gifts that I had intended to bring home with me, but now should be mailed. It takes over six weeks for packages to go home from here, so they would arrive too late if I sent them today. I'll bring them home anyway and if I'm very late, I'll write and tell people what I have for them.*

*I'm writing this by candlelight. Our generator goes out for overhaul every now and then. Icy winds and cloudy skies have chased us indoors. Every morning we can see that the snow line on the mountains has descended a little more. Soon it will be down here on the flatlands.*

*Some of us are planning a trip up in the mountains again. Chaplain "Chappy" Cooper, my old buddy Dickman and "Harry the Horse" are the hardy souls who will brave the cold conditions with me. Of course, we will take winter flying clothes and everything we will need to keep warm. Harry is bringing his four legged friend along. We intend to take another crack at the trout and wild boar.*

*I flew another mission recently, making a total of seventy-three. This week and next I am Engineering Officer, taking Capt. Stoler's place while he is in Cairo. It keeps me busy and requires my presence all day and some of the evening.*

*The pen that you gave me sure writes nicely. I guess it hasn't had enough use to wear it out these three years. Our mail service is very intermittent and your letters come in bunches. It increases my anticipation.*

*Probably you will receive this about Thanksgiving Day. I understand that we will have turkey and stuffing. I'd sure rather eat C rations on a boat headed home.*

*Some of us filled out a questionnaire recently concerning postwar plans. Do you think you would like to be an army wife? You would likely be jerked around from one corner of the earth to another. I told them I might be interested in a peace time commission. It depends on what they would have to offer.*

*Say hello to any and all that you might see during the holidays, and very special respects to your family.*

*I love you, Dale*

Capt. Nathan, our squadron surgeon had heard many sad stories and sorted through many subterfuges concocted by airmen eager to end their deployments. He acted as unofficial psychologist for the squadron and sometimes wrote letters in support of legitimate claims. I mentioned before that he handled a number of nonmedical duties for the squadron. He authored all of the mission write-ups that supported medal awards for squadron personnel. I credit him for accurately describing the situations that air crew faced.

My stoic exterior was starting to exhibit some cracks. In some ways the demands of combat missions distracted me from the loneliness that all soldiers on Corsica felt. In the closing days of 1944 there were plenty of pilots who wanted to accumulate more missions. Those of us who had managed to complete the magic seventy missions flew less frequently. This reduced our sense of mission and increased our frustration. The nonsensical insistence that we remain overseas to receive medals only magnified the situation.

Without a goal of asking for any special consideration, I talked to Capt. Nathan. It was not until many months later that I saw the following three letters in my personnel file.

November 24, 1944

486th Bombardment Squadron

340th Bombardment Group
Subject: Rotation of Combat Crew Personnel.
To: Commanding Officer, 486th Squadron, 340th Bomb Group
1. In accordance with memorandum,
Headquarters AAF/RTO,
Subject: Relief of combat crew personnel

I hereby certify that Capt. Satterthwaite, Dale J. has completed seventy-three combat missions totaling 198 hours and 40 minutes as Pilot, and has been on foreign duty since 15 December 1943.

2. Capt. Satterthwaite has flown regularly since his entry into combat many months ago, and is now in a state of chronic operational fatigue. He has given the absolute maximum effort, always willingly with the attitude that he must go as long as was possible. The greatest majority of his missions have been as flight leader, in which he took his regular turn and even more when other flight leaders were not available. It is the opinion of the Squadron Commander, the Squadron Operations Officer and myself that Capt. Satterthwaite has reached the limit of efficiency.

3. I recommend that Capt. Satterthwaite he returned to the States for rehabilitation and reassignment.

Charles R. Nathan
Capt., Med Corps
Squadron Surgeon

201-Satterthwaite, Dale J. (Off)

November 26, 1944

486th Bomb Squadron, 340th Bombardment Group
To: Commanding Officer, 340th Bombardment Group
Subject: Capt. Satterthwaite, Dale J.

1. The statements of the Squadron Surgeon concerning Capt. Satterthwaite, Dale J., 080-

4516, presents a true and accurate analysis of Capt. Satterthwaite's condition.

2. I concur with the recommendation of the Squadron Surgeon in that Capt. Satterthwaite be returned to the United States for rehabilitation and reassignment. Capt. Satterthwaite has been awarded the Distinguished Flying Cross, the Air Medal and eight Oak Leaf Clusters thereto. He has been recommended for the first cluster to the Distinguished Flying Cross.

Robert M. Hackney
Major, Air Corps, Commanding

November 27, 1944

To: Commanding General, 57th Bombardment Wing:
Subject: Capt. Satterthwaite, Dale J.

1. Approved.

2. It is believed that the return of this man to the Zone of the Interior for rehabilitation and reassignment would be in the best interest of the service.

3. Final action has been taken on all recommendations for awards.

W. F. Chapman,
Colonel, Air Corps Commanding

**I credit the unusually high regard and respect for Capt.** Nathan which gendered prompt action on his recommendations. Later generations would probably diagnose my condition as PTSD. My stoic side continued to internalize rather than share much of what I felt. Writing letters to Eleanor were as close to honesty as I would come.

I remained in Corsica until December 11, but did not fly missions other than training. In March the elusive First Cluster for DFC award was finally presented to me. You can judge for yourself how that interminable delay in Corsica would have affected me. The weather continued to be sour. Here are some notes about the last weeks of my tour.

November 21 The steady beat of rain on our tents and buildings has been unremitting. Some roads were nearly impassable, and torrents which rush down the mist enshrouded mountains have completely overrun the roads. The airfield is closed and activity in general is at a low ebb. We are equipped to face the elements better than we were last year at this time. Our offices and living quarters are better housed, and we have more clothing to withstand the cold and dampness.

November 22 For a change there is no rain, but it has been bitterly cold with a high wind. The planes that launched today were tossed about the sky like a boy's kite. We ran a mission to a rail bridge north of Trento, Italy. For three hours those crews flew in subzero weather, but to no avail. The primary target could not be located because of ground haze. The alternate target was not bombed for the same reason.

November 23 The first snowflakes of the season came in on a cold and cruel wind which swept down from the north. The mountain barrier to the west is a solid white in its winter garb, and the skies are overcast. Just a few days ago we were issued sleeping bags. These are standing us in good stead now. We crawl into one, zip up the side, pull on the hood and are virtually locked out of the cold.

November 24-30 No changes to the situation.

December 1 Eighteen airplanes departed to Villavernia to bomb a bridge just outside of town. The bomb pattern, instead of covering the bridge, fell directly across the town. The inhabitants paid dearly in destruction of property and loss of life as a result of the town's fateful proximity to the bridge.

December 2 Before our airplanes finally got into the air, there was much uncertainty as to what the target would be. Originally the crews were to bomb a bridge in the Po River Valley. They were called back to operations and directed to hit a target in Yugoslavia. Then at the last minute, a mission to the Canneto Railroad Bridge in northern Italy was ordered. Twelve cold crews headed out to that target. Clouds limited an accurate damage assessment.

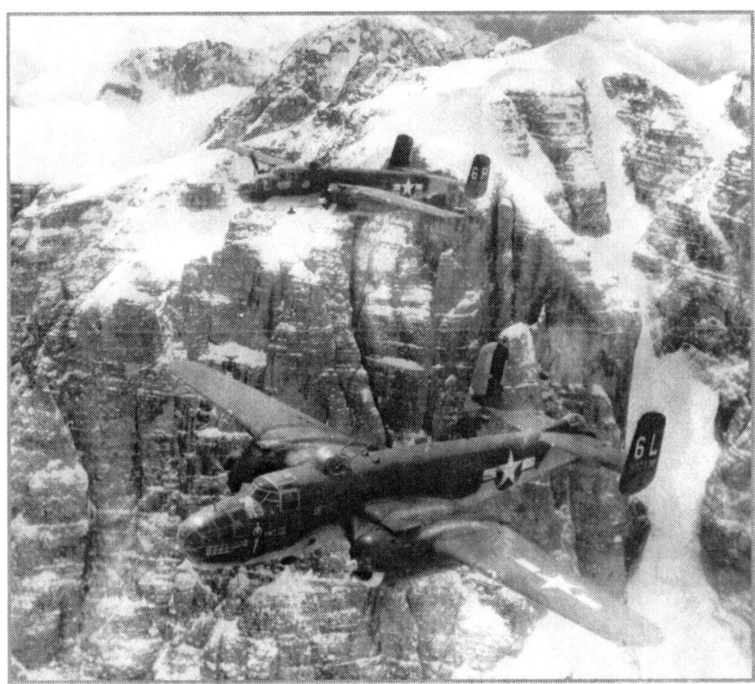


(Courtesy Daniel Setzer)

*December 2, 1944*

*Sweetheart,*

*I received a most welcome letter from you after more than a month with no mail. You somehow manage always to say what I want to hear. The new direction our lives will take upon my return has of course have been filling my thoughts of late. I know I would like more than anything else for us to be married as soon as possible. However, I am not going to make any definite plans until we are able to discuss the situation. Anyway, things look pretty good right now and I might even make it home by the first of the year. My heart and the rest of me yearns for you more than I can say.*

*The house that I spoke of is near one that my folks recently bought. I dream of us spending my leave there. The thought of it makes me so restless that I can hardly finish this letter. The lights are going out in just a minute, so I must say good night.*

*I love you, Dale*

**December 3-9 Scattered training flights and little else.** There were lots of celebrations going on for those of us who had received orders to go home. On the 5th our football season ended with the "C Ration Bowl" with the Gunners playing the Headquarters men. The game ended in a 12 to 12 tie making the Gunners All Squadron champions with six wins, one defeat and one tie.

Forty bags of Christmas mail arrived to much jubilation. Major Cassada did a little early morning duck hunting and bagged three. On the 9th an enemy reconnaissance flight flew over with vapor trails passing directly over us. One of the intelligence officers identified it with binoculars as a jet powered airplane. Quite a few fellows brushed the cobwebs from their slit trenches this afternoon in response to the overflight.

December 10 My last full day in the squadron. It was Sunday and the mission to northern Italy was rough. About six planes were holed, and one ship made a single engine landing at Pisa. One of the gunners was seriously injured.

I would like to include several other DFC awards that found their way into my file for missions flown after I departed.

## Distinguished Flying Cross Awarded

Fred L. Cormack, 076-5469, First Lieut., 487th Bomb Squadron, 340th Bomb Group, for extraordinary achievement while participating in an aerial flight as bombardier of a B-25 type aircraft area on 4 February 1945, Lieut. Cormack flew as flight bombardier in a formation attacking a railroad bridge at Lavis, Italy. Fragments from a near shell burst shattered the Plexiglas nose of his airplane and hurled him from the bombardier position. Displaying great courage and utmost determination, Lieut. Cormack quickly returned to his bomb sight and guided his pilot on a perfect run over the objective. With all bombers releasing on his sightings, many direct hits in the target area heavily damaged the bridge, thereby blocking a vital link in enemy communications lines. His outstanding proficiency in combat and steadfast devotion to duty have reflected great credit upon himself and the Armed Forces of the United States. Columbia, SC.

Edward W. Oviatt, 044-4530, First Lieut., 487th Bomb Squadron, 340th Bomb Group for extraordinary achievement while participating in an aerial flight as pilot of a B-25 type aircraft on 4 February 1945, Lieut. Oviatt flew as flight leader in a formation attacking a railroad bridge at Lavis, Italy. Upon the approach to the target intense antiaircraft fire enveloped the formation, wounding several crewmembers and damaging a number of B-25s. Displaying great courage and superior leadership in the face of this accurate barrage, Lieut. Oviatt maintained his plane in lead position for a precision run over the objective. With all of the bombers in his flight releasing simultaneously on the target, direct hits in the target area heavily damaged the bridge, thereby blocking a vital link in enemy communication lines. On sixty combat missions, his outstanding proficiency and steadfast devotion to duty have reflected great credit upon himself and the Armed Forces of the United States. East Haven, CT.

Ivan Olson, 067-3932, First Lieut., 486th Bomb Squadron, 340th Bomb Group for extraordinary achievement while participating in an aerial flight as bombardier of a B-25 type aircraft on 8 February 1945, Lieut. Olson flew as lead bombardier of a large formation attacking an enemy troop concentration near Cisterna Italy. Displaying great courage and superior professional skill, Lieut. Olson guided his pilot on a perfect run over the objective in the face of intense and accurate antiaircraft fire. A devastating bomb pattern covered the target area, inflicting many casualties upon personnel and destroying or damaging vital military supplies and equipment. On more than fifty-five combat missions, his outstanding proficiency and steadfast devotion to duty have reflected great credit upon himself and the Armed Forces of the United States. Bethany, OK.

There was a mid-air collision between two B-25s from the 340th over Italy in mid-January. The accident caused one of the planes to crash with all crew lost. The other plane managed to return to base somehow. The tail gunner was killed.

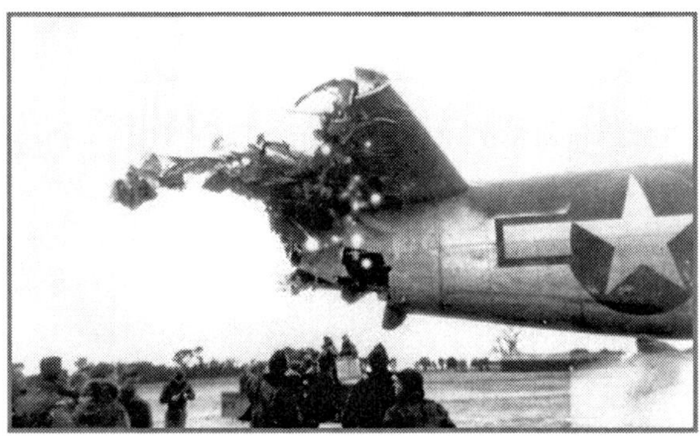

(Courtesy Bing Images)

**Air action over Italy intensified in early 1945. The 340th** attacked dangerous mountain fortifications in preparation for the final assault against Bologna. Of course losses took an expected jump during that period.

On December 11, six of us flew over to Naples and we billeted with forty men who were also heading home. I was in Naples for thirteen days and toured around the area, snapping pictures with my camera. Naples had a newfound energy, and it was fully recovered from the pounding it received when Mount Vesuvius erupted.

After buying a few more Christmas presents, I boarded the USS General M. C. Meigs on Christmas Eve in Naples harbor. We set sail for Bizerte, Tunisia and also made a stop at Oran, Algeria, picking up returning GIs in both places. I wandered through the streets of Bizerte, viewing the many destroyed buildings. The shattered downtown area was a silent reminder of the intense fighting that earlier 340th Group airmen had been party to. We had time to enjoy some wonderful Algerian food in Oran. One of the biggest European populations in Africa resided there and we received a warm welcome with many smiles.

On board with us were 450 German prisoners of war. This new American ship was built for the purpose of transporting troops and had a capacity of 5000. During our voyage there were only 3000 on board. The layout on board was like an ocean liner. At the conclusion of the war, several of these vessels were refurbished for civilian use.

Three double bunks were in the state room that I was assigned. Two of the officers on board were returning fighter pilots and they were Tuskegee airmen. I enjoyed conversing with these educated and experienced gentlemen. They were wearing many decorations and had some interesting experiences to share.

Also on board was a fighter pilot named Jack Griffin who told me that he had flown forty missions in B-26 bombers before transferring into F-4s, the photo reconnaissance variant of the P-38 fighter. He told me that he was flying over the Austrian border and was jumped by an ME-262 jet fighter. His plane was heavily damaged but still flyable, and he sought refuge in a cloud. When he emerged from the cloud several minutes later, the jet was out of sight and he limped back to his airbase. The damage to his plane was extensive from the 30 mm cannon hits and he was commended for getting that plane back. Jack told me that not bailing out was an act of self-preservation. He said the P-38 had to be turned into an inverted position when the pilot bailed out or he could hit the tail. His commanding officer told him that he was done flying missions.

Passing out of the Mediterranean, we were impressed with the enormous heft of Gibraltar. Considering it was January, we enjoyed reasonably pleasant seas and weather. On the nice days we gathered on the deck where a record player spun jazz tunes. About midway in our transatlantic trip, the weather worsened and the seas often crested the bow.

We docked in New York on January 11 and I gladly exchanged my sea legs for the wonders of Manhattan. In the evening a train took us up the Hudson River thirty miles to Camp Shanks. This enormous base was the main jumping off place for soldiers who went over for the D-Day invasion. After several days I was issued my happy stateside orders. They allowed me three weeks travel time to my new duty assignment in Santa Ana, California. In addition to that time, I was also granted leave for thirty days. I could not quantify my joy at this news. An overnight train brought me to Detroit.

A slightly dry Christmas tree greeted me in the front room at Eleanor's house. They were determined to not open packages until I arrived. The amazing warmth of those moments contrasted sharply with the sadness that I felt learning that Gayle Newman, the husband of Eleanor's sister was missing in action. He was a B-29 flight leader flying missions to targets in Japan.

Eleanor's parents had separated at an early age, and it was not until my return that I spent much time with her father. A first generation Irishman who survived the San Francisco earthquake, John Hailey had a remarkable countenance. Possessing a bulldog neck above a nearly destroyed face, his nose was broken in several places and sat squashed between fierce brown eyes. Fat cauliflower ears sat on either side of his enormous head.

John had been a prize fighter in bare fisted matches. During World War I he served as a medic and was inspired to become a doctor. John had no money for such grand plans and so he turned his fisticuff skills toward earning enough for medical school. All of his earnings were sent to his sister for safekeeping. When at last he had saved enough to enter school, John asked his sister for the money. She confessed to him that the money had gone elsewhere. He never spoke to her again.

John became the coroner for the city of Detroit. From that vantage point he knew some fairly notorious gangsters who at that time ran much of the city. His stories about gang activities gave me new insight into the history of Detroit. Chicago had much in common with Detroit in those days. The Purple Gang ran the city for many years. His Irish Catholic roots defined John, and I did not imagine that he befriended many fellows like me who had an old English name. Nevertheless, we hit it off and I always enjoyed being in his company.

One afternoon we were sitting on stools in a café and John had brought a squirt gun with him. Quietly leaning around the fellow to his right, John directed a spray at the waitress behind the counter who was turned away from us. She whirled and pasted the poor victim in the chops, which knocked him off his stool. John's innocent eyes were a thing to behold.

On January 18, Eleanor and I boarded the train for Chicago to meet my parents and pick up my car. My folks did a number of things to that car while I was overseas. They had it repainted and also replaced the convertible top. The car looked like it had just rolled out of the factory when I came back. We made a classic Route 66 trip to California, arriving there in early February.

Ted Wheeler and I had kept in touch, and we were stationed nearby each other at Santa Ana, California. One weekend we were out cruising in my convertible Ford and stopped at a gas station. An attractive young lady was working the fuel pumps and Ted struck up a conversation with her. He made a date with her to see Glenn Miller who was playing at the Palladium that night. That evening Ted, Eleanor and I returned to the gas station and picked up the young lady. It was the night before Eleanor and I were married, so we had a lot to celebrate.

We were married in a little chapel south of Long Beach. Thereafter we enjoyed pleasant days and nights, full of prospect and satisfaction. Eleanor's joy and happiness dispelled my wartime blues, and I was just another young man with a new bride.

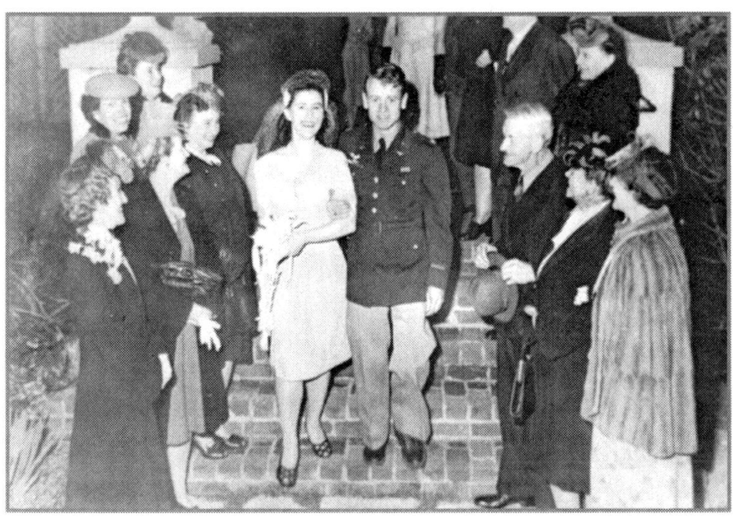

**Early March saw us reassigned to Vance Army Air Base** near Enid, Oklahoma. Pilot training was winding down, and Vance was one of the few remaining centers where bomber pilots were trained. My official non-flying job title was "Rubber Conservation Officer!" Despite the enormous buildup of war supplies, tires were in short supply because the Japanese controlled so much of the world's rubber output. It was my job to ensure the TB-25s had enough tires on hand and that old tires were quickly recycled. I flew enough hours to keep my flight status active, but little else challenged me there.

Eleanor and I decided that a career in the service meant long separations from each other that we could not bear. Had I been unattached, I would have applied for test pilots school. A friend of mine in Corsica once made a comment, "Well, we'll finish up this war but at least we won't have to fight the next one." I wasn't so sure about that. On May 15th I made my last flight. We returned to Detroit where I entered engineering school at the University of Detroit. It was the end of my military career and the start of my connection with many interesting aerospace projects.

While in school I helped a friend build a dirt track sprint car which he successfully raced in local events. This experience generated some home based business as other racers asked me to build engines for them. I would mill their engine heads to increase compression and rework the valve trains. Years later, I modified a Chevrolet Corvair engine which produced nearly twice the power of the Porsche engine it replaced.

In quick succession our family grew to three children and I had several jobs while attending school. One of the Detroit bowling alley owners placed pin ball machines in his establishments and I repaired them. One Christmas, I made two strings of lights from the pinball machine bulbs which decorated our Christmas tree. I also worked as foreman on a crew assembling awnings on commercial buildings. One of our jobs was on a building near the downtown airport. One foggy day I was on a tall ladder and heard a plane approaching on downwind. I looked up just as a DC-3 broke out of the fog. The pilots misjudged their position. There were too close to the runway to turn on to a base leg. Nevertheless, the plane sharply banked toward the runway and stalled. It fell toward the airport, and the next thing I saw was a huge fireball. No one survived the crash.

After graduating, I worked for General Motors, but quickly moved on to a start-up firm named the Aeronautical Icing Research Laboratories. The company had contracts with the Air Force and Navy to develop airborne anti-icing equipment. The test gear was mounted inside a retired B-24 which they flew from Willow Run Airport near Detroit.

I participated on a number of flights as a test engineer rather than pilot. We deliberately flew into severe weather conditions while evaluating the effectiveness of the new designs. Some of the thunderstorms we encountered tested the strength of that airplane. Hail often battered the plane like flak and the severe up and down drafts made seatbelts essential. Sections of the plane that were not equipped with anti-icing would accumulate thick ice. There was definitely an element of danger in those flights.

We also tested the equipment under severe icing conditions on the ground. These tests were conducted at a facility on the top of Mt. Washington, New Hampshire. This mountain is acknowledged to have the highest winds and coldest temperatures in the contiguous U.S. In wintertime, winds frequently exceed 100 mph with temperatures occasionally reaching thirty degrees below zero. They constructed a long shed which was open on both ends and installed a jet engine to power a wind tunnel. During winter we would spend months at a time at the facility. Artic clothing was a necessity to avoid frostbite. The staff was a fun loving bunch and created such oddities as beer parties combined with chocolate fudge to pass the time.

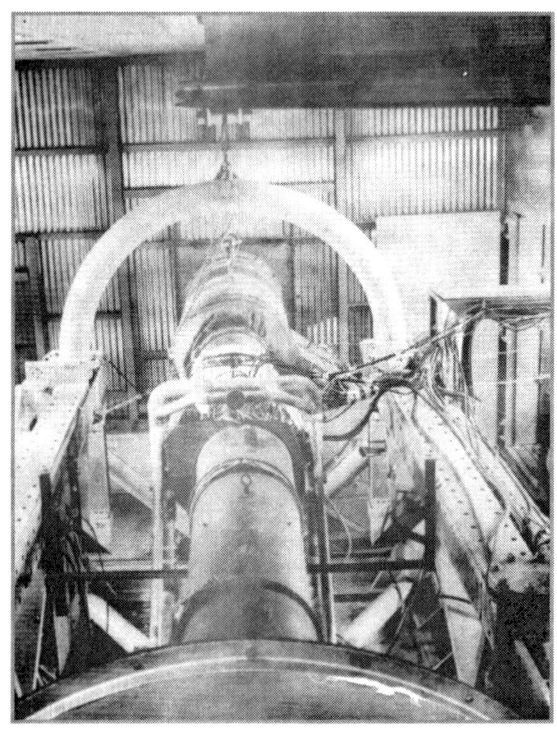

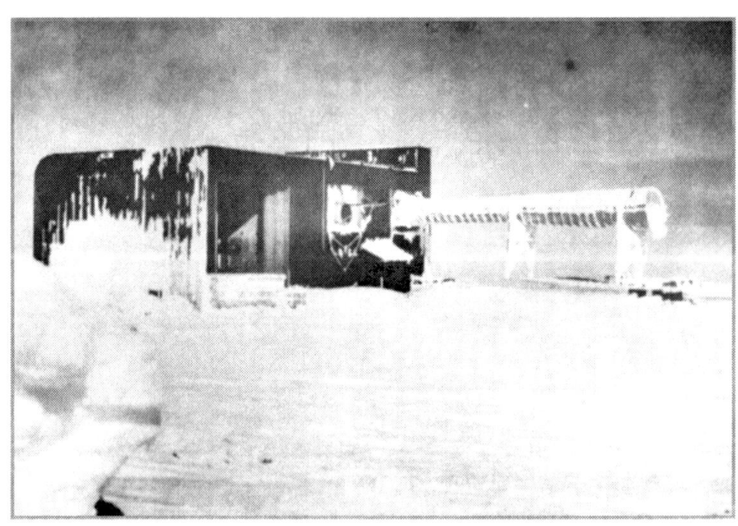

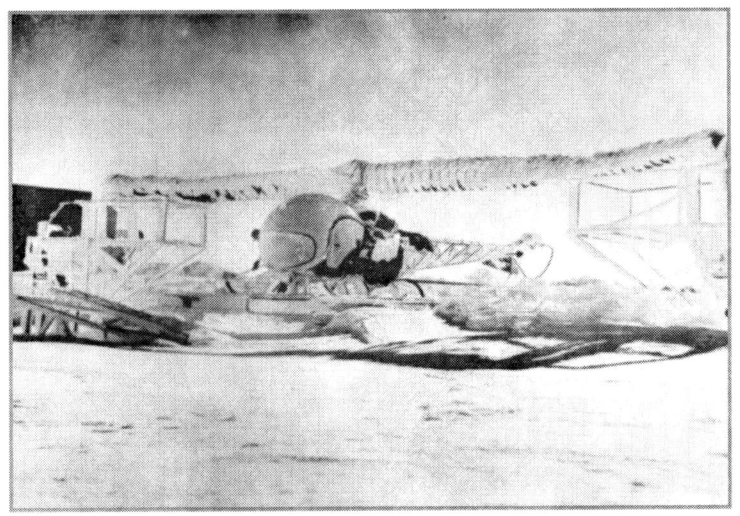

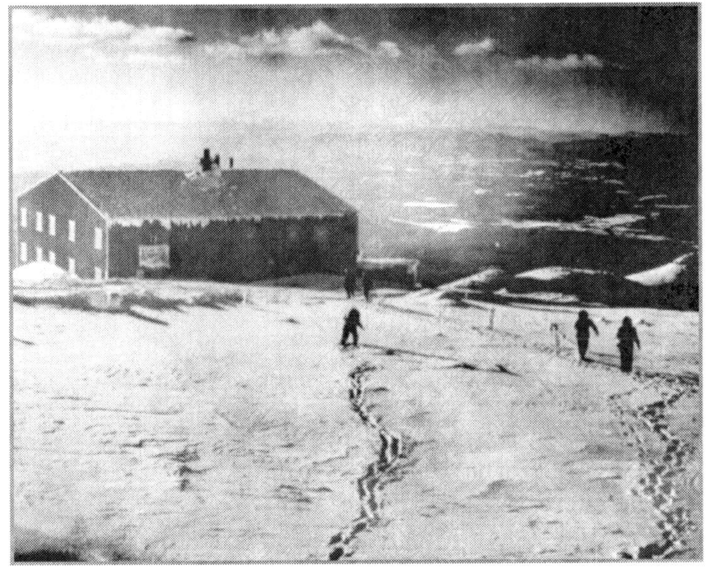

**Aerojet Company, the producer of jet assisted take off (JATO)** engines was selected to develop one of the first large rocket booster engines. This Sacramento based firm faced enormous challenges developing an engine that could produce 125,000 pounds of thrust. I accepted an offer to work on the test firing stand during the early test firing phase. A large gantry was assembled in the desert, and our monitor telemetry was placed in a bunker nearby. The time demands of the project required us to work many nights in preparation for a firing. I again wrote letters to Eleanor telling her about the beautiful nighttime desert scenery. We observed coyotes pursuing jack rabbits which sometimes hopped into view. The early test firings resulted in short burns with spectacular explosions. However, in the short interval of six months the engines were firing for more than two minutes. This was an amazing accomplishment.

Usually our work week would end about midday on Friday and the fellows would frequently hit the casinos at Lake Tahoe or go fishing in nearby rivers. My '56 Chevy Bel-Air was damaged in an accident on the freeway and for temporary transportation I purchased a Crossley. This tiny station wagon was the great, great grandfather of the Mini Clubman and was so ugly that it was kind of cute. One Friday afternoon I came off shift from the test range and my car was not where I parked it. I walked back in to my office and found the car wedged sideways where my desk had been! I had to buy the first round that afternoon as a bribe to have a car returned to the parking lot.

Lundy Company near New York City was another small engineering firm with Air Force contracts. During the late '50s they made chaff dispensers that became operational equipment on B-52s. I helped the designers go from concepts to usable products. These machines ejected hundreds of rolls of Mylar film a second from the tail of the airplane. When the Mylar unspooled from the rolls it would create huge false radar images. The purpose was to misdirect radar guided missiles and guns. This was the same defensive strategy we had used while attacking German targets, but this equipment was far better.

I also was assigned primary design duties on a Lockheed subcontract to convert the C-130 cargo plane into a commercial airliner. Ultimately, the project was scrapped because of the high noise level inside the airplane.

Martin Company in Littleton, Colorado was developing the Titan ICBM/booster rocket series and I joined them to work on special projects. In the evening they often tested rocket engines at the test facility located in the hills above the town and the blast could be seen and felt from my home. Perhaps the most interesting project that I was connected to was a system to remove monkey poop from the air in a zero G space capsule.

Hoping to find a more constructive challenge, I relocated to Bellevue, Washington where I helped develop the first cockpit heads-up displays for Sundstrand Company. We flight tested our equipment on light aircraft based at Boeing Field in Seattle and I participated in some of the on-board flight evaluations. Wintertime conditions in Seattle provided plenty of overcast days.

Helicopters were also equipped with the displays. I was along for several flights in instrument flight rules (IFR) conditions where the pilots needed instruments to fly. Helicopters are particularly difficult to operate in these conditions. The pilots assigned to these tests left me with a very favorable impression of their flying abilities. On one occasion, we emerged from the clouds and found ourselves uncomfortably close to a commercial airplane on approach to Boeing Field.

After the Sundstrand project, I connected with Dr. Dean Crystal, a well-known Seattle based cardiac physician. He wanted me to assist him designing a heart pump. The system would be used during cardiac surgery operations. This new design filtered and recycled the blood back to the pump. Earlier heart pumps did not have this capability. Consequently, heart operations were very expensive and wasteful because the blood went through the body and was discarded. We jointly developed a system and it performed well during several heart operations that Dr. Crystal performed on dogs. He asked me to assist him with these experimental surgeries. The diaphragm pump was controlled by an electronic wave pulse generator. It was capable of providing pulse rates from 50 to 200 beats per minute.

The need for cleaner coal fired power plants led me to Air Pollution Systems, a contractor for the government during the early days of the Environmental Protection Agency. The E.P.A. wanted to design and install equipment that removed pollutants from coal smoke. The initial plan was to experiment with power plants located in the Tennessee valley. We created what were called bag houses inside the smoke stacks. The equipment included devises called precipitators. These machines sprayed water through the smoke to eliminate more that ninety-five percent of the ash going out the stacks.

As this project drew to a close, Eleanor and I purchased a heavily wooded property located on a steep hill near the sleepy village of Preston, Washington. With the help of my sons we cut a road up the hill and sold the firewood to pay for their college expenses. A year round stream cut a canyon down the middle of the property and I built a small hydroelectric plant on the stream. It produced enough power to sell some surplus back to Bonneville Power.

My final full time position was with Venus Company, a fiberglass specialty firm that designed layup equipment. Some of the products were chopper guns which spray the resin mixed with fiberglass fibers into molds. They also marketed turn-key assembly lines to the Chinese to make auto bodies. I developed computer controlled machines to make large fiberglass parts.

Venus Co. acquired an Aerostar, a twin engine piston airplane which was high performance. I renewed my pilot certificate, and occasionally flew as copilot in this beautiful aircraft. We made a cross country flight to Washington DC for a presentation which increased my log time by twenty hours.

I was a full time employee commuting to work until age 75.

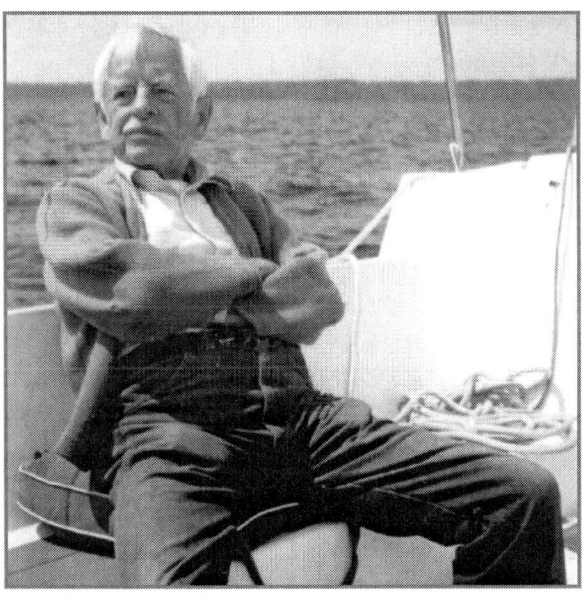

**Before….** **Some stories about my life before the military.** I also share my experiences serving in the Army Air Corps as a P-40 crew chief and early pilot training.

I was an average student in high school getting C and B grades. My folks learned of a technical school near our Detroit home named Wilbur Wright Academy. The electrical and mechanical training in the school really got me motivated. Graduates of the school could count on having jobs with the big three automakers. The trainers were very capable people who had worked in industries for years. There was an excellent drafting course and I did well. They also taught all aspects of electric motors and oscilloscopes. They had courses in printing, assembly line design and steam engineering. They graduated repair technicians for teletypes, typewriters and automobiles. I was a student there through my senior year.

There were about 1000 students enrolled in school. Classes ran through the middle of August. The other technical school in town was Cass Tech. The two schools were in a sense rivals. Cass Tech was a larger school with a bigger campus. The only shortcoming of Wilbur Wright Academy was that it had no gymnasium. A math teacher coached our football team and they trained at a nearby high school. We were never able to put together a strong team. I didn't play football, but was fast enough to do well in track events. My father was a like me of short stature, and he as a very good quarterback. He also ran relays with the national youth team and was a pitcher for baseball league play.

My folks met in 1914 at the Detroit Bell phone company where my mother Veda was an operator and my father Albert was a lineman. Dad was a self-taught engineer who quickly branched out into instrumentation and eventually became chief of blast furnace controls for Ford Motor Company. My mother was very attractive, and won the Miss Detroit contest. They built their first home together from wood which was salvaged from an old barn. While inside the barn, my mother was injured when a beam fell and hit her face. The cosmetic damage healed, but she had her teeth replaced by dentures.

To augment my father's income, my mother became one of the first female real estate agents in Detroit. She was successful, and my dad invested her earnings in the stock market. The 1929 crash wiped out most of their savings, but they were still relatively comfortable with their salaries. My mother continued in real estate and made money buying distressed properties.

One day she came home with a beautiful Gibson steel guitar purchased from a store going out of business. I liked the instrument and became pretty good with it. On weekends there was a radio show from Detroit with a group that played Hawaiian guitar music. I went down for an audition and was accepted in the group. I learned to play the slide guitar which was one of the first electric instruments.

My twelfth birthday gift was a big German shepherd and I named him Smokey. He was an excellent dog, but I had to be careful when my friends were near because he was very protective of the family. Pop went fishing one day and threw the perch that he caught in the sink. When he came back later the fish were missing and no one knew anything about it. About a month later I was playing hide and seek with the daughter of a family friend. She hid behind the couch but yelled in surprise. I looked behind the couch and saw the skeletons of the missing perch! Smokey had eaten them back there.

Mom bought a baby grand piano and I was home when the movers carried it up to the second floor of our house. They were half way up the staircase when Smokey saw them and charged with fangs fully bared. Dropping the piano down, they ran out of the house! Fortunately, the dog was corralled before inflicting any damage and the piano came to rest against the banister and didn't fall far. Shortly after that I was at a car wash with my mom and Smokey was in the back. One of the fellows at the car wash admired the dog and my mom said, "Do you like this dog?" The fellow said, "Yes." Mom said, "Okay, he's yours."

They bought a home in Redmond which is a suburb outside Detroit. There were beautiful pastures and fields around the house. I bought a 22 caliber rifle and mounted a scope on it. I spent most of my pocket change on ammunition. With the scope I could be accurate some distance out, and several times made head shots on pheasants from a block and a half away. For my sixteenth birthday dad gave me a 20 gauge shotgun. A stray collie started hanging around the house and my mother said he could stay. I named him Bing and he was a wonderful hunting dog. He knew how to expertly circle around a pheasant and flush it up. Mom seldom bought chicken at the market because we had a ready supply of pheasant.

Several weeks after we moved into that house, a young woman wearing a foul weather gear knocked on the door and introduced herself as our neighbor. In those days it was common for neighbors to introduce themselves, and she was making a courtesy visit. She invited me to go to church with her and I accepted. I went to several youth meetings held at the church, and it was at one of those meetings where I met my future wife. There was an immediate mutual attraction between us, and Eleanor invited me to her mother's home where I used my mechanical aptitude to repair household things. As the school year progressed, our fondness for each other increased. My mother, fearing that this relationship was growing too strong, arranged for me to work on my grandfather's farm for the summer.

Grandpa Wayne was a successful farmer who didn't like the country life and moved to Iowa where he started a grocery store. He also owned a repair shop for train wheels where several people were employed. The store and repair businesses did well and as a side investment he purchased a beautiful 320 acre farm in Minnesota. The farm had a ten acre vegetable garden, large barn, a chicken coop, big pig pens, and a gravel pit. It sat on 500 feet of shoreline.

His businesses in Iowa quickly failed. The railroad shut down the wheel repair shop. Then a Kroger grocery opened up his town. Until then there were no other markets in the area. There was a herd of cows on his Minnesota farm and in 1932 he went back to dairying and farming with my uncle Perry Satterthwaite. When he lived in the city, he was about forty pounds overweight. In the summer of 1939 when I worked with him, he was 150 pounds and a little over six feet.

Of course, the main job with dairy cows is milking them. When I first got to the farm my wrists were so weak that I wasn't a very good milker. By the end of the summer I had a really nice firm handshake. After milking the cows, we would separate the cream and put the milk in the well to keep it cool.

To fertilize the fields they used a manure spreader, and it was really something to watch. When that thing got going, manure flew all over the place. Grandma told me about a four-year old cousin who came to visit the farm. When he saw grandpa operating the manure spreader, he ran back inside and said, "Grandma, Grandma! Grandpa's spreading shame on you all over the field!"

There was an old swayed back horse on the farm that was left out to pasture. My friend Herb had come with me to the farm and Grandpa gave us permission to ride him. There was no saddle, but we did have a bit and lariat. That horse was a smart old fellow. When I got on him, he walked to the center of the paddock and wouldn't move. Herb and I did manage to get him some distance out in the pasture. I mounted the old stallion, and we headed back toward the barn. Suddenly, the horse took off and headed straight toward the barn gate. The top part of the door was closed and I had to bail off the horse as he went through!

We had one outing that summer for recreation. We milked the cows in the evening and hit the road at first light. Our destination was a state forest that was at the headwaters of the Mississippi River. The forest was very beautiful with enormous oak trees that lined the banks. The Mississippi River was about fifty feet wide, and adventurous types could step across the river on rocks. After returning from the park that evening, we milked the cows.

The folks were not religious, but there were some house rules. Card playing was not allowed except for the game "Pit." Since there was no electricity, kerosene lamps provided the house lighting. Grandpa was pretty stingy with kerosene, so it was usually early to bed and early to rise. The house was very dusty and when we set the table we always put the plates on the table upside down. Dust would quickly coat any dishes left right side up.

Grandpa fed the pigs with skim milk, and one of our jobs was pouring the milk into the trough. The pigs caused all sorts of trouble and jostled us when we tried to fill the trough. I came up with a plan to fix that situation. I removed the battery and a spark plug from a Model A that was not running. The floor of the pigsty was very wet of course. I put a piece of dry wood underneath the trough so that it was raised up and insulated from the ground. A wire from the battery connected the spark plug to the trough. Another wire was connected to a metal stake driven into the ground. I put water into the trough, and open the door to let the pigs in. After they began drinking, power was applied to the trough. After jumping back, the pigs squealed and ran out.

That evening when Herb and I fed the pigs, they came in and stuck their noses in the trough. I applied the power to the trough and the pigs squealed, but they kept on drinking. The next day they made a lot of racket, but waited until we were away from the trough. There was one other thing about pigs that was interesting. When grandpa wanted to move a pig, he would put a bucket over its head and push them backwards where he wanted them to go.

*October 20, 1939*

*Dear Eleanor,*

*It's been a week since my last letter, but I have been so very busy. Last week we started to harvest and I have been working long days. It's been very hard work and I am going to go to bed right after dinner. Yesterday, we took the harvester over to the clover field which is a mile away. It wouldn't go through the gates with the four horses hitched up. I was asked to ride through the gate bareback while pulling a horse behind me. They were then going to pull the harvester through the gate with the other two horses. "Billy" is a black western quarter horse who won't follow a lead. I managed to board Billy, and he began to buck and act wild. It took both my uncle and granddad to restrain him. I got off him and rode the other horse "Babe" while pulling Billy through the gate. I really had fun riding a wild bronc.*

*It's a beautiful evening. Earlier tonight there was a nice half-moon, but now its pitch black except for the airway beacons which I can see plainly flashing even though they are from ten to fifteen miles away. It was quite warm earlier, but now there is a cool breeze blowing across the lake. It smells like rain.*

*How I wish I were home, but it won't be long now. I'm getting a little homesick.*

*Good night, Dale*

After returning to Detroit, I went to work at the RL Dentman Company. It was good job for me, and I was sort of a jack of all trades. In addition to drafting duties, I was the shipping clerk. My pay was $15 a week which was very good for the time. I managed to save $65 and bought a 1932 Ford five window coupe. The car was in reasonably good shape. The body looked good and I wish I had that car today. It was the first year that Ford made V-8 engines, but my car had the four cylinder power plant. While this was nice car, it wasn't the '32 deuce that everyone loves today.

The timing was slightly off on the engine, and the main bearings were sloppy. Looking back on it, I should've milled some bearings for the engine myself. One day the car wouldn't start. My dad was on his way to work and agreed to give me a push. Dad had a large Plymouth, and he had no trouble getting my car rolling. After the initial push the cars separated a little and I put the car in the second gear. Just then, dad slammed into the back of the car and the impact destroyed my transmission. I managed to drive the car to my office and the boss graciously allowed me to bring it in to the shop. We pulled out the transmission and I found another one in a junkyard for $12.50.

Ice boats were a common sight on White Lake where we sometimes spent winter weekends. These graceful boats were capable of great speed. After constructing my own ice boat from catalog plans, I waited until the conditions were right. Unfortunately, the trim and rigging on the boat needed some adjustment which limited its speed.

My father also had an ice boat and it was beautifully rigged. On several occasions we had that boat above seventy miles an hour. One day dad was riding near the outrigger and a friend was the helmsman. As we approached another iceboat, the friend made a sudden correction and dad fell off! He slid at least 300 feet, but was not hurt. On another occasion we slid onto a section where the ice was a little thin and we started to push the ice boat to the shore. The ice cracked all around us. We pushed like mad and managed to get the boat back on solid ice.

Dad had a fishing boat and he gave me a 16 hp. motor from that boat. He didn't like the engine because it didn't idle down for trolling. I found a nice small runabout made of cedar and put the motor on it. It had a steering wheel and would plane quite nicely. In order to get the boat on a plane, the driver had to stand up and lean way up on the bow. One day I was out with that boat and saw two girls sitting on an island in the lake. I thought a show of speed would impress them and accelerated the boat. As the boat was about to pass by the island, I realized that the steering was not working correctly. I pulled back the throttle, but the boat turned and bounced up the island beach. It came to rest close to the girls who looked on in wide-eyed amazement.

I saved my money and eventually had $150. I went shopping for a '37 or '38 Chord. Used cars were plentiful in Detroit. These beautiful cars sold for as little as $350. Although I found some nice cars, I wasn't able to finance them because the draft was about to start. Potential soldiers were not good credit risks. In April, I found a guy who would sell me a '37 Oldsmobile. The two door coupe was really nice car. In July, 1941 I was drafted and the car was put up on blocks at my parents' home. After I converted from a one-year enlistment to three years, my mother convinced me to sell the car.

*July 24, 1941*

*Dear Eleanor,*

*Having been well cloaked and reasonably well fed I have little to complain about at this time. We have had a full day and it hardly seems that it was only this morning we were stepping off the train for our first view of Camp Grant. They are very efficient here. By 3 PM we were dressed in army clothes, had two meals and classified for our military jobs. One of the officers said that I had the highest mark he had seen lately in the IQ test. They want to put me in officers' school. Where I will be sent for training depends on where there is an opening, but it may surprise you.*

*I have a bunch of swell fellows in my company, and the sergeant must've been a Boy Scout leader at one time. The excuse for the poor penmanship is that the inoculation made my arm so sore I can hardly write, but I think you would rather have a letter than a card.*

*Love, Dale*

On a warm July morning I reported to the Detroit train station with dozens of other inductees. We traveled down to Camp Grant, Illinois on a train pulled by a slow steam engine that emitted thick black smoke. Our lunch on the way to Camp Grant consisted of one grayish slice of bologna between two dry pieces of bread. We arrived late in the evening and were fed cold tomato soup before heading to a dusty barracks. The next morning we were awakened at 0400 hrs. for KP duty. Meals at the giant mess hall were unpalatable.

They gave an intelligence test. Those who scored above eighty were given the opportunity of enlisting in one of three services for three years; Air Corps, Signal Corps and Cavalry. I urged some of the people who came down with me to enlist in the Air Corps. Most of them refused to do so, thinking they would serve their one year draft obligation out and go home.

After one week at Camp Grant, I left for my Air Corps assignment. My base was Selfridge Field, Michigan, which was thirty miles from my home. We traveled there on a streamlined train with good meals served in the dining car. Arriving at Selfridge, we were quartered in permanent brick barracks. At breakfast the next morning, we ate from china plates. As we passed through the chow line, the cook asked me, "How do you like your eggs?" I knew I had made the right decision to join the Air Corps. Monthly pay was increased from $21 to $30 upon enlistment.

I became good friends with Herman "Herm" Grub, a Cass Tech graduate. We were moved from the permanent brick barracks as more recruits arrived. Our new quarters were in a large hangar on the flight line near the field. Rows of bunks and lockers filled the hangar. The doors at both ends were usually wide open in warmer weather. My bunk was near the headquarters side. In the morning an artillery piece was fired just outside our hangar door during reveille. All of us were quickly on our feet after that blast.

Tests were administered to determine eligibility for schools such as communications and aircraft mechanics. Meanwhile, we were given work assignments based wherever possible on our previous experience. I was assigned to the Communication section of the 50th Pursuit Group. We had thirteen aircraft of which twelve were P-35 pursuit ships and one was a BT-13 two-seat trainer.

The work consisted of communicating with the control tower every morning to determine whether the airplane would be used for local or cross-country flying. We would physically change out the radios every morning according to the aircraft's assignment. No frequency selection was available on the radios which had only one channel.

The old timers in the section were sent away for training on new high frequency equipment which was coming into use. I became a temporary Section Chief of Communications after only six weeks in the Air Corps. Since the field was only thirty miles from home, I had a car parked outside the base and went home on weekends. In September, Herm was sent to school at the Chicago Aeronautical University for training as an aircraft mechanic. I expected to go to communication school at Chanute Field. My orders came through, and I was surprised to learn that I was also being sent to train alongside Herm.

During the period at Selfridge Field there was an undercurrent of talk about the opportunity for experienced people to join the forces of Chiang Kai-shek. The pay was rumored to be very attractive, with bonuses being offered to pilots for shooting down Japanese aircraft. Aircraft mechanics were also being sought. I don't know if anyone actually accepted that offer from our unit.

*September 15, 1941*

*Dear Eleanor,*

*We arrived in Chicago after a pleasant trip on a Twilight Limited train out of Detroit. A short bus ride brought us to the YMCA. By 10 PM we were checked into the small cubicles which will be our home for six months. I am happy to have a space that is my own, and have no complaint about the size of the room. Having individual rooms permits us greater ease of movement. It is no longer necessary to tiptoe in after 9 PM to avoid waking others.*

*The atmosphere is pleasant, especially in the mess hall. The food is the best I've eaten in the army. We are called cadets here, and we have enough expense money to take care of everything and leave between $15 and $20 per month. We are close to the museum, beach, planetarium, a brewery, the park, tennis courts and the small boat harbor. The very heart of Chicago," the loop" is only a fifteen minute walk. At the YMCA there are various kinds of amusements and recreations including dances in the roof garden.*

*There will be plenty to keep us busy. School is eight hours per day, five days per week. We have lots of homework. There is enough time for study, with bed check at 11 PM. Herman was happy to see me and as I write this letter he sits at the next desk writing up electrical experiments. He has spent hours on these assignments. I'm looking forward to my classes.*

*Love, Dale*

*November 7, 1941*

*Dear Eleanor,*

*I was somewhat overwhelmed when I opened your package Saturday morning. I knew nothing about a "sweetheart" day until then. Herm said that I hit the jackpot. I think so myself. I was just about to buy a pipe myself, but I did not see one that I liked. You certainly must have known what I wanted. I read the letter last and it was the best of all. It really raised my spirits.*

*I am studying a little more than most of the other fellows. Friday, our ignition instructor wanted to know why I could answer all his questions and the rest of them couldn't. The other students wasted no time telling him that I had studied electricity before. Now, I believe he will expect more of me. He is that kind of person. I might have had it a little easier if he had not found out. From now on, I think I had better know the answers to all of the questions.*

*Today I sent you a package with a couple of items that I saw in an interesting shop nearby. They deal in all kinds of handmade jewelry. I was particularly attracted by their sterling stuff. I wonder if you like it. The "little man" charm is the God of laughter. He is made of cherry wood. The snake is sterling, with coral eyes. I thought it was solid silver when I bought it, but found out afterwards that it was not. I couldn't insure the package. I hope it arrives okay.*

*Love, Dale*

*December 12, 1941*

*Dear Eleanor,*

*Well, I beat the boys again this time, but marks in instrument class were low and I finished with 88, my lowest mark so far. I also scored well in the carburation course with a 90 average, but the fellows are hounding me. My total average is now 93, and the nearest to me is 90 3/4. I am now studying ignition and it requires much writing and study. I'll have to keep hitting the ball.*

*Herm and I nearly always celebrate the completion of a course. We went to see the play "Native Son." Perhaps you heard about it. It was directed by Orson Welles and is a very powerful story. The tickets were complementary, and were surprisingly in the front row. It was a very well spent evening. I enjoyed myself and met some interesting people who subsequently had me to dinner and tea Sunday. They are elderly people, and they have a son in New York who is being treated well. As a friendly gesture they reciprocate in this manner. Therefore, I have a new "Uncle" Bob Anderson.*

*It will only be a week before I will be home again. I wish the holidays came more often. We had Armistice Day off, but not the Monday before, so no one got away last weekend. There were some beautiful displays here and parades, but luckily we did not have to march.*

*I am glad to hear that your nursing examinations have been okay. You have my best wishes and thoughts.*

*Love, Dale*

Every morning we walked about a mile from the YMCA to the school. We arrived at the school about 0800 hrs. and had a half-day of instruction followed by hands-on mechanical work. They had some airplane engines which were located on the eighth floor, and we would open all the windows and run the engines. Our school, the Aeronautical University, was a private institution that the military contracted to train mechanics. The largest engine that we ran there was a Curtis Concorde. It was a V-12 and made about 400 hp.

The crew chief training program was twenty-two weeks long. In the final twelve weeks we took a morning bus to Chicago Municipal Airport. Most of the planes that we worked on there did not have wings. The army provided three pursuit planes for our training. There were two P-12Es and one P-40. These planes were kept in a separate hanger about a quarter of a mile from our work area. Every morning we would get them out and push them up to our hanger. During December and January, the city known for wind greeted us with blustery gales or eerie white twilight. Any kind of heat was our friend and we shared the warmth of a Zippo lighter. Returning the airplanes to their hanger was particularly frigid work, and we all prayed for warmer permanent assignments.

One day a group of three students and I changed out an engine on a P-12E. After we finished the engine swap out, we rolled the airplane out of the hangar and drew straws to see who would start the engine. I won. There was quite a bit of snow and ice front of the hanger. Instead of regular wheel chocks, we used two big pieces of 2 x 12 with a large timber of 8 x 8 bolted to the ends. We rolled the wheels up on the 2 x 12 planks and nested the wheels against the 8 x 8 chock. I got the airplane started and warmed up the engine. Then I put my head down in the cockpit to watch the magnetos and tachometer.

I was really focused on what I was doing, but suddenly felt a vibration in the airplane. A sensation of movement startled me, and I looked up to see the plane moving towards the hangar door! The 2 x 12s were acting like a couple of skis. I kicked the rudder and the airplane slewed around just in time. I looked back at my classmates who were yelling and jumping up and down. The engine made so much noise that I couldn't hear them. Fortunately, no one observed this except the four of us. After that, I was a little more careful about engine run-ups.

*January 14, 1942*

*Dear Eleanor,*

*Herm and I went to the Aragon ballroom last Saturday evening. I am going to take you there someday. It is a beautiful place. Sunday we attended a quiz broadcast at one of the recreation centers and I won two dollars for telling the colors of the top and bottom stripes on the flag. It was a very inexpensive weekend. They offered soldiers free tickets to the ballroom. My final mark in test stands was a little lower than my accumulated average, but I still beat the boys, so they call me "Professor" again. I lost the title in the last course by two points.*

*I expect to come home the weekend after next on the 24th, and since we are scheduled to go to school Saturday, I will fly home. If I can make the 5:30 PM plane, I would like to meet you with Olive and Al at the airport and we could go out from there. The plane arrives at 8:20 PM. You must write me and let me know if that will work. Of course you can never tell in advance in the Army. A change in our training schedule that week could make me early or late. When I am sure of my arrival time I will send you a wire.*

*Love, Dale*

*January 30, 1942*

*Dear Eleanor,*

*I arrived back in Chicago Monday morning about 6 AM. I hitched a ride to Ann Arbor a few minutes after we parted. The next train to Chicago from Ann Arbor departed about sixty minutes later, but I didn't mind.*

*I was pretty tired Monday, so I climbed into the fuselage of one of the planes and slept for a couple of hours. It's not an uncommon practice and is perfectly okay as long as the instructor doesn't catch you. The weather has been sub-zero, and we are working with the eighth floor with the windows open and the motors fanning the breeze around us.*

*You know I rather looked forward to this unsettled life, but I know that I will be away for many months. It is nice to go to new places and meet new faces for change, but even new faces get boring after a while. There is nothing I would rather be doing right now than sitting by my own fireside with my loved ones near.*

*Love, Dale*

*PS Please finish that sweater before I shiver myself to a frazzle.*

**In February 1942 I graduated from mechanics school as a** crew chief. While I was training, my unit based at Selfridge Field, Michigan moved to Meridian, Mississippi. Most of my graduating class was also assigned to the base at Meridian, and they took military transportation. I elected to take civilian airlines with the thought that I could spend a day or two in Detroit. On the day of my departure from Detroit to Meridian, the entire east coast was socked in and there were no airplanes flying.

*February 20, 1942*

*Dear Eleanor,*

*I arrived at Key Field, Meridian Air Base at 6:30 this morning. My trip was rather long and tiresome. I "thumbed" part of the way, rode a bus part of the way and flew the rest. Connections and travel were very poor. Technically I was twelve or more hours overdue, but nothing has been said. I was assigned to "C" flight and I will start tomorrow adjusting an engine on a brand-new fighter of which there are quite a few here. The weather is cold, although they tell me it was summer-like yesterday. There is grass growing and some frogs chirping in a swamp nearby. Hopefully, these things indicate an early spring.*

*The field is in a flat valley surrounded by rolling wooded hills. The earth here is a red sticky clay and airplanes cannot land on it. They have to stay on the runways. The barracks are all wooden, and are similar to the temporary ones at Selfridge Field. My bunk is right next to Herms'. There seems to be a pretty good bunch of fellows in this outfit. Food is good. There are about 4000 men here.*

*We have heard rumors that we will be leaving within two weeks. So far the rumors have been pretty accurate. The story is that we will be allowed rations for four days travel by rail. I can't figure out where we might be heading.*

*PS I am enclosing a letter of recommendation in support of my application for flight school. I would like to have your mother draft a letter and send it to my superior officers. Please have her use my letter as a pattern, and have her sign it. Her recommendation would really improve my chances. I must get some action on my application for pilot before we move.*

*PPS Include the address with the signature.*

*Private Dale Satterthwaite*
*10th pursuit squadron, 50th group*
*Key Field*
*Meridian, Mississippi*

*To whom it may Concern:*

*I recommend Dale Satterthwaite as a young man of excellent character. His friends and neighbors respect him as an honest, ambitious and serious minded citizen. During the four years I have known him he has shown sound judgment. Although his personality is inclined to be quiet and retiring, he is confident of his own ability. He makes many friends and is well-liked by the young people of his group as well as his elders. His reputation has been excellent.*

*Eleanor, I could go on like this, but your mother will no doubt want to express her own thoughts.*

*Love, Dale*

All of the classmates who took military transportation arrived days ahead of me. Upon arrival, they were all promoted to PFC, but I missed that promotion. They put me in for promotion the next month, but I remained behind the group in promotions. At the base they were assembling new aircraft which came in crates. These planes were P-40Es. When the planes came out of the crates, the mechanics would attach the wings. My group was not working on that part of the assembly. It was our job to adjust the engine valves and get the planes ready to fly after the planes were rolled out on the flight line.

Valve adjustments for the Allison engine were supposed to be done while the engine was cold. The flight line was damp and chilly, and it was a miserable place to work. We would run the engines until they were warm. After shutting the engines down, we would quickly pull the valve covers off and make the adjustments with a slight correction for the heated parts. Our rule bending did not seem to affect the performance of the engines.

The base was used to transition pilots from trainers to fighters. These new single seat pursuit ships were being flown by pilots with little or no stick time in the aircraft. Consequently, there was a lot of excitement while flight operations were going on. One day I saw a P-40 on downwind, and it was trailing a wire at the back of the aircraft. I thought it was some kind of tow plane. The plane landed and quickly taxied over to the hard stand. The pilot got out of the airplane and knelt and kissed the ground!

A section of high tension cable was caught between the fifty caliber machine guns on the wing. The cable extended across the fuselage of the plane and was caught on the tail with part of it trailing behind. This sturdy power line cable was aluminum line wound around a steel core. After snagging the line while hedge-hopping, the pilot climbed the plane to 10,000 feet and tried to shake it loose, but he couldn't do it. He got into a spin, and wasn't able to recover until he was very low. I don't know if they grounded him for doing that.

*February 28, 1942*

*Dear Eleanor,*

*Well, I guess I am settled here now. I was pretty tired when I last wrote and my letter didn't say very much. I have not been off the field so far and I haven't found much incentive to go into town. Meridian's only attraction is a movie theater. We have been assigned dirty yard bird work since arriving here. Herm is pretty fed up with it, but I think things will change soon. It doesn't take $2000 worth of education to wash trucks and tractors.*

*This field has been set up as an assembly plant. They have been turning out three or more pursuit ships per day, but the new pilots have been smashing them faster than they are being built. So far no one has been hurt seriously, but these machines cost over $50,000 each.*

*Some of the boys who transferred to the 10th squadron have been made crew chiefs already. George and Mac, the lowest standing graduates in our Chicago class each have two planes to care for -the fortunes of war. George's plane came in on its nose yesterday, and he went running to the line and asked if it was his fault. Everyone laughed. Last Thursday was Washington's Birthday and I was not scheduled to work. Our Master Sergeant asked three of us to prepare a new plane for its first flight.*

*Therefore, I have this afternoon off while the others work. Sunday is just another workday for us.*

*It was warm today and we are getting sunburned. The birds are singing, still, it does not seem like spring. The trees know better. The leaves are not out yet. Everyone has left base except for a couple of us who are writing letters.*

*I guess I didn't tell you much about my trip down here. I hitchhiked down to Cincinnati arriving there at 4 AM Tuesday. A bus ride put me in Louisville, Kentucky at 9 AM. I boarded a plane heading to Jackson, Mississippi, but had to leave it at Nashville, Tennessee because the space was previously reserved. I hitchhiked from Nashville to Memphis arriving about 7 PM and took another plane to Jackson. It took me from 10 AM Wednesday to 6 AM Thursday to travel the ninety remaining miles to Meridian. It was an interesting trip, but I don't want to do it again.*

*You know every time I see you it is harder to leave. I often think of the day when I'll not have to be away from you and we are always together.*

*Love, Dale*

*March 2, 1942*

*Dear Eleanor,*

*This Sunday afternoon has been warm and a trifle cloudy. Several of the boys are lying on their bunks recuperating from a "rugged" Saturday which was not only a holiday, but also a payday. Nearly everyone was celebrating their promotions. The atmosphere is unlike any other place, and I am unlikely to ever forget it.*

*I finished up my assigned duties by late morning, and with a friend wandered into the wooded hills which surround the airbase. I am comfortably tired now after walking all afternoon, and feel quite at peace with the world. My mood has improved now that the flight school application was submitted to the cadet examining board. Once they have received my papers, I cannot be moved outside the boundaries of the US until they have been acted on.*

*Yesterday we were notified that our unit will be moving to Orlando, Florida. We started packing up all of our tools and parts today. They will be loaded in the thirteen box cars that are on the side rail. Some of the bundles being loaded weigh over 1000 pounds. We will work night and day to pack everything. From now on we are going to eat out of mess kits. Our chow all goes into one metal dish, so no matter what we have to eat it turns out to be hash! We will subsist on sandwiches and coffee until we arrive there.*

*Today we packed our clothes and personal belongings. We had to turn in our foot lockers, which were the ones we've had since Selfridge Field. Our belongings went into two barracks bags which will hold about a bushel each. It is no small achievement to get all of our clothes, private articles, radios, gas masks, blankets, shoes, etc. into those bags.*

*My promotion to PFC came through today, and my pay was increased to $36. I am still sore about my crew chief* *rating being held up. The travel problems effectively meant that my name was placed on the bottom of the roster. I still hope to make it next month. If the choice were presented to me again, I would still go home though. My thoughts are with you at this moment. My love and my best regards to everyone, and my special love to you.*

*Dale*

*PS Please have some pictures taken with your nurses' uniform on. I will send you some of me one of these days.*

*March 24, 1942* *(Orlando FL)*

*Dear Eleanor,*

*Well, I am pretty well settled again. We were just getting used to our new barracks, but we were told to pack up and relocate next door. We sleep in double bunks. Herm is down and I am up. I have to be careful not to jump out of bed before I am thoroughly awake, or I will start walking about four feet too soon! The weather is quite warm. I am writing this note while sitting on a blanket on the lawn. There is an orange tree on one side of me and a palm on the other. I have no shirt on, and am enjoying the sunshine. The town is beautiful, and the people are friendly. It is about the nicest place I have seen. Parks, lakes, beautiful homes, etc. I hope I spend some time here.*

*Herm and I are going to buy a car I guess. We can afford it, and we will get one that we can resell easily if we should be moved.*

*I suppose that after these few lax days that we will work like dogs next week. I don't mind though. It makes me eat more and put on some weight. I wish you were here to share this weather and beautiful Florida scenery. I expect I will be brown as a nut before long. I love you.*

*Best regards to everyone,*
*Dale*

In Orlando, they gave me the cadet examination and I passed with a very good grade. The Schneider medical test was also no problem and I was all set to enter flying school. I was finally crewing P-40s, and we had an excellent work schedule there. Our on-duty shifts were forty-eight hours, followed by seventy-two hours off. Often I could get a night's sleep while on duty. Sometimes a plane would come in late in the evening. We would service and fuel it. There were usually no other duties until 0700 hrs.

We were still a pilot transition group. One of the pilots did very well with the airplane, but he didn't know how to drive a car. Some of the other pilots were teaching him how to drive on his off-time. The seventy-two hour breaks gave us time to see a lot of the state. The main impediment to that was gas rationing and fuel cards. We only had an "A" fuel ration card which allowed us to buy two gallons of fuel a week.

Before a P-40 was cranked up, we were supposed to dump about a gallon out of the fuel lines to ensure there was no water getting in the engine. Most of the guys would just dump that gallon of 100 octane fuel on the ramp. I thought it was a terrible waste, the so I started collecting one gallon hydraulic oil cans. When I dumped that fuel from the airplane, I would save it in a can. We could buy kerosene for about ten or fifteen cents a gallon, and we would mix the kerosene with the 100 octane gas. A car would run pretty well on that mixture.

Herm and I bought a 1932 Chrysler coupe for $55. We found a rumble seat for $20 and replaced the one that was in the car. We had a nice car for $75, and our fellow mechanics were often with us on excursions. With the long hood most people assumed that had a big V- 8 inside, but it was just a flathead six.

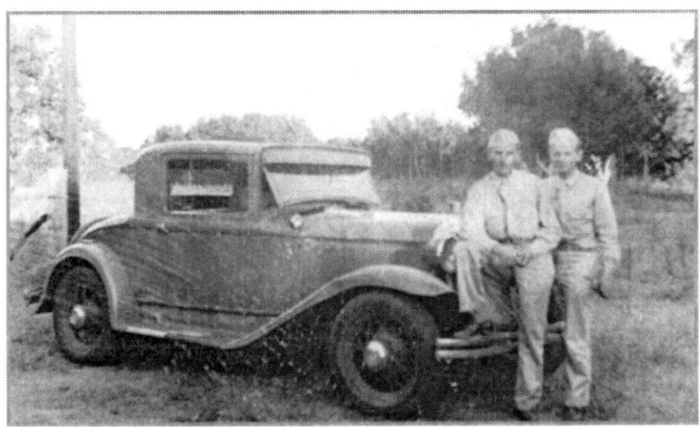

Herm had made friends with some people down in Kissimmee, Florida. He wanted me to meet these new friends. We headed down there on a three day break. I was surprised to see horse hitching rails up and down the streets with horses tied to them and many of the townspeople wearing western clothes. One of his friends told me that Florida was the third largest beef raising state. Cows could be raised on just one acre because the grass grew so quickly.

Herm's friends had a fifteen acre ranch outside of town. The family had a thirteen year-old girl and a seventeen year-old girl who was engaged to a G.I. The house was small and simple. They had a grove of lime trees on the property. There were fifteen head of cattle and two nice horses that we could ride. The man of the house was a postal worker who delivered mail on a bicycle. He would finish his route everyday about 3:30 PM. Then he would crank up his boat and we would go out fishing for bass in the big lake. The girls would come along and bring a picnic lunch with them. After fishing for a while, we would stop at an island to eat lunch and swim. It was a real nice situation.

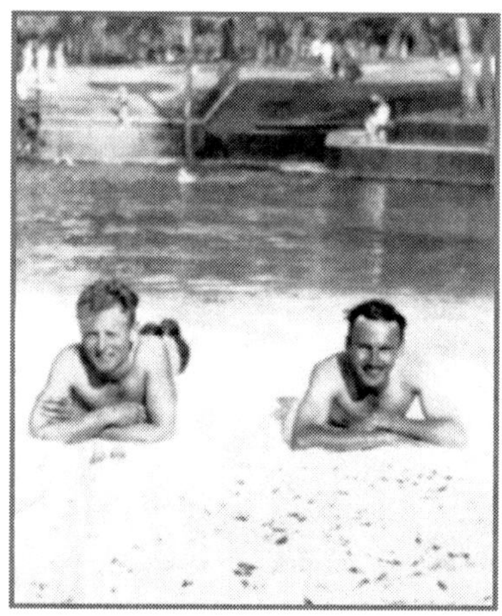

**The thing that we didn't know about 100 octane fuel was** that it was an aromatic fuel that tended to eat up rubber seals in an automobile fuel system. On our return trip from Kissimmee, we left with plenty of time to arrive before curfew. About midway to Orlando the engine started missing and we pulled to the side of the road. We guessed that it was a fuel pump problem, so I cut off the end of the air hose on a tire pump and shoved the air line into the gas fueling pipe. We caulked the tank opening so that the pump would pressurize the tank, thereby forcing fuel into the carburetor. I jumped in the rumble seat and pumped air into the gas tank while Herb drove. We made it back to the base just ahead of curfew.

*July 1, 1942*

*Dear Eleanor,*

*I took the sunshine just a little too fast, and the skin on my face has a sort of mottled appearance where I peeled from sun exposure. Other than that, I am in first-class shape. I was on KP again this last week. The First Sgt. doesn't seem to be giving me a break on that. I have a black eye that is a beauty. I was carrying a gallon of catsup when one of the boys banged it with his elbow. The can edge hit me in the eye and it rapidly turned blue. Everyone is giving that guy a hard time for picking on the littlest GI on KP!*

*On Wednesday I was assigned as the crew chief for a P-40. I wasn't excused from the KP duties, so the line chief took care of that plane for the rest of the week. The plane was the newest and fastest one here. On the evening that I finished KP, my assigned plane crashed while attempting a landing and was destroyed. There are no other planes without an assigned crew chief, and I have done very little work since the accident. I've been transferred to another outfit, but have not moved yet. My address remains the same.*

*The dog racing season ended last week, and one of the greyhounds was given to our outfit for a mascot. Its name is Spot Caprice, and it is really a pretty thing. I took him for a long hike the other morning. If I run as fast as I can, it just sort of lopes to keep up. I took some pictures which I will show you.*

*Four of my buddies and I are planning on chartering a cabin boat for a day of fishing. I am told that you can spear fish from the deck of the boat. I'll let you know if that is really possible in my next letter.*

*Love, Dale*

*August 13, 1942*

*Dear Eleanor*

*Yesterday I went for a flight in a bomber with some new equipment. We were on a training mission to see if fighters could intercept us. We flew out over the Gulf at high altitude and cruised for about an hour. Two P-40s attempted to intercept us, but they had trouble getting on our tail because we were so high. Our pilot throttled back so that they could get a "shot" at us. All the crewmen in the bomber were wearing English type helmets and oxygen masks. I can tell you that it was very cold up there.*

*A new order has come through from Gen. Walch to the effect that all enlisted men will have priority in flight school enrollments, and that we will all be gone by the end of September. This news makes me feel better. We were forming a school on our own here. We were going to have classes in meteorology, airborne radio, theory of flight and navigation. I was going to teach airborne radio to about 150 men. Since the new order came through the plan was partially abandoned. I still teach about a dozen fellows for half an hour in the morning and half an hour in the evening. I get quite a bit out of it myself. We have two periods of calisthenics in the morning totaling about one hour. I am doing weightlifting every other day at the officers gym, and also swimming or playing ball. I will be in better shape than ever when we finish this training.*

*In my last letter, I mentioned that we would try to catch fish by spearing them. We did see quite a few big channel cats, but nobody succeeded in spearing one. We did catch a few of them using big trebled hooks.*

*I wish you were here with me to share these blue skies and balmy evenings. The sun burns down, but there is a constant breeze blowing in from the ocean. It is always cool in the shade and hot in the sun. Every day it rains for just about fifteen minutes. The dry earth soaks up the rain and is again dry a half-hour afterwards.*

*Be good.*

*Love, Dale*

I was placed on a two week leave because all the flying schools were full. There was a possibility that orders for flight school would be issued before the fourteen days were up, so I remained in Florida. Herm received his orders for flight school and sold the car. Shortly after my leave ended I received orders to go to Decatur, Alabama for primary flight training.

*September 13, 1942*

*Dear Eleanor,*

*Much has happened since I last wrote. I was on KP you may recall and on Friday I snuck away from the mess and played a little black jack. I won eighteen dollars in about ten minutes and returned to the kitchen. At 10 o'clock we finally received our orders for flight school. Two of us dropped our mops on the floor of the mess and ran.*

*We boarded the streamliner at 3 PM the next day and had a car to ourselves. After a full day on a train, we reached our destination which was Nashville. We were immediately transferred to the Army Air Force Classification Center.*

*We have been poked, prodded, injected, scratched and minutely inspected. We were psychoanalyzed and our IQs taken. They tested our nerves, reactions, eyes, etc. We held a nail in a small hole and endeavored to keep it from touching the walls while a man screamed at us that we were physical and mental wrecks. Meanwhile, an electric counter scored the number of times our hands shook.*

*These tests are over now, and we will know in a week or so whether we qualify for pilot, navigator, or bombardier training. We will probably get our new uniforms next week. They are really nice. It feels good to be treated with a certain amount of respect by officers and sergeants. We are called "mister" which is an improvement over private.*

*The place is quite huge. It is called Berry Hill Gardens on Thompson Lane, but it does not live up to its fancy address. The buildings are all temporary structures made of tarpaper and clapboards. They are better than the shacks at Orlando, however. Altogether my outlook on life is much better and my appetite is improving. The fact that I am closer to you and home helps as well.*

*I expect that a letter will come from you soon. Of course, it takes some time for mail to go clear to Florida and back here. I'll be looking forward to hearing from you.*

*Love, Dale*

*September 25, 1942*

*Dear Eleanor,*

*I will attempt to tell you something about the life here in preflight school. Since I don't have much time, this letter will be written in stages.*

*The upperclassmen are our senior officers, and they carry their authority as far as it will stretch. Of course, there are various customs which underclassmen must observe, such as walking the rat line when we fall out for formations. This line is an imaginary one between the barracks and the parade ground. Lower cadets must walk the rat line in an exaggerated position of attention at a very rapid pace. There are about ten formations each day. Shoes must be shined between each formation and the upperclassmen make minute inspections of our uniforms. Our eyes are always focused on an imaginary point at eye level. "Gigs" (demerits) are handed out freely for any discrepancy in dress or behavior.*

*At dinner the seating positions alternate with one upperclassman seated between an underclassman. While eating, our eyes must be focused at the center of the table and at attention. To have something passed to you, you say, "Sirs, would anyone care for the sugar?"*

*Last night the upperclassmen had "open post", and we were allowed to eat dinner at ease. It certainly felt good for a change. At breakfast this morning, I sat at attention at the end of the meal as usual. One of the nasty ones in the upper class put me in a brace for no reason. A brace is a strange position of attention which causes the face to change to various tones of red and blue and cuts off one's breath. One of the decent upperclassmen gave me an order to rest. When the first upperclassman saw me, he put me in a brace again. The second one again countered this order, instructing me to rest. A disagreement ensued between the two upperclassmen. The first one said that he would gig me. The second one, a cadet sergeant, said he would gig him if he gigged me. They argued violently about this and nearly went to fisticuffs. It seems as though I have a friend in the upper class now. He says I am "on the ball".*

*Love, Dale*

*October 19, 1942*

*Dear Eleanor,*

*We were officially made upperclassmen last Wednesday. We will get our first open post sometime this week. It will have been about seven weeks since I last stepped off an army post. The old class will be moving out Monday and Tuesday, and the new class will come in immediately afterward.*

*It is unlikely that I will have to leave the southeast for the remainder of my flight training. It seems that once you are in an area, you remain. I'm hoping that most of my training will be in Florida. That is the only state in this part of the country that is worth anything in my opinion.*

*I can let my hair grow now, and we only shine our shoes once a day. I get enough sleep, and I don't have to worry about being gigged every time we fall out for a formation. There are some swell fellows in the barracks, but I miss the friends I had in Orlando.*

*Since it doesn't look as if I will see you soon, I'm going to go to bed now and dream up a magic carpet. You can expect me in an hour or so! Until then, good night sweetheart.*

*Love, Dale*

*October 26, 1942*

*Dear Eleanor,*

*Just enough time for a short note before lights out. I went to Birmingham yesterday and stayed up all night. A number of us went; perhaps twenty-five. We took over the best hotel in the city. One of the boys took his wife and we all enjoyed her company. Liquor flowed freely, but I was very conservative as usual. The party was sobered somewhat by the news that some of the boys had been hurt on the way. They demolished a new car, and were lucky to come out of it with cuts and bruises. The curves on the mountainous descent into Birmingham are sharp and treacherous. Our group had a nice ride through the country, with the foliage on the rugged hills already red and yellow.*

*We are wearing winter uniforms since this morning, and the weather has been cool enough so that the change is welcome. I sure hope I can come home to see you in my new clothes soon.*

*Love, Dale*

*December 16, 1942*

*Dear Eleanor*

*The last week has been a very busy one. My studies went late every night for finals in navigation, meteorology, engines, airplanes, etc. We are through with ground school now. I finished with a 95 average. We have been going to school both morning and afternoon instead of flying. This allows the upper-class cadets to finish their flying on time. The schedule change means that we will probably have to take flying lessons on Sunday and also on Christmas Day. Our flight training is progressing rapidly. Maybe I will solo next week.*

*The weather has been warm, but very wet. Our field is worst possible place to take off and land airplanes on. The mud flies in all directions when you open the throttle. The meteorologists say we will fly tomorrow, though at this minute there is a heavy drizzle outside. It shows no signs of a break.*

*Please give our friends and your family the warmest Christmas greeting from me.*

*Love, Dale*

**My primary flight training at Decatur was very demanding.** Forty percent of our class washed out. My instructor, Mr. Lock, would chew on me from the moment I got in the cockpit until I got out. Flight time with him was really tense. Each instructor started with five students and typically they would quickly wash one out to lighten their workload. This instructor got all five of his students through. That was very unusual.

Sometimes he would test us with some kind of forced landing scenario at the end of the lesson. One day while we were flying along, he pulled the throttle back and said "forced landing." I looked around and there was no place to safely put the airplane down. Then I saw two fenced fields that didn't meet. There was a space between the two fields that gave me enough room to set down. I made a good approach to that space before he took the airplane back. In my mind I think those few minutes of flying are what led to my graduation. Military pilots made periodic check rides with us and I didn't do well on those check rides until the very last one. I buzzed through the final check ride with no problem.

One day I was on a solo flight and cruising at 5000 feet when I saw a big turkey buzzard circling in a thermal. These birds are common in that area, and they make foul and pungent nests in the tops of the pine trees. I went down and started circling in the thermal with him. The bird suddenly made a quick turn and nearly flew through the prop on the airplane! On another day we were told that the winds aloft were very high. I was flying solo and went up to about 10,000 feet. I edged the throttle back to minimum cruise, heading into the wind. I looked down and my airplane was going backwards.

The Stearman was a fun airplane to fly. You have to be on your toes during landing to avoid ground looping the airplane because the landing gear was fairly narrow. It was a very good airplane for acrobatics. Snap rolls were very quick, and it took split-second timing to avoid rolling past straight and level into another half roll. I got checked out on snap rolls and the weather turned bad for three days. When I went back up solo, I couldn't make the airplane snap roll. After several attempts I gave up for the day. Later, I was talking to some other student pilots in my room and I told them about this. They asked me, "Which way were you rolling, to the left or right?" When I told them they said, "You're trying to roll the wrong way!" The airplane wouldn't do the roll without the torque assistance of the engine and propeller. The next time I went up, I was able to do the maneuver.

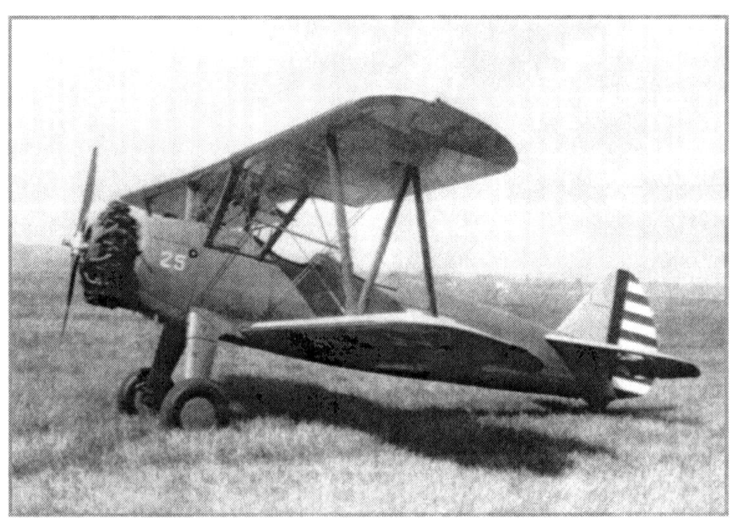

One day we were sitting near the flight line waiting for our turn to fly. We saw a Stearman on a downwind leg and the plane was flying too close to the runway. This really got our attention and we noticed that the pilot was sitting way up high in the cockpit. We knew who it was from the size of the pilot. He was the only guy in the squadron who was that big. Suddenly, the plane banked steeply and got lined up for a landing halfway down the runway. As he passed us, we could see him really working the controls. The airplane went off the runway and through the fence at the end of the field. We all ran over to see if he was all right. It turned out that the propeller had become disconnected from the crankshaft. The propeller would windmill with no resistance, and obviously would not propel the airplane. He flew the close downwind leg to ensure that he got onto the runway. The plane wasn't damaged much. There were some scratches on the wing where he went through the barbed wire fence.

*January 15, 1943*

*Dear Eleanor*

*I suppose you're back in the groove from your Christmas break as I am. We fly every possible minute now that the weather is better so that we can catch up. I am supposed to get at least four hours a day. Flying is quite enjoyable. It is really a most wonderful feeling to go high above earth alone where you can move the whole universe with pressure from two fingers. It is hard work though, and I'm usually tired enough to enjoy eight hours sleep if I can get it.*

*Perhaps I told you that Herm is in primary flight training in Florida, not far from Orlando. He flies in a light weight jacket while I bundle in sheepskins. For recreation, he swims and plays baseball while I play rugby, the roughest game ever invented.*

*Tomorrow I will take my forty hour check ride with the squadron Commander. Last time I rode with him I did not do so well, but I expect to do better this time. Our training involves precision maneuvering and is really hard work. After four hours of it I would just as soon bust rocks with a hammer. If the check ride goes okay, I will start practicing the more difficult aerobatics - snap rolls, slow rolls, loops, Immelmanns, split S's and vertical reverses. I went through some of these maneuvers today and found that I was not quite prepared for them. Various articles such as pencils, etc. fell out of my pockets while the plane was inverted. I did not tighten my safety belt sufficiently, so I hung out flapping in the breeze.*

*We have had no excitement to speak of since we came here. One ship hit another while landing, but no one was even bruised despite the fact that an instructor was standing on the wing of the parked plane and both its wings were torn off.*

*One of the boys apparently became lost the other night. To help him hopefully locate the landing field, they turned on the lights and the beacon. The Commanding officer went out in his plane searching for him. The missing plane turned up later in a cotton field a dozen miles away. It was out of gas, and they told us that the fuel gauge was stuck.*

*We will be leaving here in a couple of weeks. I don't know where we are going, but I suspect it will be Arkansas. Write soon.*

*Love, Dale*

*January 25, 1943*

*Dear Eleanor,*

*Well, primary training is all over, and a big celebration party is planned for Wednesday. Tomorrow, I will go on a cross-country trip and a short dual ride. After those flights I will have the sixty hours required for this training segment. We still don't know where we are going, but it is likely we will ship out next week. My instructor has dropped his stiffness, and it is easy to get along with him. I have to give him credit for pulling five of us through the course. The squadron Commander told me that I was Mr. Lock's best student. That was good to hear. He certainly never allowed me to think that way for a minute while I was training with him.*

*They have turned the lights out now, so I'm going to finish this letter in the phone booth outside. Our ranks are somewhat depleted now. It is quite noticeable at mealtime. About 110 remain of a class of 180. None of the students got more than a scratch while training even though we have demolished two airplanes and damaged about ten others in varying degrees.*

*I liked the Artie Shaw record that you sent me. I was rather surprised though and so was the crowd whose record player I used.*

*Love, Dale*

**I took my basic flight training at Walnut Ridge, Arkansas.** Herm's training field was close to mine, and we saw each other frequently. The population was about 500 people and the only activity in town was a bowling alley with two lanes. We transitioned from Stearman biplanes to BT-13/BT-15 monoplanes which were very similar. Both of these closed cockpit airplanes had fixed landing gear and were powered by a 450 horsepower radial engine. They cruised at about 135 miles an hour. The planes were made by Consolidated, and we called them "Vultee Vibrators." The entire airplane would vibrate when it approached the edge of a stall. There was no way that a pilot could ignore the onset of a stall.

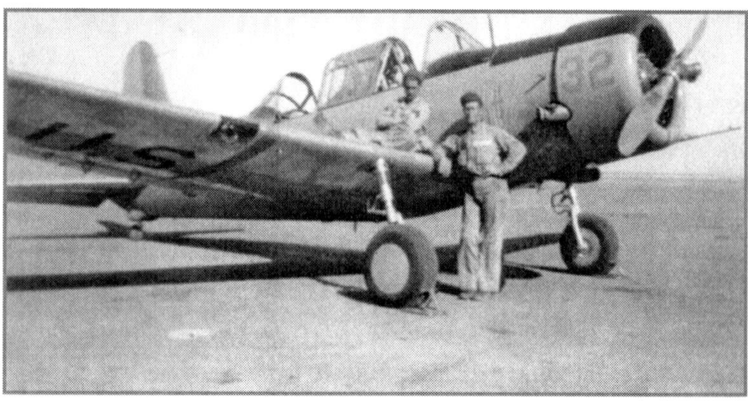

One day on a solo flight, I went out to a remote training field and practiced takeoffs and landings. I forgot to put the propeller in low pitch on one takeoff. The plane felt very sluggish to me, and did not break ground until the end of the runway. Fortunately, there were no hills to avoid as plane slowly gained altitude. Afterword, I gave myself a good talking to about performing preflight check lists.

We practiced nighttime flying at the main airfield. As night fell the ground crew would illuminate the runway with flare pots that glowed dimly. In winter it was really dark in that part of Arkansas. We often used the railroad tracks as navigation aids. The only thing we could see sometimes were the green lights at intersection markers. Often we would shoot night time touch and go landings. On one approach I turned from base to final, and I became aware that there was another airplane close to me. I craned my neck around and looked up. Another BT-13 was on final just above me, and was coming down on top of my airplane! I did a diving turn and went around for another approach. The Army wasn't using tower controllers at that airfield.

After a training flight, one of the students went off the end of runway and nearly hit a barrier. Our instructor was watching this approach from his office, and saw that the flaps were up on that plane. I happened to be in his office at the time. The instructor sent word to the flight line that the offending student pilot should report to him immediately. When he reported, the instructor asked him if he had completed the cockpit check list before landing. The red-faced student admitted that he had not completed the check. The instructor said, "Well, I have a new check that you will perform before any landing. Take hold of your right ear with your right hand. Now take hold of your left ear with your left hand. Pull down!"

*February 2, 1943*

*Dear Eleanor,*

*Another short letter. Nearly every night they find something extra for us to do in our "free" time. The night before last we filled out personal history forms. Last night we set up our new maple beds. They look a little out of place in these shacks, but they are much more comfortable. It was so comfortable this morning that I overslept and was caught asleep at breakfast formation. So I was gigged.*

*Today I began formation flying. It is the most nerve-racking work I have ever run across. An hour and a quarter of it rather bushed me. Next week I will begin night flying. I am beginning to get acquainted with the ship now. Of course, every type has different characteristics and it takes a while to learn. I have about eighty hours now altogether. In another week I will be halfway through.*

*The candy you sent was a real treat. I eat a good deal of sweets here. It seems to depend on the quality of the food. At Decatur I had almost no sweet tooth at all. I also received your very good letter. I look forward every day to mail call, and resolve to find time to write myself.*

*Love, Dale*

*February 12, 1943*

*Dear Eleanor,*

*This may be my Valentine to you. There isn't even a card in the PX, and we won't have a chance to leave the post until Sunday. What a desolate country this is. I wonder that people have stayed here and tried to wrest a living from the poor soil. It seems to me that it would be a very bleak existence before the recent advent of radio and electricity.*

*It is no place for a flying school. Despite our southern location, the winter weather reminds me of Chicago.*

*Navigation is difficult because the terrain offers few geographic clues. The fields are muddy which makes it impossible to make a forced landing safely. Despite this, I think I am going to like it all right. I am now doing some solo flights. On other training flights there is an instructor aboard and I fly the plane on instruments. They put a hood over my eyes on those flights, so I must use the navigation instruments without looking out of the cockpit. We will also be taught cross-country navigation, night flying and formations. I like the airplanes, and my instructor seems a good egg.*

*It is clear and cold out tonight. The wind whistles around the corners and makes the tarpaper rattle like myriads of mice running around in the walls. The stove in the "parlor" is putting out waves of heat and a soft red glow. Every minute or so a ship comes by with a wide open engine, shaking the windows as one of the boys begins a night flight.*

*The radio is on. Benny Goodman's orchestra is playing, and I always wish you were here to share it with me. Good night.*

*Love, Dale*

*February 22, 1943*

*Dear Eleanor,*

*I don't remember how many times I started to write this letter. I have to save enough time this evening to plot a cross-country course. It will be a long flight; nearly all day if the weather remains good.*

> *It was beautiful last night. I was up there for three hours and watched the reflection of the moon on the highways, water and wings. Someday we must do that together. It was so bright we made a number of landings without the lights. We finished at about 2 AM and had to fly again this morning. That winds up our flying here, except for the cross-country tomorrow. We will make that flight on instruments, and will make our cross-country night flight on the first good night.*

*Tomorrow is the first day of spring; my favorite part of the year. I hope I am able to come home. It is just about a year since the last time I came to Detroit. It has gone by very rapidly, but I am glad that I'm looking back on this time rather than forward.*

*I must close now. Please find enclosed all the love that one envelope will contain! I'll hold you in my dreams.*

*Dale*

The instructors at Walnut Ridge were pretty good, and didn't wash very many students out. Ninety-five percent of our students passed basic flight instruction. My class graduated in late March and I was sent off to Seymour, Indiana for advanced flight training In AT-10s.

The AT-10 was a plywood and fabric twin-engine airplane with retractable landing gear. It would've made a nice five place civilian airplane. It was manufactured by Beech and had room for three seats behind the pilots. I really enjoyed flying these planes which cruised at 160 mph. They had fuel ratio analyzer gauges which were used to maximize range. I can still remember the takeoff checklist - flaps down, trim for takeoff, mixture full rich, props full forward, friction brake set, tail wheel locked.

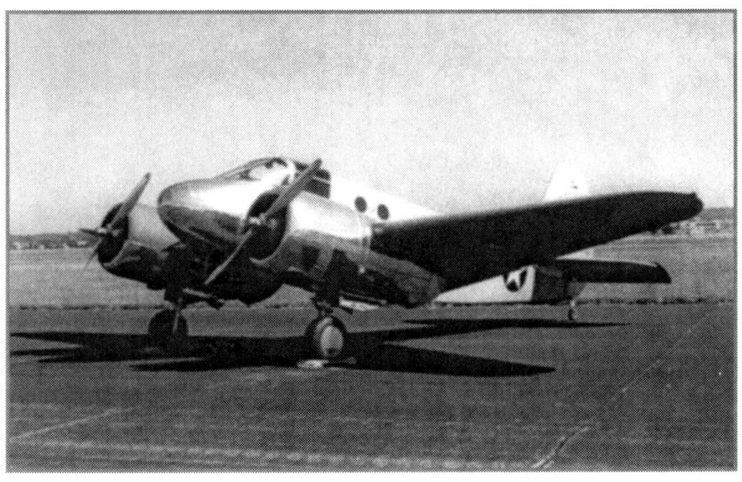

*April 9, 1942*

*Dear Eleanor,*

*I went to the dance last night. It was swell. If Detroit weren't quite so far away, I would've had you come down. A fine orchestra played and the singers were excellent. Some of the cadets made an arch with their sabers, and the dancers passed under them! It made me very lonesome for you.*

*Yesterday, I took a trip with my instructor to northern Ohio and then down to Lexington, Kentucky. On our way back we passed over Dayton, Cincinnati and other cities. We had to be rather careful because the area is covered with restricted regions and in some places there is just a narrow alley to sneak through. These restricted areas are explosive factories and proving grounds, etc. Tomorrow another student and I will go on a longer trip;*

*one that is not as pretty I think. None of our planned flights will take us to Detroit. They haven't issued any maps covering that area. We don't carry quite enough fuel to get there and back and still have a reasonable safety factor.*

*I have been wondering what kind of weekend you have planned. It has been in the back of my mind that we might get together somewhere between here and Detroit. It depends on the weather here. If it is good and we're ahead of schedule, we might get overnight passes. If it is bad, we will fly every day to make it up.*

*It certainly gave me no end of pleasure to see the green hills as we came up to Indiana. I hope I never have to go back to Arkansas. It also made me happy knowing that I'm going to be closer to home and you.*

*I would like to take you for a ride while you are here. The AT-10 would be a good airplane to take you up. It has side-by-side seating. What kind of copilot do you think you would make?*

*Talking to you on the telephone has brought you even more into my dreams and thoughts. It increases my anticipation of seeing you.*

*Love, Dale*

Seymour was a nice place. During that time of year the weather was pleasant nearly every day, with small puffy clouds overhead. We went on some fairly extended cross-country flights. On one of them, we flew from Seymour down to Louisville, then west to the Mississippi River, then north to Chicago and back to Seymour. On the leg from Louisville we were flying at about 9000 feet on top of a cloud deck. A small hole in the clouds allowed me to see objects on the ground. It became clear that we were bucking a strong head wind. I leaned the engines out with the help of the fuel ratio analyzers. The more efficient fuel use gave the plane increased range and we made it to Chicago without refueling. There were about eighteen airplanes on that trip, and a third of them had to stop somewhere enroute and take on fuel. In Chicago, I called my father who was working there on a Ford Motor Company project. He came down and we had a chance to visit before I headed back to Indiana.

One day I took off in an AT-10, and I heard something rattling under the left seat. I put my hand under the seat and came up with a fistful of blood and feathers! This really puzzled me, and I told the crew chief about it after the flight. He said, "Oh, I know what happened. You hit a bird while you were taking off." There was a hole two inches in diameter on the leading edge of the wing. A passage from there went through the heat exchanger which was connected to the exhaust manifold. It continued through the wing to the cockpit where it vented under the seat for heat. The bird hit the airplane squarely on that hole and went all the way through that tubing to wind up under the seat!

*May 7, 1943*

*Dear Eleanor,*

*I'm kind of tired tonight. Our days are longer here and we are up at 5 AM. We go straight through till dinner at 7:30 PM. This evening I was measured for my officer uniforms. I ordered $220 worth of tailor-made clothes. This leaves quite a bit that still must be bought. Insignia,* *accessories, etc. Our $250 allowance will just about do the job.*

*I haven't been able to get in town to see about a place for you to stay. It will probably be at one of the hotels. I don't know what they are like. The town is rather small, about 10,000 population, and it hasn't much to offer. There are a great many soldiers around, and I am afraid I am going to have to lock you up someplace between my open posts.*

*Of course, this is my party. I think it would be wise to make train reservations as soon as possible. I will send you a check in my next letter. If you must travel at night, take a Pullman if you can get it.*

*Wednesday will be here before we know it! I will send you a telegram or special delivery letter with instructions about where to go when you arrive. Chances are I won't be able to meet the train. Best regards to your folks. See you soon!*

*Love, Dale*

## THE END

## A NOTE FROM DALE'S SON:

Dale was a modest man who never spoke about his war experience unless someone asked him to. He was never interviewed or recognized for his wartime accomplishments except by friends and family. In 2002, Dale and I attended the Oshkosh airshow with my brothers David and Mark. While strolling through the parked WWII aircraft, we came upon a B-25. He began talking to several crewmen under the wing of the plane. In less than ten minutes, an audience of about one hundred gathered around to hear his conversation with the pilots. He spoke for about a half hour with the listeners straining to hear every word. I knew then that his story was worth telling.

He was an inspiration to me, and I was fascinated by flight as a youngster. I soloed at age seventeen. However, my vision disqualified me for military pilot training. I served as an Army air traffic controller from 1968 to 1971. Following our Oshkosh trip I dreamed of going to Italy and Corsica with Dad to see the area first-hand. Unfortunately, the cost of a European trip exceeded both of our budgets. We could however afford to go to Thailand which was about half the cost.

Dad spent three weeks with my wife and me touring the lovely southern Thailand beaches of Koh Samui and Phuket. I brought along a micro cassette recorder and made many tapes of his life experiences while we rode in airplanes and while sitting near the beach.

Most of this book is based on those conversations. I hope that some of his personality and humor comes across, but what is harder to convey is the strength and warmth of his character. The people who knew and loved him will agree with me that we never looked into more clear, honest and intelligent eyes than his. Dale passed away in 2007 and was buried with full honors at the military cemetery in Covington, Washington. It is my honor to help him present his memoirs as a book.

Paul Satterthwaite

CPSIA information can be obtained at www.ICGtesting.com
Printed in the USA
LVOW06s2346120814

398778LV00001B/118/P

9 781480 804845